PRAISE FOR
Jim Naughton's

TAKING TO THE AIR

more . . .

TAKING TO THE AIR

THE RISE OF
MICHAEL JORDAN

JIM NAUGHTON

WARNER BOOKS

A Time Warner Company

WARNER BOOKS EDITION

Copyright © 1992 by Jim Naughton
All rights reserved.

Book design by H. Roberts
Cover design by Mike Stromberg
Cover photo by Focus on Sports

Warner Books, Inc.
1271 Avenue of the Americas
New York, NY 10020

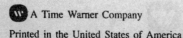 A Time Warner Company

Printed in the United States of America

Originally published in hardcover by Warner Books.
First Printed in Paperback: February, 1993
10 9 8 7 6 5 4 3 2 1

for Liz

1

The frosty breath of city kids rises and dissipates in the dark sky above Chicago Stadium. Tonight's game is still two and a half hours away, but already a crowd of three dozen has bunched at the barricades beside the players' parking lot. They have come to hustle tickets and hunt autographs or simply to stand for a moment in the aura of good fortune that seems to emanate from professional athletes.

One by one, the members of the Chicago Bulls basketball team pull through the gate, borne above the crowd in high-riding, four-wheel-drive vehicles. It is hard for the kids to establish contact with the young celebrities who sit behind tinted windows in a warmer world. Every once in a while, though, a player has extra tickets and this is where he chooses to give them away.

Last week such a gift was bestowed on Antwan Peters, admitting the street-toughened teenager into an evening-long dream. For Antwan not only witnessed the excitement; as a contestant in the Bulls' nightly shoot-for-cash promotion, he became part of it.

Eighteen thousand people watched as he strode onto the court his heroes had just vacated. With a 30-second clock ticking, he began firing up the jump shot honed on a dozen city playgrounds. The first one dropped in and the crowd cheered politely. The second one dropped in too. So did the third. When he sank the jumper that won him the money, the building rocked with loud applause.

"I won $1,000, and you can ask anybody in there if that isn't true," Antwan says. He speaks in the defensive tone of a young man whose assertions are not always accepted as fact.

For half a minute that night, Chicago received him as though he were a ballplayer himself. But on this night he is back at the barricade outside the players' entrance with a friend who calls himself the G Man. The boys are watching for Bulls forward Horace Grant, who is also known as G Man. The young G Man says he and Horace have an understanding regarding some tickets. Whether Horace is aware of this understanding is not entirely clear.

The conversational hum at the gate intensifies, then ceases when a familiar Chevy Blazer rounds the corner and approaches the gate. Kids surge to the barricade. Security guards move forward to hold them back. Everyone waves and shouts greetings as the car rolls into the lot and pulls to a stop near the battered red Stadium door. A strange silence descends as the driver emerges—the sound of 40 kids rising on tiptoe.

Michael Jordan, a leather bag slung over his shoulder, hands his keys to an attendant and crosses the short stretch of blacktop to the door. The full-throated chorus of "Myyykuuul" has just begun to build when he disappears inside the building. Nothing visible has transpired between himself and his audience, yet the kids seem oddly satisfied when Jordan is gone. Boys congratulate each other on having caught a glimpse of him. Legs splayed, tongues wagging, they pantomime his trademark dunks. Even Antwan and the G Man, professionally jaded, become momentarily giddy.

"I seen his gray Porsche once," a kid says.

"The Porsche is black," another snaps.

The excitement dissipates almost as quickly as it arose. In the lull that follows some of the younger kids head for home. Antwan and the G Man amble to the corner, hoping to head off Horace before anyone else sees him. Inside the Stadium, Jordan has just begun the gauntlet of admiration that awaits him each evening.

Everywhere Michael Jordan goes, the world rises up to meet him. He is a political candidate at an endless victory party, a rock star touring sold-out stadiums, a soldier perpetually returning from a brief and glorious war. There is such a surfeit of good feeling for the Bulls' star that he can sample it only momentarily. His last unrestricted public appearance drew more than 5,000 children to a Dallas mall where he signed autographs for an hour and a half, and still met only a fraction of a crowd that overwhelmed security and overran the mall.

Yet nothing seems to dampen the public's enthusiasm for the 29-year-old legend in progress. Fan mail floods in—a new 1,000-letter torrent each week. Can Michael come to a bar mitzvah? A wedding? Can he take my daughter to the prom? Some supplicants, aware perhaps how unlikely their requests, offer substantial sums of cash. Others offer different sorts of inducement. A Chicago dentist whose name also happens to be Michael Jordan says he receives "very interesting" if misguided letters from ardent young women. "They send pictures," the middle-aged Michael Jordan says. "And numbers to call if I'm ever lonely."

The mail brings more innocent tribute too. Friendship bracelets, drawings, poems, school projects from the wood and machine shops. Kids in religion classes compose prayers to thank God for making Michael. Rap songs in Jordan's honor are left on the answering machine at his charitable foundation. A German boy sent him a piece of the Berlin Wall.

Jordan is, by any measure, the most popular athlete in America and perhaps the best-known sports figure in the world. What Babe Ruth was to the 1920s and Joe DiMaggio was to the 1930s and '40s, Jordan is to the here and now. Talent, timing, personality and style have combined to make him the most significant athlete of our era, the one whose packaging and popularity have opened a window on myth-making and hero worship in the 1990s.

It was only ten years ago that Jordan, then a college freshman, made his initial impression on a sizeable portion of the American public. With time winding down, he swished a 17-foot jump shot that gave the University of North Carolina its first NCAA basketball championship in 25 years. Since that night he has shown himself to be the most exciting player ever to pick up a basketball. He is also the most successfully marketed athlete in the history of team sports; the public encounters Jordan's image more often than that of any other athlete. But the roots of Michael's mystique are neither purely visceral nor purely commercial. He is also among the nation's most admired men and among young people's most frequently mentioned role models.

The breadth of Jordan's popularity would be less intriguing were he white. As a black man, playing a game dominated by black men, he overcame obstacles to public acceptance that a white superstar would never have faced. His story is not simply a romance between personable athlete and appreciative public, but an illustration of how magnetism and the marketplace surmounted racial prejudice and created an icon. It is a story of how that icon is interpreted, about black pride and ambivalence and about white fascination and fear. Finally, it is a story about being that icon, about the conflict between self and symbol.

Two and a half hours before game time, the Stadium should be almost empty, but when Jordan sweeps through the door of the players' entrance, a platoon of children materializes before him. Abdomen high and autograph hungry, each is equipped with a program, a pen and a pair of eyes wide as his mouth.

"How's everybody doing?" Jordan asks, his expression

rueful. The boys raise their writing implements and intone the magic words "Michael, can you please..."

Jordan generally obliges signature seekers, but today he is nursing a sore thumb and a sour mood. So he is not altogether disappointed when a squad of late-arriving security guards rounds a nearby corner and shoos the boys away. It is the guards' job to spirit him unhindered toward the Bulls' locker room, but along the way they whisper entreaties of their own.

"Sign one for the boss's kid, Mike?"

Jordan writes as he walks, taking long strides and eventually outdistancing his escorts. The hallway is empty before him now and his relief is palpable, if short-lived. Hurrying up from behind is an elderly usher, armed with a cocktail napkin and the hope of impressing his nephew. When the man lays a hand on Jordan's elbow, the ballplayer flinches just perceptibly. But any trace of surprise or irritation has vanished when he turns to take the napkin and jot his good wishes.

The usher falls back, thanking Jordan profusely, and Michael turns toward the stairs that lead down to the locker room. Perched at the railing stands a young woman wearing high heels, baroque hosiery and an equatorial hemline.

"Look, Michael, look," she calls to him.

"I'm looking," he says. But there is less of the lustful than the merely polite in his reply. In a moment he has entered the relative tranquillity of the locker room.

Jordan accepted long ago that there would be very little uncontested space in his life. But he is still sometimes startled by the magnitude of his fame. "I never knew it could be like this," he says. "In high school you have people who know you and who appreciate your game, and then in college that gets broader. But I never knew it could be nation-based—or, if you want, world-based."

But Jordan underestimates the depth of his popularity if he thinks it flows solely from his athletic accomplishments. His life has special resonance because it is a modern retelling of that most cherished American myth: the story of the self-made man. The elements are familiar: a boy of modest background, God-given talent, unceasing industry, blind luck. We have only to watch as the world rewards him, as we would like to believe it must, with riches, and with fame.

It is a narrative encountered increasingly on the nation's sports pages, as is its frequent sequel, the story of innocence corrupted by success. This occurs not simply because athletes are earning enormous salaries, but because sports, for better and worse, functions as a long-running public morality play. In an increasingly fragmented society, sports provides a common language in which to speak of good and evil, promise and disappointment, authenticity and fraudulence, justice and revenge.

Sports, in some ways, are uniquely suited for this role, not least because they are so exciting, offering the spectator an intensity and clarity often lacking in his daily life. For the bored, the lonely, the underwhelmed, sports are a way of trafficking in unseen worlds and dormant emotions. For the addled, the world-weary and the overworked, they are an opportunity to slip out of the self and follow the fortunes of others.

Athletics makes this possible because its excellence is easily understood. It takes a particle physicist to evaluate another particle physicist's work, a tax attorney to appraise the performance of a professional colleague, but when Jordan picks off a pass at half court, reverses his dribble past a defender and soars down the lane to dunk, everyone who sees understands.

Popular entertainment, especially music, can be equally exciting, equally accessible, but it lacks the moral component. Sports, unlike entertainment, functions as a meritocracy. Standards are well-established, evaluations fairly objective and other considerations—looks, connections, family background—entirely extraneous. More importantly, the competition at the heart of sports forces fans to choose one team over another and justify the choice. There has to be some reason for following a team, some sense that this group of players deserves our allegiance more than any other.

Our loyalties may be based on something as simple as where we live or went to school, but we seldom defend them on those grounds. Instead, we portray our choice in moral terms, projecting onto our heroes the virtues we most admire, transforming these athletes into our surrogates and their games into a metaphor for our own daily struggles.

It is not individual athletes alone who are invested with this symbolic weight. Athletics, historically, have served as a narrow avenue on which ethnic minorities fought their way into the American mainstream. The victories of Irish boxers, Polish fullbacks, Jewish point guards and Italian outfielders were interpreted not simply as athletic achievements, but as testaments to the worthiness of their race. Athletics, because its practitioners were poor and ethnically suspect, became the arena in which the drama of assimilation was played out. Acceptance in sports presaged and sometimes facilitated acceptance in the culture at large.

This is what gives the story of Michael Jordan and his contemporaries much of its appeal and complexity. Black and poor—or, in Jordan's case, working class—they seem characters of a latter-day Horatio Alger, men whose success allows us to believe what we wish to believe: that in this country, have-nots can still become haves; that the American dream is still working.

Yet acceptance in athletics has not done for blacks what it did for other groups. For them, this symbolic display of excellence has not been taken as a sign of racial worthiness, but as a sign of genetic peculiarity. Rather than facilitating their inclusion in the broader economy, it has led to their segregation in the gilded ghetto of sports. The truth that many blacks excel in athletics has been perverted to hold that blacks excel *only* in athletics. Several years ago, when protestors marched through a Brooklyn neighborhood after the murder of a black teenager, white residents, in mockery, spun basketballs on their fingertips.

The demolition of this stereotype falls to Michael Jordan and others like him, men who can capture the public with their athletic abilities while demonstrating what civil rights activist Roger Wilkins calls "the beauty of being a whole black man." Michael is better suited for the task than most. His huge commercial success indicates that he has a knack for disarming the kind of people who show up at civil rights demonstrations with banana peels and basketballs.

Friends say Jordan "transcends" race. The larger question is whether he causes other people to transcend it in cases other than his own. Is he helping to reshape white Americans' image of young black men, or is his breakthrough purely a personal one? Were Jordan to throw his considerable prestige behind cause or candidate, would he forfeit the universal acceptance on which that prestige is based?

How much good can Michael Jordan do?

A Bulls game brings gritty vitality to one of the most desperate neighborhoods in Chicago. Scalpers in ski jackets and scully caps dot West Madison Street holding signs that say "I need tickets." They don't add "to sell at a tremendous profit," but that is what is going on in front of the west entrance of the Stadium, where an exceedingly well-fed gentleman in an expensive sweater has stopped his Oldsmobile to talk terms with one of the local sales force.

The Bulls audience, or that segment which can afford to attend games, is overwhelmingly white and largely suburban. Tickets begin at $14 for a seat near the ceiling, run through a $25 and $45 mid-range, and top out at $200 for a spot at courtside. It is a mark of Jordan's popularity that, even at those prices, the Bulls have sold out every home game since November, 1987. The team's waiting list for season tickets is over 5,000 names long. At $3.25 million per year, Jordan remains an excellent investment for Bulls owner Jerry Reinsdorf, whose team is worth perhaps seven times the $16 million he paid for it in Michael's rookie season.

Nor is Jordan's drawing power a hometown phenomenon.

His presence generally assures a full arena, even in towns that have forsaken their local teams. The National Basketball Association won't disclose what percentage of its profits derives from Michael's popularity, but after the 1986–87 season the league estimated Jordan was responsible for one-third of its increase in attendance. The unfortunate consequence of the league's resurgence is an escalation of ticket prices that all but insures that games will seldom be attended by children from the inner-city neighborhoods where basketball means so much.

Other players are still arriving when Jordan and Scottie Pippen—his most valuable teammate—climb the steps to the court and weave their way through cheerleaders who are practicing a new routine. Standing some 18 feet from the basket, with Jordan on the left wing and Pippen on the right, the players begin a routine of their own. From each of five spots around the perimeter—the corners, the wings and the top of the key—they fire up jump shots—10, 12, sometimes 15 from each station before moving on.

Even in practice there is something striking about the grace and precision of Jordan's movements. Each shot begins with his shoulders square to the basket. His leap into the air is almost perfectly vertical. He elevates the ball quickly—reflexively—above his head, but well in front of his body. The elbows flex. Steadied by his left hand, the ball is poised on the fingertips of his right. At the peak of his trajectory Jordan launches the shot with a powerful flick of his right wrist. He lands where he leapt. The net dances.

Fans are trickling into the building now, congregating at courtside to watch Jordan work. He is comfortable from the perimeter and just beginning to sweat. Moving closer to the hoop, Michael sets up along the baseline, turns his back to the basket and begins working on his inside moves. He takes pass after pass from a solemn-faced ball boy and spins right to shoot; spins left to shoot; spins right and drives beneath the basket, for a reverse layup; spins left and leaps to the rim, slamming the ball through.

When Jordan has completed his routine from the left baseline he crosses the lane and repeats the drill from the right. When he feels comfortable on the right side he jogs out to the foul line and practices his free throws. When he feels comfortable at the free throw line, he wends his way back through the cheerleaders and begins the entire process at the opposite basket.

Jordan has won the Most Valuable Player award twice, in 1988 and 1991, and is widely regarded as the best player in the NBA. Basketball people assume the superlative when they appraise him. The only questions are of qualification.

Is he the greatest talent?

"I don't think I've ever seen anybody have the physical skills that he has," says Jerry West, the Hall of Fame guard who is general manager of the Los Angeles Lakers.

The greatest scorer?

"He is one of the toughest, if not the toughest man in history to do something about once the ball is in his hands," says Red Auerbach, the basketball legend who is president of the Boston Celtics.

The greatest ever?

"Pound for pound I have never, ever, seen a better ballplayer," says Paul Silas, assistant coach of the New York Knicks, and one of the game's all-time leading rebounders. "Whatever he really concentrates on he can master. At times he seems to toy with the game and with players because of the extent of his mastery of the game."

Fred Carter, assistant coach of the Philadelphia 76ers, suggests divine intervention. "When God decided to create the perfect basketball player and send him down here, he gave him to the Jordans."

Michael's proficiency with a basketball, prodigious as it is, can't fully account for the electricity he generates. It is not so much the fact that he excels which captures the imagination, but the way in which he does it, for Jordan exploits an opportunity unique to basketball. While baseball has its high fives and football its end zone strut, only in basketball can celebration transform scoring into self-expression. Only in basketball is the game itself enlivened by the players' joy. This is the beauty of the slam dunk with its vengeful, high-flying sense of release; it is at the aesthetic heart of the falling-on-your-face layup, the somewhere-from-the-sheetops scoop shot and the sleight-of-hand pass.

All are part of what essayist Stanley Crouch calls "a percussive ballet." And no one has ever danced like Jordan. His game is a marvelous combination of leaping ability, body control and split-second creativity. But Michael not only jumps higher than anyone else, he twists his body into such unusual shapes, slips through such minute openings, gauges the trajectory of such improbable shots, and accomplishes it all with such startling speed that he not only succeeds, he confounds.

"He plays with disciplined audacity," Crouch says. "That's what Americans have always liked. The improvisational hero is the great American hero. Louis Armstrong, Fred Astaire or Michael Jordan conceiving some sort of remarkable play while in motion. That idea is in the air of this culture, that there may be another way to get it done, an alternate vocabulary of possibilities."

By the time Jordan has finished his pregame warm-up, sweat runs in rivulets down his head and across his face. As he leaves the court, a man from the Bulls front office staff whisks him aside to have a quick picture taken with the family that baby-sits the man's children. Jordan, who dislikes being interrupted during his pregame workout, obliges them with a wordless smile, then bounds down the stairs to the Bulls' dressing room. His cubicle is the first one inside the door on the right-hand side, but before the game, while his teammates are warming up, he pulls his chair into the middle of the room and begins lacing up a new pair of sneakers.

It is one of his few quiet moments in the locker room. After every game a four-and-five-deep circle of reporters and cameramen surround his cubicle, waving microphones, scribbling notes and blocking the doorway. His comments are valued so highly that the circle assembles even before Jordan returns from the shower and the crowd must part to grant him access to his clothes.

In the last few years, Jordan has cut back a bit on his accessibility to the media, but before a game he is still extremely cooperative, assuming he has not disappeared into the trainer's room. Tonight, he is being courted by a University of Georgia student in town during a school break. The young man is just learning how to conduct an interview and seems most interested in getting Jordan's views on the Georgia basketball team. It is a subject about which Jordan knows little, as his vague, polite answers make obvious. Yet the young man presses on, fueled at least in part by the momentous shock of talking to Michael Jordan.

"Would you mind," he asks, after the last question has been answered, "if we take a picture so my friends will believe this?"

"Sure," Jordan says.

And then as they are about to snap the shot, "Can I put my arm around you like we are buddies?"

"Sure," Jordan says. And after the shot has been snapped: "Have a safe trip back."

When the young man departs Jordan turns his attention to deciding who will get which of the many complimentary tickets he hands out for each game. While he studies the seating arrangements Pippen mentions that the weather is supposed to turn even colder.

"You better stay here then," Jordan says cryptically.

Pippen asks what he means.

"I heard they don't have indoor heat in Arkansas," Jordan responds, getting a dig in at Pippen's home state.

"Arkansas is God's country," Pippen responds with mock indignation.

"North Carolina is God's country," Jordan says. "Arkansas is pig country." He laughs at his own joke.

One of the reporters who has come down for a quick pregame interview says that he drove through Arkansas once.

"I hope you drove fast," Jordan says. "Arkansas," he adds, shaking his head, "that's great pig country." By now, even Pippen is laughing.

The room grows quiet again and Jordan seems to retreat a bit from those around him. In a few moments, tickets disbursed, Michael heads for the trainer's room. He will be taped for tonight's game. He will slip into his uniform, and then he will wait to be summoned to the court.

As always, he will be the last player to trot across the darkened court and into the white circle of the spotlight. And as always, the fans will cheer so loudly that he will not hear the announcer speak his name.

2

It is quiet on the golf course. Even when he is playing before a gallery, there is silence in those moments when he stands above the ball. The game offers the opportunity for solitude and self-improvement, and Michael Jordan craves both. Intensely competitive, he insists that he is going to retire from basketball in the next few years to pursue a career on the PGA tour. In the meantime the golf course is his haven, one of the few places where he can move freely in public, where he knows that the world will recede for several hours and he can pretend he is living a normal life. Michael uses that phrase often—"a normal life"—mostly to describe what he can't have.

"If I want to go to a movie, I go to the late show," he told Bulls broadcaster John "Red" Kerr in 1988. "If I want to get my hair cut I go to a place where the barber closes at night and then opens up again so he can take me. If I want to go to a restaurant, I call ahead and see if they have a booth or a table in the back."

But even these strategies don't work anymore. Michael

14

can seldom leave his home without attracting a crowd. On the road, even his hotel room isn't safe because maids and bellhops keep showing up with towels, pillow candies, and oh, can you sign this for my son while I'm here.

Jordan bears these intrusions with an equanimity that exacerbates his problem. "It's nothing for him to be in his room and people are sliding business propositions under the door," says his friend Fred Whitfield. "They wouldn't take that chance with another celebrity, but they do it because they know a guy like Michael is not going to blast them."

Much of Jordan's phenomenal appeal is grounded in the public's perception that fame has not spoiled him, that he believes himself a "normal" guy. His outgoing commercial image shrinks the distance between himself and his fans. Jordan cannot make friends with all the people who love him, but he gives the impression that he'd like to.

"He seems like he'd be really easy to get along with," says Bakari Baker, a thoughtful teenage fan from the west side of Chicago. "If he didn't play basketball and you met him on the street, he seems like he'd be real nice."

Yet the notion that a celebrity of Jordan's stature can remain a normal person excites a frenzy that precludes his doing so. People simply want too much from him, and so he is forced into self-defeating attempts to reconcile fame and normality. Once revered for his openness, Michael must now enter buildings through the back door. Proud of his spontaneity, he must live a rigorously scheduled life. Even something as simple as walking down a public hallway forces him to make difficult choices. Does he meet a person's eyes and oblige the request for an autograph, knowing that a crowd may quickly assemble? Or does he walk quickly by, knowing he's disappointed someone?

"The good part about being me," Jordan says, "is being able to stretch myself and meet people and help people. The hard part is every day you've got to be in a good mood because that is what people expect from you."

Though he is famous for satisfying those expectations,

Jordan often exhausts himself doing so. One can't help feeling, after a few times in his presence, that the best thing one can do for him is leave.

But of course, no one does leave. The hunger to know Jordan is too great. One recent summer, he was appearing in Memphis at a charity golf tournament for St. Jude's Children's and Research Hospital. The previous year, at the same event, he'd had to turn away several thousand disappointed people after signing autographs for over an hour in almost 100-degree heat. This year, in an attempt to be fair, Jordan wasn't signing.

Still, a huge throng followed him around the course. Men kept reaching over the ropes, proffering Michael posters with $100 bills attached, begging for autographs. A woman who worked for Jordan's host asked for the opportunity to touch Michael, and she lightly laid a hand on his arm as he walked near the ropes around the 12th green.

On the 14th hole Michael finished the apple he was eating and tossed the core into the woods. A squad of adoring boys tore after it. "Please, please don't do that," Jordan yelled, but to no avail.

Michael knows what he means to these children. "I think people want a big brother for their kids or a good example," he says. "And that is my whole intention, because a lot of kids don't have that in their lives and it helps get them over the hump."

But living one's life as America's good example is a daunting task. In a 1988 interview with writer David Breskin of *Gentlemen's Quarterly*, Jordan confessed to nightmares of self-destruction. "It's always something I've done," he said. "I have robbed a bank. Or I have done cocaine. I have succumbed to the pressure of drugs. I have felt the pressure to drink. These are all nightmares.

"They're nightmares of something terrible happening to me that would destroy a lot of people's dreams or conceptions of me—that's the biggest nightmare I live every day.

What if I make a mistake?...That's the biggest fear I face.''

The ''mistakes'' he refers to have tarnished the image of a succession of seemingly wholesome athletic heroes. Dwight Gooden tested positive for cocaine. Steve Garvey faced multiple paternity suits. Pete Rose went to prison for gambling.

Jordan has avoided these pitfalls. His reputation is such an enormous asset that he occasionally gives the sense of having suppressed his personality to protect it. "He has a great desire to burst forth and be free," one friend says. "To go out and act crazy like you or I can do without it being on the front page."

Instead, Jordan contents himself by making smaller symbolic statements, and investing them with unusual weight. In his most recent video, "Michael Jordan's Playground," Jordan joins a musical group for a little bit of lip-synching, some self-conscious dancing and good-natured fooling around. It is an amusing little performance, the video equivalent of making funny faces in an amusement park photo booth, but for Michael it was a small-scale declaration of independence.

"It is a little different than what people have seen me in," he says. "I like that because it gives me a good sense of being a normal person. I still have a normal life. I don't want to be constantly on a pedestal where I don't do these things, I don't live a normal life. I think these things show I do enjoy myself in different ways."

Yet the pedestal is there and Jordan is always mindful of it. Before the 1990–91 season he began wearing an earring in his left ear. This was not exactly a major rebellion, but Jordan realized that his wearing an earring would mean that a lot of kids would want one too, and he was worried about the family friction that might create. His wife, Juanita, who liked the earring, convinced him that even Michael Jordan was not responsible for the earlobes of young America.

Jordan lives at a furious pace. "He is fully booked [with commercial and charitable engagements] from the end of the playoffs through October 1," says his scheduler, Barbara Allen. "He takes 10 days of vacation, then the rest of summer he is on the road. If each of the endorsement companies held him to his strict number of appearances, then he probably wouldn't have enough days in the year."

Despite the exhausting itinerary, Michael has succeeded in creating a world inside his other worlds, a life whose terms are not totally dictated by fame and commercial commitments. It is a world inhabited by family and a small circle of friends. These are the people who keep Jordan's head on straight, the ones who tell him if he's made a mistake. "They kind of help me by being a backboard for whatever problems I might have in my career and my life," Michael says.

Most of the people closest to him knew Michael long before everybody wanted to. With rare exceptions, they depend on him for neither identity nor livelihood. As a result, Jordan can count on their unsparing honesty. "They'll criticize him as soon as they'd criticize anyone else," says Kevin Jones, a college friend who is an attorney in Washington, D.C.

The best-known members of this inner circle are Michael's parents, James and Deloris Jordan. "Everything starts with them," Michael has said. Mr. and Mrs. Jordan are sharecroppers' children who raised their own five offspring on hard work—much of which Michael managed to avoid—self-sufficiency and the vibrant Christianity of the African Methodist Episcopal church.

"Where his parents come from is really down home," Fred Whitfield says. "Family life is extremely important to them. I think they were careful about who his friends were and what he did away from basketball. If you look at the reasons that Michael has been so successful, one is the values that he learned from his parents."

Jordan's fame has changed Deloris's and James's lives completely. They work for him, running his chain of "Flight 23" sportswear stores in North Carolina and serving on the board of JUMP, Inc., his personal corporation. His mother appeared with Michael in Coke and Wheaties commercials and is now so widely recognized that she's cut several regional advertisements on her own. Requests for the Jordans' time became so numerous that in 1985 the couple moved from coastal Wilmington, North Carolina, to be near the airport in Charlotte.

Though the Jordans' lives are built around servicing Michael's renown, in fundamental ways their relationship with him has not changed. He still consults them on important decisions, and they still prod him to work hard, better himself and help those he can.

"Lots of parents have this feeling once you reach a certain age that, well, 'I'm done with you,'" Deloris Jordan says. "That's not my outlook. I'm still here."

In 1989, Deloris convinced Michael to establish the Michael Jordan Foundation, which the family hopes to build into a $1-million-a-year children's charity. "Whatever has a good image and seems successful everyone wants a piece of," she says. "But it is the ones who keep things in perspective—Julius Erving, Arthur Ashe—who are the leaders and are the role models." And that is what she wants for her son.

"Mrs. Jordan is a great source of positive energy," says one of Michael's business associates. "She is the one who keeps challenging him to take it to the next level."

For a man who has risen through many levels of wealth and acclaim, Jordan has remained remarkably constant in his intimates. Adolph Shiver was Michael's summertime playmate at Empie Park in Wilmington, his classmate at Laney High School and again at Chapel Hill. An aspiring nightclub owner, Shiver lives in Charlotte, but spends much of his time in Chicago. He is easy to find in the Stadium crowd because of his stylish wardrobe and his excellent seats.

A man who always looks concerned that he is missing something, Shiver's life is bound up in Michael's. Through

Jordan he's met a world of celebrities, both athletes and entertainers. At the 1991 All-Star game he put some of those connections to work, throwing Michael a huge birthday party attended by many of the game's top performers and featuring entertainment by rappers Kid 'n' Play.

Fred Whitfield, a Greensboro attorney and fledgling sports agent, met Jordan while the two were serving as counselors at a basketball camp the summer before Michael entered UNC. Whitfield had just graduated from Campbell University in North Carolina and helped prepare Jordan for student life.

"He was just a real clean-cut guy with his head on straight," Whitfield remembers. "Easy to talk to, easy to laugh and joke around with. Our personalities just kind of clicked."

Whitfield is a frequent houseguest of Michael and Juanita, and he makes it to many of the Bulls' East Coast road games. He was a college basketball player himself, and shares with Jordan a passion for other sports. But because of his law practice, Whitfield's experience of the world is more intellectual than Jordan's own, and he offers Michael a friendly discernment that the ballplayer might not otherwise receive.

The inner circle also includes Fred Kearns, an undertaker in Troy, North Carolina, who met Michael and Adolph when the three were freshmen at Chapel Hill; T. O. Stokes, a former minor league baseball player who is Whitfield's law partner; and Howard White, Nike's liaison to the athletes who wear its shoes, the man who was Jordan's almost constant companion early in his rookie season.

At the center of this network is Michael's own family: his wife, the former Juanita Vanoy, who was a loan officer at a Chicago bank before she married Michael in September of 1989; and his sons, Jeffrey Michael, who was born in November of 1988, and Marcus James, who arrived early on Christmas Eve morning in 1990.

The Jordans are "pretty laid-back people," friends say,

reluctant to be more expansive. The family is fiercely protective of its privacy. Jordan is tired of people following him home and ringing his doorbell or waiting for him outside his house in Highland Park, an affluent suburb north of Chicago. "I never want to give my total private life away for the public to make judgments," he says.

He has trouble saying no to people, he admits, but says Juanita has helped him in this regard. "She is more the stern side of this relationship," Jordan says. "And I like that."

"I have no problem saying no," Juanita acknowledged in a November 1991 article in *Ebony* magazine. "If someone didn't step up and say no, there would be no time for his family. . . . I know it makes me look like a bitch, but I can't worry about it because I am protecting what we have. If that is what I have to be, then I will be a bitch."

Juanita makes appearances for the Jordan Foundation and several other charities, but until recently, the Jordans have turned down a spate of proposed endorsement deals that would have involved the entire family. It is critical to Michael that he maintain what Fred Whitfield calls his ability to "make privacy." After the Bulls won the 1991 NBA championship, he even skipped the team's audience with President Bush in the White House.

"He has to be able to escape to a world where it is just his family and friends," Whitfield says. "If he's on the road in Washington or Atlanta, it's just us. In Chicago, it's just us. It's just our circle. We are like one big family."

And it is within that family that the "real" Michael Jordan spends whatever time he can.

The Jordans are building a home on eight acres in suburban Highland Park. The new mánse and guest cottage will reportedly contain 26,000 square feet, an area slightly greater than half a football field. In the meantime, the family's current quarters offer a glimpse into the life of a man who has embraced wealth while using it to re-create an idyllic version of his younger days before he had money.

The Jordans' present home is an intriguing blend of excess and modesty, not as palatial as the new one, but roomy, well-appointed and marked by the tastes of a man striving to stay in touch with his childhood. Some of the excess stems from the public's urge to give Michael presents. Jordan owns about a dozen cars, many of which were given to him or came through commercial contracts. The automotive livery includes a Ferrari, a Porsche, a BMW, a Z, two Mercedes, several Corvettes and a few Chevy Blazers for the rough weather. It is a flashy collection, but nothing compared to his wardrobe.

Michael is a partner in a new venture with the owners of Bigsby and Kruthers, Chicago's top men's store, which will market three new lines of clothing—formal wear (23Night), business suits (23Day) and weekend wear (23Relax)—designed especially for Jordan. This connection accounts for much of Michael's impressive holdings in suits, slacks and blazers. But he also receives donations—custom-made and entirely unsolicited—from tailors in Italy and California eager for the free publicity Michael can generate. These gifts have become so numerous that Jordan has taken to giving them to whichever friend he thinks they will fit.

This unneeded charity, however, does not account for all the luxury in Jordan's life. He's got over 100 pairs of shoes of the nonathletic variety, likes to surprise Juanita with jewelry and occasionally indulges his own taste for gold. But the real extravagances in Michael's home are his game and media rooms. He is a man who can't get out much, so he has tried to make it just as exciting to stay in.

The basement features a six-hole putting green complete with breaks, plus billiard, Ping-Pong and poker tables, suggesting the tastes of a man who can now afford to re-create the community rec centers of his youth. Michael's predilection for state-of-the-art home entertainment equipment also seems to have sprung from a childhood fantasy of instant riches.

Jordan loves popular culture. He rents movies by the dozen and devours pop music with an almost indiscriminate joy. His tastes range from the country of Kenny Rogers to the jazz of Grover Washington, and he likes to blare something upbeat and inspiring when he is dressing for a game.

About the only childhood passion he has not been able to import is a pair of golden arches. Jordan has never outgrown his taste for McDonald's food, and says one of the things he misses most is being able to eat in the restaurants without being mobbed. During his early years in the NBA, he'd sometimes show up at the drive-through window in a chauffeur-driven limousine, but now he sends friends to pick up his order.

As his basement suggests, Michael is a man obsessed with games. Even by the standards of professional athletics he is an unusually competitive person. It is not simply that he likes to win—who doesn't?—but that he loves the confrontation. One business associate said he thought he could talk Jordan into a game of full-contact checkers. "If he finds you can do something he can do, he likes to show you that he can beat you," says Lacy Banks, a sportswriter with the *Chicago Sun-Times* who used to play cards with Jordan on the team's bus and plane.

Golf, as he has pointed out a time or two, is his game of choice. Jordan plays whenever he can and talks about it the rest of the time. Charity tournaments are a favorite summer-time activity, and he's more likely to embrace an endorse-ment deal if the "appearances" in his contract are actually golf dates. Asked at the 1991 All-Star game what he liked best about the NBA's festive weekend, Jordan said it gave him the chance to get in at least 18 holes a day.

"Magic said he enjoyed being a fan himself," a reporter told him. "Watching the slam dunk and the rest of it."

"Well, he can't play golf," Michael said.

Jordan has been golfing since his junior year at North Carolina, when he was introduced to the sport by Davis Love III, his Carolina classmate who is now a professional golfer. Jordan's handicap hovers between five and 10, but he likes to test his game against better players.

At a recent pro-am, Jordan, with his handicap for a spot, took on touring pro Andy Bean. Bean let Michael hit from the shorter tees, and for a while Jordan was holding his own. But after several holes his pride got the best of him and he moved back to the pro tees. Bean won the bet.

Lacking a convenient golf course, Jordan will play whatever is available. One afternoon before a Bulls road game, Lacy Banks took a $400 lead on Michael in their long-running game of Tonk, a variation on poker. That night, on the flight back to Chicago, Banks was sleeping in the coach while the team sat up in first class.

"I felt a tap on my shoulder and it was Michael," he says. "And he said, 'Let's get at it, ho' [as in homeboy]. So we started playing, and I got up another $100. His eyes began to glitter and sparkle and he said, 'Now I got you where I want you.' And I'm thinking, 'I'm in command. I'm behind the console.' And he said, 'I'm going to walk you down.'

"We kept on playing and playing. He was not going to stop. When we got off the plane I was only up $50 and I felt like the biggest fool."

Banks had a similar experience in Ping-Pong. Playing for $25 a game, he once had Jordan in the hole $125, but today Michael is so good that they can't play anymore. The one thing left is conversation, and here too Jordan likes a little combat. "He loves to debate," Banks says. "He hates to lose a point. He will argue, argue, argue."

Jordan's sense of humor is pugnacious. "With his friends and people who are close to him, Michael will see something and ride you and crack on you," says Rod Higgins of the Golden State Warriors, who is Jordan's best friend in the league. "To deal with him, you have to go right back at him just to make the night not so long." Cracks about how he's lost most of his hair are generally effective, Higgins says.

"If you make a mistake, he'll let you know about it," says Buzz Peterson, Jordan's college roommate. "He'll laugh and laugh. He *hates* to be embarrassed. He can't take that. He can dish it out all the time, though."

Beneath this verbal sparring, friends say, is the thoughtful Jordan who has romanced a nation of fans. Several summers ago, after playing for two days in a McDonald's charity golf tournament in Greensboro, Jordan chartered a plane so he could make it to Fresno by 7:30 that evening for Rod Higgins's charity basketball game. That same summer, after the Bulls had been bounced from the playoffs, Jordan took his father, Shiver, Whitfield and Kearns on a 10-day cross-country trip that he paid for. "Once you are friends with him he really works at keeping that friendship and nursing that friendship," Higgins says.

Kevin Jones, a college friend to whom Michael gave one of his tailored tuxedos, says these gifts are Jordan's way of making sure "his buddies don't get left behind." And they don't seem to. That may be because Jordan draws as much from these friendships as "his buddies" do, finding in them a way to keep in touch with the young man he used to be.

"He doesn't go to these different cities and start hanging with the big wheels," Whitfield says. "Basically what Michael has done is take his North Carolina upbringing and take it to Chicago during the season and then he's back down here in the summer."

Several years ago, Michael was one of the ushers at Buzz Peterson's wedding. "Some of the guys were nervous, but they figured Michael's made all these public appearances, he'll be all right," Peterson says. "Well, he was more nervous than I was. He was shaking. I said to a couple of guys in the wedding, 'I bet you $10 Michael Jordan will come down that aisle chewing gum.' Because when he gets nervous he starts smacking gum.

"So I'm standing up there and here he comes down the aisle smacking gum. I made about $30."

But this notion that Jordan is "the same old Michael" can be easily overstated. This is also the man who his peers say has the most sophisticated fashion sense in the NBA, who keeps up with a large, diverse investment portfolio and who was deeply involved in the planning of his new restaurant. Michael is skillful at switching gears, at knowing who people need him to be. "Wherever you are coming from, he can get there," Fred Whitfield says. "He can walk into a roomful of white people and get along with everyone in there, from somebody who is in the Klan to the most liberal person in the room. And he can walk into a room of black people and do the same thing, from the person who is the most bourgeois to the person who is the most streetwise."

There are, however, limits to Jordan's empathy. "I know this will sound crazy, but I thought if I ever had a chance to come back in a second life, I'd like to be a woman," he told Red Kerr not long after Jeffrey was born. "I used to think I'd like to experience what they go through in becoming a mother, but after watching my son being born, I think I'll skip it, because the mother goes through more pain than I'd like."

When he first came to Chicago Michael played several games with the Wilson sporting goods employee softball team and shot a few rounds of golf with some local businessmen. Ken Cohen, who owns a suburban Chicago clothing store, remembers meeting Jordan in a Las Vegas coffee shop in 1986 and receiving a 5:30 A.M. invitation to join Michael for his 8:30 tee time. It was easier in those days for Jordan to invite people into his life, especially if they were young children.

Toddlers offer Michael something older people can't. Because they are innocent of his fame, he knows that they like him for *who* he is, rather than *what* he is. Such knowledge is hard to come by.

Adam Schifrin, whose parents belong to the health club where the Bulls practice, met Jordan in the fall of 1987 when Adam was two and a half. "Michael took a liking to him," Adam's mother, Jodi, says. "He took him out on the court and held him up so he could dunk. He had him to his house, asked him to come over and watch the games on TV. He gave him his unlisted phone number.

"And Adam certainly was not affected by who Michael was. To him Michael Jordan was another guy. I still don't think he realizes he's an international sports figure."

While Jordan has cleared an island of tranquillity on which to live his personal life, casual relationships—like the ones he had with the guys on the softball team or at the golf course—have become casualties of his fame and his new family. "He's become more elusive and reclusive," Cohen says. "He's had to." And so he turns down invitations he once might have accepted for golf dates and backyard barbecues.

Jordan used to be a churchgoer, but he can't do that anymore either. "It doesn't seem like church, because everybody stares," he told *GQ*'s David Breskin. "It's more or less, 'Well, Michael's here today, let's have him speak for us.'"

One day after practice, Bulls coach Phil Jackson dispatched the team to the health club wading pool for a little "hydrotherapy," a new part of Chicago's training regimen. "How about some life jackets?" asked Jordan, who can't swim and doesn't like the water, even when, as in this case, it isn't deep enough to wet his navel.

It was a weekend afternoon and a small crowd assembled outside the glass-enclosed pool. Michael was one of the last Bulls to strip off his T-shirt. He stood on the edge of the pool for several seconds, grinning a self-mocking grin.

There is something unsettling about watching grace and self-assurance dissolve into anxiety, which is what happened as Jordan lowered himself gingerly into the thigh-high water, never loosening his grasp on the side of the pool.

Someone else might have been able to pass this small personal trial in private, but not Jordan. The crowd outside was getting larger as he took his first unsteady paces toward the other end of the pool. It was a distance of no more than 50 feet. Michael covered it slowly, as though he were walking on sharp stones. When he reached the other end he turned awkwardly, never looking up into the wall of people— who were glad, at least in that moment, to be someone other than Michael Jordan.

3

The Bulls used to practice in an old Catholic school gymnasium on the northern edge of town. Now they, like most NBA teams, have taken the city game to the suburbs. The Deerfield Multiplex sits in one mall that is adjacent to another and just down the street from a third. The players live in nearby Northbrook and Highland Park, communities that make Lake Michigan's north shore one of the most affluent areas in the country. Arriving for practice each day, the Bulls park amidst tanning salons, wallpaper boutiques and the branch offices of regional banks. They enter the facility the team shares with suburban parents pounding around the jogging track, yuppies lost in the repetitious torture of Nautilus and seniors deep in water aerobics.

The season that these Bulls believed would make them champions began late on the afternoon of October 4, 1990. For veteran players this was not so much a day for business as for catching up with teammates who had gone home for the summer, chatting with the media about the season ahead and having their pictures taken by the Bulls publicity peo-

ple. Some of the free agents whom the Bulls had signed just
to have a few extra bodies in camp were hooked up to
futuristic machines that measured their quickness and tested
their hand-eye coordination.

Of all the worlds in which Michael Jordan moves, this is
the one he affects most deeply and immediately. It is a world
populated by teammates who work in his shadow, coaches
and front office people who seek to channel his remarkable
gifts and devoted fans who wait near the court accumulating
casual encounters with Chicago's star. Here he is at his most
combative, and fans who come expecting the carefree Jordan
of television commercials may find his businesslike intensity
off-putting. Michael's first six years in the league have
tempered his ebullience. He understands better than he once
did the mental toughness required to win an NBA championship and wants to impress that toughness on his teammates through the rigor of his own example.

Everything about Jordan indicates a fastidious, even com-
pulsive approach to the game. His practice clothing is
color-coordinated—red bicycle pants beneath black extra-
long shorts; a black knee brace; a red wristband worn well
up the elbow; white sneakers trimmed in black and red. His
expression is intent, even when involved in something as
simple as throwing a chest pass. He leads the Bulls through
most of their sprints and laps, plays in-your-shirt defense
during dribbling drills and maintains a deep silence through
much of the workout.

"During the first drills and everything, that's when I
figured out he's so competitive," said Cliff Levingston,
who joined the Bulls just before training camp in 1990. "I
said to Craig [Hodges], 'Is he always like this?' He said,
'Man, he hates to lose. Hates to lose. And you can't give
him anything. Don't let him have his way with you or he
will look down on you.'"

Jordan's competitiveness is only one facet of perhaps the
most closely analyzed game in basketball. His mastery of
the sport is such that he attracts basketball experts the way

Shakespeare attracts literary critics. His is the work that studied closely enough promises to yield the essence of the art form. Yet identifying Jordan's virtues as a ballplayer is an easier feat than emulating them, because as experts around the league point out, his game begins in his gifts.

Positioning: "I think one outstanding aspect is he's always playing the game low," says Pete Newell, the former college and professional coach, who is still regarded as one of the game's great teachers. "He's always in a flexed-knee position. A flexed knee is the beginning of movement. His ability to accelerate and to stop are two things that are better than anybody. Anybody I've seen, anyway. He's always got the gun cocked."

Hands: "Great hands," says Bill Fitch, coach of the New Jersey Nets. "If Nike made gloves, they'd make a lot of money."

Quickness: "I think technically he is doing some things we don't realize until we study the films," says Dick Versace, former coach of the Indiana Pacers. "When you are watching the films you might say, 'Boy, when the defender came flying at him, I didn't see him adjust the ball six inches to the left and still dunk it.' Because in person it just looked like a quick dunk."

Body control: "We were watching the tape of a game they played against Portland [in December of 1990] and he had the ball on the right wing about 30 feet from the basket," remembers Del Harris, head coach of the Milwaukee Bucks. "He put it on the floor and went through all five guys. I said, 'Hey, rewind that,' and we watched it again. All five guys on the best team in the world had a shot at him, but you would hardly have noticed. He made one of the most unbelievable shots look easy.

"On the ground or in the air, I think his body control is the best I've ever seen, and I've been coaching since 1959."

Strength: "Dr. J. [Julius Erving] was pure finesse with

his body control," says Earl Strom, who recently retired as dean of the NBA's officiating corps. "Michael is able to include not only the finesse, he uses his powerful body as well as anyone I've seen. When Michael drives to the basket he draws a crowd, but he powers right through them. He powers through the big men who go up to block his shot."

Leaping ability: "They talk about his vertical jump," says Frank Layden, president of the Utah Jazz. "We have a lot of guys who have great vertical jumps. *He* has a great vertical *and* horizontal jump. He's like a broad jumper. Except that this guy is traveling through the air and his feet must be five feet off the ground."

Attitude: "There are a lot of guys in the league who perform spectacular feats," Fitch says. "They do it once. Michael does a steady diet of it. Every game, every practice. There is a consistency. In this day and age, one of the big drawbacks is players who become lackadaisical, self-satisfied, content. They put some of that in everybody, but his doesn't seem to have a switch."

Intelligence: "He has the sensational flair to appeal to the masses," Versace says. "Yet the purist sees the unselfishness, the high percentage shots that he takes and makes, the good choices and good decisions."

Endurance: "The way he goes flying through the air, gets knocked down," Layden says, "his first season in the league I said, 'Come April and this guy is going to be dead. He won't have anything left in the playoffs.'

"You know what? He's better in the playoffs."

The Bulls know. They know that since 1984 they have possessed the most explosive offensive weapon in basketball. And for all the years since then, they have been trying to figure out how best to aim him.

Phil Jackson moves along the sidelines at a Bulls practice with an amused expression, as though he were constantly on the verge of making a witty, if sarcastic, interjection. He is a tall, thin, slightly lopsided man dressed in an old white polo shirt and loose black pants. The hitch in his stride is a result of a spinal fusion operation, the gray in his hair at least partly the result of the years he's spent coaching in the Continental Basketball Association and now in the NBA.

Jackson has deep-set eyes, a broad mustache and a deliberate way of speaking that makes him seem more pensive than the typical can-do coach. A former New York Knick and New Jersey Net, his nickname is those days was "Action" Jackson. Long-armed and long-legged, he had a knack for causing commotion when he entered a game. The commotion was not always productive, but it was inspiring, and that, coupled with his court sense, was enough to see him through a 13-year career.

As a reserve forward on the Knicks' 1973 championship team, he was the quintessential team player on a squad that made team play its hallmark. Those Knicks were a cerebral, quick-thinking group whose members knew each other's movements, compensated for each other's weaknesses and fed each other's strengths. In the process they made team-work look exciting, and breathed a little flair into the drab virtues of hitting the open man and moving without the ball.

When Jackson joined the Bulls staff in 1987, Doug Collins, who was then the head coach, asked him to talk with Jordan about the philosophy behind those Knick teams. "He kindly received my advice," Jackson says wryly.

In his playing days, Jackson was the Woodstock nation's ambassador to the NBA. His jock autobiography was not the story of sexual and athletic conquests, but of a spiritual journey through Christianity and Eastern religions. Now in his mid-40s, Jackson is a bit more the polished and professional basketball man. Still, one's conversation with him flows from the pick and roll to Japanese fiction and back again. When a strategic fine point proves difficult for his listener to understand, Jackson diagrams it, in ink, on the tablecloth in the Chinese restaurant where their conversation is taking place.

Unlike Jerry Krause, the Bulls general manager, Jackson has had no public skirmishes with Jordan. Nor is their relationship as complex and tormented as the one Michael had with Collins, who coached the club from 1986–87 through 1988–89. Instead, Jackson has cultivated a benign detachment from his star. He seems more appreciative than Jordan's previous professional coaches of the paradox posed by Michael's talent.

"Michael Jordan is a coach's dream and a coach's nightmare at the same level," he says. "He knows that there are ways for him to shortcut things and beat the system. So for every incredible thing he does, he does something that defies the rules of the game. Like when the double team comes at him, instead of passing the ball, he *beats* the double team."

"This has its tendency to be good," Jackson says—for Jordan has often carried the Bulls deeper into the postseason than they deserved to go. But it also, Jackson adds, has "its tendency to be ill," because it inhibits his teammates from developing offensive identities of their own.

Jordan is not a selfish player, nor is he incapable of playing within a strict offensive system. He excelled in Dean Smith's system at North Carolina and in Bobby Knight's system on the 1984 U.S. Olympic team. His problem with the Bulls has been learning to trust his teammates. Or, as Jordan might put it, learning *whether* he could trust his teammates.

Early in his career Michael was likely to conclude that he had a better chance of scoring at that moment than anyone else in a Chicago uniform. And he was likely to be right. But in playing the game possession by possession he often wore himself out, played into the hands of specially designed defenses and undercut the self-confidence of his less-accomplished teammates.

Jackson says his project for the 1990–91 season is fielding

a more fully integrated team. To accomplish this he has committed the Bulls to assistant coach Tex Winter's controversial "triple post" offense.

The triple post is a scheme built on the pass rather than the dribble. It makes the ball-handler less an artist and more an analyst, forcing him to read the defense and make the proper pass, rather than simply trying to rocket past his man. One side effect of the new offense is that it is likely to slow Jordan, Pippen and Grant, the three fleet Bulls who favor a more free-flowing style.

If it works, Michael will score his points more easily and finish the season fresher, and the Bulls will become a more well-balanced team. If it doesn't, Jackson will be guilty of putting the game's greatest improvisor into a script-reading straitjacket. He thinks the risk is worth it.

"Ultimately, Michael has to know he can rely on other people to pick up some of the scoring," he says. But before training camp began, Jordan indicated his unwillingness to participate in a season-long experiment with an unproductive offense. "If we are losing, I am going to start shooting," he said. His coach's challenge for the season will be channeling Michael's rage to win, keeping it in check long enough to let the new system take hold.

"Michael is a little bit of a shark," Jackson says. "He's competitive to the extent that he'd like to beat you for your last cent and send you home without your clothes too. Dr. J. was competitive. He wanted to take your last cent. But he wouldn't send you home naked and without your car."

After three seasons of losing to the Pistons, Jackson thinks Jordan will be willing to give the new game plan a chance. At least for a while. As the coach finishes speaking a waiter materializes with a couple of fortune cookies. "Do these count?" Jackson asks.

He cracks a cookie between long, thin fingers and pulls out a fortune that sheds no light on the future of the triple post.

* * * *

More than any player in the NBA, Jordan's performance determines how completely his team will succeed. Even Jackson's plan to make others shoulder some of this burden depends on Michael's willingness to relinquish it. The hunger for information about the man is insatiable, as all his teammates can attest.

"What is it like to play with Michael Jordan?" says Stacy King, the chunky second-year forward. "Not a day goes by I don't get asked that question. It took a lot of pressure off me to do well right away. It takes a lot of pressure off all of us. When we make a mistake, it's like it's okay because he is there. But if he makes a mistake, he has to face the critics and the press."

Playing beside so accomplished a teammate is not without its drawbacks, though. "You are used to being The Man," King says. "Now you are in another environment with someone on your team who is All-Mr. Universe. He gets all the attention and you are on the bottom of the totem pole. Sometimes you feel like you are not part of the team. That's one of the mental challenges. You feel like no one is paying attention to you and you say, 'I'm going to quit.'"

Horace Grant, the Bulls' leading rebounder, worked through similar feelings. "My first season it was a great thrill to answer that question," says Grant on the eve of his fourth. "Now it gets tiring sometimes. The media projects that it is only Michael's show, but we know within ourselves that it is not. And he knows."

And yet one sometimes senses the audience for this and similar remarks made by Grant's teammates are the speakers themselves. "Coming from college, where you were the Michael Jordan, in a way, to here, where you are the 12th man on the bench, it is tough on your ego," Grant acknowledges.

"The question is, 'Is Michael stuck-up?' No, Michael is not stuck-up. Michael is Michael," he says ambiguously. "You accept that he is there. There *is* room for everyone."

Perhaps, but Jordan has definite tastes in teammates and

he is not shy about expressing them. In 1988, when the Bulls traded Charles Oakley—Michael's close friend and the team's best rebounder—for veteran center Bill Cartwright, Jordan criticized the deal publicly and spent much of the 1988–89 season playing as though the capable but awkward center simply wasn't there. After Chicago dropped two quick games to the Pistons in the 1989–90 playoffs he questioned the masculinity of an anonymous teammate whom everyone understood to be Horace Grant. Grant responded with an equally public request to be traded, anywhere, "even New Jersey."

When the Bulls were finally eliminated from those playoffs after seven epic games, Jordan said he hoped the club's management realized that championships weren't won with children, an obvious reference to the disappointing postseason performances of first-round draft choices King and B. J. Armstrong. But, when Jerry Krause traded a pair of draft picks for third-year guard Dennis Hopson, the man he thought would push the club over the top, Michael made it known that he was not impressed with Hopson's game.

Whether these pointed criticisms arouse much by way of indignation in their targets is hard to calculate. After three seasons together, Jordan and Cartwright seem to have established a professional relationship. The storm with Grant passed quickly. Michael's less secure targets have remained silent, understanding the central fact of life on the Bulls. "You have to gain his respect and confidence as a player," says John Paxson, the point guard who has played beside Jordan since the 1985–86 season. "Because this is his organization right now."

That is not precisely true. The man charged with building the Bulls into champions is Jordan's frequent adversary, general manager Jerry Krause. He is, in many ways, the perfect foil for his star—short and round where Jordan is long and lean; secretive where Michael is straightforward; gruff, even rude, where Jordan seems approachable and occasionally warm.

Michael's virtues—a straight-arrow lifestyle, his devotion to children and a willingness to play through pain—are the stuff of marketing campaigns. Krause's virtues—a reverence for age, his fondness for underdogs and a willingness to work around the clock—are less well-known. The general manager, as a result, is on the losing end of his many skirmishes with Jordan, at least where public opinion is concerned. Questioning his intelligence is a favorite pastime of Chicago sports columnists, who have labeled him a "gerbil," a "chowder brain" and a "bobo."

Nor was he among the league's most respected general managers when he took the job seven years ago. "They [basketball insiders] had a perception of me as a short, stocky little guy who didn't dress very well," Krause told the *Chicago Tribune* when his appointment was announced. "I know there were probably a few snickers around the league. I'm not in their little fraternity."

A man in his early 50s, Krause is, in many ways, an anachronism. A former two-sport scout, he flourished in the days before scouting combines made the profession more bureaucratic and efficient, back when a knack for finding talent in the hinterlands was invaluable. One of the talents Krause spotted at an obscure Southern college was a young guard named Earl Monroe.

A Chicago native, Krause worked for the White Sox, the Cleveland Indians, the Oakland A's and the Seattle Mariners, as well as the Baltimore Bullets, the Phoenix Suns, the Los Angeles Lakers and the Philadelphia 76ers. He served a brief and disastrous stint as the Bulls' director of player personnel in 1976, exiting ignominiously during a controversy over whether he had reneged on an offer to make De Paul's Ray Meyer the team's head coach.

In that instance, Krause found himself on the wrong side of a public dispute with one of Chicago's best-loved sports figures, and it cost him the job he had coveted most of his life. But, when White Sox owner Jerry Reinsdorf bought the Bulls in 1985, he offered Krause a second chance. Reinsdorf was no stranger to public vilification. Several years earlier he had fired beloved baseball broadcaster Harry Caray, and has never quite lived it down.

In the six years since he resumed control of the Bulls, Krause has entirely rebuilt the team. Jordan is the only player who was on the roster the day he took over. Krause was named the NBA's Executive of the Year in 1987–88, when the Bulls won 50 games for the first time in over a decade, yet his numerous critics say that Jordan would have already brought Chicago a championship if the general manager had managed to surround him with better players.

His frequent public clashes with Jordan only reinforce the notion that Michael is driving the team forward while he holds it back. Krause realizes it would be counterproductive to return Michael's fire during these disputes, so he never does, seeking instead to underplay any dissension between them. He says things like: "In five years I've seen him mature greatly as a person. The rough edges have been worn off."

And: "We understand each other better now. We talk. I think I like Michael more now than I did then. I've grown to respect his thoughts. He's a bright, bright kid. I don't think people realize how bright he is."

Krause even suggests that the friction between Jordan and him is a by-product of their mutual esteem. "We needle the hell out of each other," he says, and recounts that in 1990, Jordan called him long distance from Comiskey Park to gloat about the $200 he'd just won from Krause by hitting a couple of batting-practice home runs. "You don't needle somebody you don't like," Krause says. "We bet on my weight; he's beaten me a few times on that."

And while he admits that Jordan probably exerts as much influence over personnel moves as any player in the league, Krause wants it understood that he runs the team. "Could he get somebody fired? No," he says. "Could he trade somebody? No. We talk to him. He has influence here, yeah. He has a good, large influence."

The only hint of how Krause feels about the public scourgings he has taken from Jordan surfaces when he speaks of a seven-year-old controversy. After Michael broke his left foot in the third game of the 1985–86 season, Krause and Reinsdorf wanted him to sit out the rest of the schedule. But Jordan insisted on coming back. In the clash of wills that followed, Michael charged that the Bulls' management was losing games on purpose, kissing off the season in hopes of acquiring a better draft pick.

Remembering that incident on the eve of the 1990–91 season, Krause says: "My dad is buried here. He never lived to see me do what I really wanted to do in life. I want to win real bad here. That's why when we were going through that stuff about my not wanting to win it really boiled my ass. Nobody wants to win here more than I do."

With the possible exception of Jordan. And it is Krause's recognition of Michael's desire that keeps the relationship between the two men from rupturing. Jerry Krause respects great natural talent, but he is not enamored of it. His favorite basketball players are not the game's most gifted stars, but its outstanding journeymen, men whose ferocious work habits helped them transcend their physical limitations. His ideal is Jerry Sloan, the former Bulls guard who now coaches the Utah Jazz. It is a measure of his respect for Jordan, a player with all the talent Sloan lacked, that Krause sees a lot of one in the other.

"You set the standards by Sloan," he says, "and Michael is as good or better in practice than Jerry Sloan. Michael gets everything he can out of himself."

An evening practice at the Multiplex. After a long night of ball-handling drills, Jackson breaks the team up into four groups for an intrasquad scrimmage. As if to underline the need for Michael to trust his teammates, he sends Jordan onto the court with three free agents who have no chance of making the team, and one who may earn the privilege of warming the Bulls bench. Jackson matches this marginal bunch against three Chicago starters and two top reserves.

The result is ugly. Jordan's teammates cannot execute the Bulls offense; they are getting hammered on the boards and embarrassed on defense. In a matter of minutes the score is 18–2 and Michael is seething. He calls for the ball again and again, whistles passes into the chests of unsuspecting teammates and makes it clear that these are not his idea of basketball players. The final tally is 20–10.

From a coach's point of view, this is an encouraging development. In Michael's rookie season, coach Kevin Loughery played him on one team until it built an enormous lead, then made him switch sides. More often than not, Jordan's second team won. The fact that he's got tougher teammates this season isn't too comforting to Michael right now, though. He breaks away from the scrubs and sits by himself behind an unused basket, from where the Bulls starters no doubt look like an impressive group of guys.

In the Multiplex weight room, arrayed along the window that overlooks the court, sits a passel of children wearing jackets that proclaim them the Wilson Park gymnastics team. They've spent most of the evening talking with one another about whose autographs they want most, but there is one five-year-old who is having trouble understanding how the transaction works.

"I'm going to give Michael Jordan my autograph," he says.

"Give him your picture too," says an equally confused young friend.

Their older companions roll knowing eyes. Almost teenagers, they are much more sophisticated about how these things work. Several of them wear Bulls' caps or Air Jordan sneakers. Michael's image is on every T-shirt that doesn't say "New Kids on the Block." But it isn't so much Michael the ballplayer they are interested in. They've watched the scrimmage with only mild interest. It is Michael the celebrity whom they love. For them, he is less a colleague of

Magic Johnson and Charles Barkley than of Madonna and the New Kids. The Bulls winning a championship is less important in their minds than Michael's personal progress, which is almost as important as his signing their autograph books and smiling for their cameras.

As practice draws to a close Jordan slips through the glass door that separates fans from players and is quickly surrounded by anxious children bearing ballpoint pens. On another evening their presence might seem an inconvenience. But at the end of this frustrating practice, the ballplayer seems at least momentarily grateful to be the toast of Wilson Park.

4

Before their youngest son became famous, James and Deloris Jordan were in the midst of their own more modest success story. A sharecropper's son from the tiny town of Wallace, North Carolina, James began work as a forklift operator for General Electric, rose to dispatcher and retired as a supervisor. After her children were in school, Deloris took a job at the drive-through window for United Carolina Bank. She worked her way up to head teller and retired as chief of customer service.

Michael Jeffrey was his parents' fourth child and the youngest of their three boys. He was born on February 17, 1963, in Brooklyn, New York, while his father was attending a G.E. training school, but the family soon returned to Wallace. North Carolina's cities had just begun to churn with racial unrest as black residents embraced the tactics of civil disobedience in their struggle for equal rights. Away from the fray in rural Wallace, the Jordans tried to raise their children color-blind and self-assured.

"You just didn't judge people's color," Deloris says.

"Even if people were ignorant and said racial things, you just looked beyond that. Either you could let it affect you or you could struggle against it and move on. And that's what I did."

The children—James Ronald, Deloris, Larry, Michael and Roslyn—grew up "normal like everybody else," she says. "Maybe they couldn't get away with what some kids get away with out in the street. They couldn't do that." But Michael had a knack for finding his way into mischief, and the accounts of his boyhood have the feel of a *Tom Sawyer* send-up. Jordan talked about the funniest, and most frightening, of these episodes during a 1989 appearance on the "Late Night with David Letterman."

Letterman: So you're out one day, you're chopping wood, now is this a true story, you're out one day chopping wood and what happens?

Jordan: Well, I was being bad, first of all. My parents told me not to mess with the axe. So, I'm out chopping wood . . .

Letterman: Did they tell you don't go out there to chop wood?

Jordan: "Don't bother with the axe. You're too young to be playing with the axe. It's a very dangerous instrument."

DL: How old were you?

MJ: I was about, I'd say, five.

DL: Five. Yeah, six is about the cutoff. Six and above you can play with the axe.

MJ: So I was playing with the axe. I don't have any shoes on.

DL: Oooh! Oh my.

MJ: Being from the country you don't wear shoes outside. So I'm chopping little bits and pieces of wood, and being hardheaded, and I accidentally missed the wood and I caught half of my big toe.

DL: So, now you've got an emergency here.

MJ: Well, it was an emergency. Here I am, a little kid, five years old, I'm yelling, screaming, don't know what to do. So I run home and my mother and my father say, "Well, let's go down and see this lady who is supposed to be the neighborhood doctor."

DL: Somebody who knows . . .

MJ: But I never saw the certificate, so I don't know whether she was a doctor or not. But the first thing she says is, "Well, we need to do something to take away the pain." So she pours kerosene over my toe.

DL: Kerosene?

MJ: It took away the pain.

DL: Yeah, I guess it would. So it's amazing that as a young kid, if this had been a worse accident, you might not have even been able to walk and now you're like the greatest basketball player. . . .

MJ: Every time I fall now my father keeps telling me, "You shouldn't have played with that axe."

In 1970, his toe intact, Michael and his family left Wallace for Wilmington, a small port city in the southern part of the state. James built the family a brick split-level home and bought enough land so the children could play ball, ride bicycles and race the secondhand motorcycle that would one day pitch 13-year-old Michael into a ditch.

Wilmington was a racially charged environment when the Jordans arrived. A now-celebrated civil rights case—the Wilmington 10—had split the community black against white. The schools were still not fully desegregated and Laney High, the integrated school that Michael would attend, had yet to be built.

The Jordans' lives in those days were organized around their children's sports. "It was baseball, football, track," Deloris says. "They were always saying, 'Hurry, Momma, we're gonna be late for the game.' And I was always saying, 'No, honey, you're not gonna be late for the game.' Not only with Michael, but with all my children."

With such a large brood, the family's home quickly became a meeting place and playground for neighborhood kids, one of whom was Adolph Shiver. Deloris Jordan says Michael was the most outgoing of her children, "the one who liked people more." He was also the biggest handful.

"If there was something to be tried he was the one to try it," she says. "If someone needed to be disciplined more, he was the one who needed it. He was going to test you to the end."

Jordan learned about the world by challenging those closest to him. It was a secure if contentious way of learning his own limits and it allowed him to give full range to his competitiveness without risking any real damage. In sports he challenged his brother Larry, who was one year older than he. In academics he competed with his sister Roslyn, who was one year younger. In other matters, he challenged his parents.

"Michael was always . . . testing us," James Jordan told Red Kerr. "If we told him the stove was hot, don't touch, he'd touch it. If there was a wet-paint sign, he'd touch the paint to see if it was wet.

"All the kids had chores and sometimes Michael would get into one of his moods and purposely mess them up. That used to drive us crazy. . . . One time I found out that he was taking his allowance and paying other kids to do his chores. That really got me."

Jordan admits he wasn't much for physical labor. "I was lazy about some things," he said. "I never got into mowing the lawn or doing hard jobs." While his siblings worked part-time cutting tobacco during the harvest season, Michael strained his back on the first day of work and never returned.

"One summer my mom said, 'You just got to work,' and she got me a job as a maintenance man in a hotel," he said. "I just couldn't do it. I could not keep regular hours. It just wasn't me. From then on, I never, ever had another job." Not that Michael was likely to have been much of a maintenance man. "If you hand him a wrench, he wouldn't know what to turn with it," his mother says.

The onset of adolescence only made Michael's life more difficult. Jordan was suspended three times in his freshman year of high school: once for leaving the school grounds to practice his jump shot; once for squishing a Popsicle on the head of a girl who called him a "nigger"; and once for fighting with a boy who erased the baselines he was assiduously drawing on the high school infield.

"If there was a most likely to succeed, I was the least," he told David Breskin of *Gentlemen's Quarterly*.

By the ninth grade, Jordan had developed the mocking sense of humor that he shares today primarily with close friends. Bill Billingsly, his ninth-grade baseball coach at D.C. Virgo School, remembers one road trip on which he, a first-time bus driver, had wedged the team bus into a circular drive that was surrounded by a large wooden fence.

"Michael said, 'I'll help you, Coach. I'll help you. Back up,'" Billingsly says. "So I backed up and kept backing up and—bam! There was lumber everywhere. And Michael was laughing and saying, 'I'm sorry, Coach. I'm sorry.'"

Billingsly, who is a doctoral candidate in American history at the University of California at Irvine, says that there was an unspoken understanding in Wilmington that baseball was a white sport and basketball a black one. The Babe Ruth League baseball field was in a white neighborhood where many black boys were afraid to go, he says.

Jordan stuck with the sport longer than most and was one of only three or four blacks on the ninth-grade team. "He had a real love-hate thing with the white kids," Billingsly says. "He got along with them, but he wasn't afraid to stand up for himself. He didn't take anything from them."

Michael was not so assertive with the opposite sex. He was sensitive about the jut of his ears and what friends referred to as his "little boy" haircut. "A lot of guys picked on me, and they would do it in front of the girls," he told Diane Sawyer on "60 Minutes." "They would joke about my haircut and the way I played with my tongue out and just different things. And the girls would, kind of, they would laugh at that, and right then, I was dead. I couldn't get a date with anybody.''

This led Jordan to become one of the few boys studying home economics at Laney High School, which he entered in the 10th grade. His domestic abilities have been chronicled by ''60 Minutes'' as well as *People* magazine, each of which captured him running a vacuum or sorting his laundry. While these stories burnished his image as a regular guy—and a sensitive, new-age regular guy at that—it wasn't publicity that was on his mind when he signed up for cooking classes.

''I always thought I was going to be a bachelor,'' he said. ''No one would marry me. I would end up doing my cooking, my dishwashing, my clothes washing, my dusting.'' He doesn't do as much sewing as he used to, Jordan added, but he's still capable of a ''quick hem'' when the need arises.

Like many young men, Jordan felt most comfortable when playing, thinking or talking about sports. He had been a gifted Little League pitcher, throwing two no-hitters before moving on to greater triumphs in Wilmington's Babe Ruth League. ''My favorite childhood memory, my greatest accomplishment was when I got the Most Valuable Player award when my team won the state baseball championship,'' he told Sam Smith of the *Chicago Tribune*. ''That was the first big thing I accomplished in my life, and you always remember the first. I remember I batted over .500, hit five home runs in seven games and pitched a one-hitter to get us into the championship game.''

Michael's greatest friend and toughest opponent in those years was his brother Larry. Larry worked harder at athletics than Michael did, and he possessed a startling leaping ability. His younger brother revered him. On the Laney High School basketball team Michael requested number 23, because it was roughly half the 45 that Larry wore.

This fraternal regard, however, was not immediately evident to James and Deloris as they watched the two boys trying to pound each other into the dirt of their backyard basketball court. In these initial showdowns, Larry doled out defeats that often sent his brother into a fury. The games became increasingly heated during the younger Jordan's sophomore year, when Michael sprouted to 5-foot-11 while Larry remained a shade under 5-foot-8.

In those contests, many of which ended in fights, Michael developed perhaps the essential element in his personality: a passion for competition. Jordan hates to play on the losing side in a Bulls scrimmage. He once stormed out of a practice because he felt former coach Doug Collins was not keeping score fairly. However casual a game might seem, Jordan pursues victory relentlessly and accepts almost any challenge. This can seem a bit obsessive, a bit juvenile at times, but Michael regards competition as an unmixed blessing. For him it has been the key to self-discovery.

Jordan's fierce but loving rivalry with Larry allowed him to give this hunger for victory full reign. Because they were brothers, Michael knew that regardless of what happened on the court, their bond would endure. The relationship facilitated the most heated sort of competition, but at the same time it negated competition's most destructive effects. Michael relied so heavily on this bond that he created another one like it in college.

The rewards of these backyard clashes with Larry were not as immediate as Michael might have hoped. As even the casual Jordan fan knows, Michael was cut from the Laney varsity during his sophomore year by coach Fred Lynch, who kept Jordan's taller friend Leroy Smith. "He [Lynch] works at my [summer basketball] camp now," Michael told David Letterman. "I give him all the dirty jobs."

Jordan was angry and embarrassed to be cut, but, in hindsight, it was one of the best things that ever happened to him. The embarrassment strengthened his resolve and drove him to wake at six each morning for practice sessions with junior varsity coach Clifton Herring. Beyond that, his demotion to the jayvee became an integral part of the Jordan legend. It is the fall against which his rise is measured, the test in which his character was proven. It has also been sold as the experience that allows Michael to identify with discouraged adolescents everywhere. In his latest video, "Michael Jordan's Playground," Jordan counsels a young man who has undergone a similar disappointment and helps him turn his life around.

Even in Jordan's case, however, luck was of the essence. After averaging almost 25 points a game for the Laney jayvee, Jordan grew to 6-foot-3½ when the season was over. That summer he began attending the basketball clinics at which he'd eventually make his name.

The Jordans were happy to support their son's enthusiasm, but they were unsure where his obsession with basketball would lead. "Up to that point," his mother says, "just like any other parents, we were worrying about how we were going to pay tuition." But slowly, word began to get around that Jordan might become a player yet. He enjoyed an impressive junior season playing forward with his best friend Adolph on the point. Still, college scouts were not exactly falling over one another to get a look at him.

Jordan was a late bloomer by athletic standards. Many top basketball prospects are contacted by college recruiters before their voices change, but Michael was all but ignored outside North Carolina. He didn't even make a list of the nation's top 300 college prospects published before his senior year in high school.

The lack of attention, though painful at the time, had beneficial side effects. Jordan was spared the pressure that accompanies youthful athletic acclaim. He had no reason to imagine himself a star, and felt little temptation to presume his athleticism would excuse poor grades or bad conduct. His late athletic development afforded Michael the luxury of a normal adolescence.

In the summer before his senior year, Jordan attended a

camp conducted by Bobby Cremins at Appalachian State University. Cremins, now the head coach at Georgia Tech, is normally an astute judge of talent, yet he never even realized Jordan was in his program. When Michael broke the news to him a few years later, the coach was incredulous.

After Cremins's clinic Jordan moved on to Chapel Hill, where Dean Smith, a Carolina institution, offered the most prestigious high school basketball camp in the area. Michael's suitemate there was Buzz Peterson. The two boys played the same position and played it as well as anyone in the state. Over the next two years, they would compete—first for statewide high school honors and then for a starting spot on the Carolina varsity. In the process these opponents became extremely close friends.

The local experts thought Peterson was a better college prospect. He was headed for Howie Garfinkel's Five Star Camp in Pittsburgh, where the nation's best high school players were drilled by a top-notch coaching staff and evaluated by scouts from almost every major college program in the country. Playing well there was the surest way to win a scholarship.

Jordan had not even been invited to the Five Star Camp. "No one was recruiting him at that time," remembers Brendan Malone, the Detroit Pistons assistant who was then on the camp staff. "The only people who knew about him were in North Carolina."

One of those people was Roy Williams, the Kansas University coach who was then one of Smith's assistants. He liked Jordan enough to recommend Michael for the camp in Pittsburgh. And on the strength of Williams's word, the Five Star people also offered Jordan a job waiting tables to help pay his expenses.

Michael was not invited to the first of the camp's three week-long sessions. That one was reserved for top college prospects. But Jordan made himself known pretty quickly nonetheless. "His ability to put the ball on the floor and

take it to the basket really jumped out at you," Malone
remembers.

"He just steps out on the court and he's like playing a
different game," camp official Tom Konchalski told Barry
Jacobs of the *New York Times*. Jordan leapt so high before
releasing his jump shot, Konchalski said, that "it was like
there was no defender."

Michael excelled against some of the most sought-after
young players in the country and was named Most Valuable
Player two weeks in a row. He also realized for the first time
that he might have a future in the game. "It was as though
somebody had tapped me on the shoulder with a magic
wand and said, 'You must emerge as somebody—somebody
to be admired, to achieve big things,'" he said.

The camp also gave him a chance to deepen his friendship
with Peterson. "We talked on the phone all the time after
that," Peterson says. "And we made a commitment to each
other that we would go to the same school."

Jordan had always been a North Carolina State fan. He
particularly admired David Thompson, the phenomenal leaper
who led the Wolfpack to a national championship in 1973.
"Michael [tried] to emulate David Thompson, especially
how David used to leap," his father said. "I remember
seeing Michael in the yard practicing the kind of dunks he
saw Thompson do on TV." But North Carolina State was in
the midst of a coaching change and Jordan became uncertain
about his opportunities there.

Kenneth McLaurin, the principal at Laney, was urging
Jordan to consider the Air Force Academy, but Michael had
made up his mind to play for a basketball powerhouse. He
wrote to UCLA expressing an interest in the school but
never received a reply. "I know he had a strong interest in
Virginia," Fred Whitfield says. "I think he made up his
mind he wanted to play with Ralph [Sampson, the Virginia
center], Buck Williams [the University of Maryland forward]
or [James] Worthy at North Carolina. But Buck was coming
out [to enter the NBA draft]."

Jordan wrote to officials at Virginia and received a standard undergraduate application. The school never sent anyone to see him play. New opportunities, however, kept presenting themselves.

"Senior year we had people at the door," Deloris Jordan remembers. "It was sort of scary and we had a lot of problems figuring out which of the schools were looking at him as a human being and not as a basketball machine." The family visited Maryland, South Carolina and NC State. They also returned to the UNC campus in Chapel Hill.

Deloris Jordan had always been a Carolina fan, but her son could not abide the Tar Heels. "Growing up, I hated North Carolina," he says, "My mom liked Phil Ford, but I couldn't stand him or any of those UNC guys." Jordan, however, felt his options dwindling. He also found his visit to the Carolina campus more enjoyable than he'd expected.

Michael says he saw UNC "as a student, not as a recruit," which is probably about half right. However admirable and academically oriented the Carolina program might be, it is not above going all out to impress a coveted recruit. And if anyone was ignorant as to why the school coveted Jordan, he let them know in a hurry during his two-day visit to campus in the fall of his senior year.

"The first time I saw him was when he came for his visit," says Ken Stewart, a lawyer in Raleigh, North Carolina, who was then a freshman. "There was a court behind the dorm. He came out doing 360s, alley oops, slamming over people, and that was the first we had heard of him."

"Here was this guy doing stuff we'd never seen before and calling attention to himself," says Darryl Summey, who played on the Tar Heels junior varsity.

What struck Jordan's parents most about UNC was what Mrs. Jordan called its "family atmosphere." She was also impressed by the way Dean Smith recruited her son. "We talked education, we didn't talk basketball," she says. "He didn't come in making a lot of promises. He said, 'If you work hard and qualify academically we'll see about your coming onto our basketball team.' "

There was really never much doubt that Michael would wind up on the basketball team. Pushed by competition with his sister Ros, the once-lackluster student had finished high school with a B average. There was also not much chance that Carolina would keep him on scholarship if he didn't make the squad. But Smith's emphasis on academics convinced the Jordans that Carolina was interested in their son as something more than just an athlete.

Michael had other motivations. He'd heard talk around town that no one from Wilmington had ever succeeded in a Division I athletic program. People said he'd probably spend four years on the Carolina bench and then come back home looking for a job. This had the effect on Jordan that a waving cape has on a bull.

In November, 1980, Michael announced his decision to attend Chapel Hill. His sister Roslyn, graduating after just three years in high school, was going to join him. The day that the news broke, the Jordans got their first taste of what lay ahead. "Reporters were standing on our patio refusing to leave until we came out to do an interview," Deloris says. "It took time for us to adjust to people barging in."

Meanwhile, in Asheville, Peterson was in the process of reneging on his agreement with Michael. "I about broke the promise," he says. "I made a verbal commitment, in private, to the University of Kentucky. Michael called me up and said, 'Hey, I thought we were going to the same school.' I said, 'Yeah, but Mike, Kentucky is nice, you ought to go up there and take a look.' " Peterson, however, ultimately submitted to Jordan's persuasion—helped considerably by a recruiting visit from Smith.

Now an assistant coach at North Carolina State, Peterson occasionally looks back on his decision and wonders if he made the right choice. "Here I was committing to a school with a guy who played the same position as me," he says. "I guess you could say it wasn't a good decision in terms of playing time. I mean, I knew he was pretty good, but I didn't think he was going to be *that* good. I remember we were in Washington for the McDonald's [high school all-star] game and he didn't even start." Besides, Peterson had edged Jordan out for state high school Player of the Year honors.

At Chapel Hill, the two became roommates and developed a relationship much like the one Michael had forged with Larry. It was a bond based on admiration and competition. "We would go at each other on the court, but off the court we were the best of friends," Peterson says. "I'd go down to Wilmington to his house one weekend, he'd come to my house the next."

The basketball program that the two entered is one of the most distinguished in college sports. "The Carolina Corporation," some people called it, or "The IBM of College Basketball." Smith's deliberate, team-oriented offense bends the will of the individual to the demands of the system, no matter how brilliant the individual might be. After Jordan began tearing up the NBA a new version of an old joke asked: "Who's the only man who could hold Michael Jordan under 20 points a game?" Answer: "Dean Smith."

But the coach's offense has been copied nearly as often as it has been criticized, and Smith has turned out NBA stars ranging from Billy Cunningham, Charlie Scott and Walter Davis to Jordan, James Worthy and Sam Perkins. More importantly, he has earned a reputation as an outstanding moral influence. His players attend nightly study halls, abide by a strict code of discipline and are urged to get involved in community activities.

Smith's detractors say that despite his high-toned image he is as capable as the next coach of embracing an academically questionable junior college transfer like Bob McAdoo or a bad actor like J. R. Reid. What cannot be disputed, however, is that Smith's system works wonderfully for most of the young men involved. His former players, almost all of whom graduate, revere him. They speak of playing for him as one of the high points of their lives. Many keep in close touch long after they've left Chapel Hill. They return in large numbers for reunions and charity games.

Carolina's emphasis on team unity is especially beneficial for freshmen. "They don't let them be alone," Fred Whitfield says. "Somebody is always coming by to see how you are, and I think that helped Mike mature a lot. And coming onto a team that already had Worthy and Perkins, there was no pressure on him. He just cruised right through."

Smith knew Jordan was talented when he recruited him, but he wasn't quite sure how talented until the first week of practice. During a one-on-one drill, the coach realized that "we didn't have anybody who could guard him." Michael played his way onto the starting five during the fall practices—where he also earned a reputation for talking trash.

The upperclassmen voted Jordan the team's cockiest freshman and saddled him with the cumbersome task of carrying the film projector when the team was on the road. Peterson was forced to lug the somewhat lighter boom box. "It took them a while to get used to Mike," Peterson says.

It took Buzz a little while to get used to Mike, too. "Times when we were together I'd say to myself, 'I can't live with this guy.' Sometimes I'd say, 'Why do I have to listen to this guy talk and run his mouth all the time?' When we got on the court he'd tell you, 'I'm better than you. I can do this better than you.' Sometimes you hate to hear that, but you've got to have that if you are going to be a good athlete."

But Peterson couldn't help being impressed by his roommate's work ethic. "He was very conscious to keep up with his work," he says. "He was conscious of how his room looked. Everything was in its place."

Jordan's Carolina coming-out party took place on December 3, 1981, as the top-ranked Tar Heels beat ninth-ranked Tulsa, 78–70. "Freshman Michael Jordan came out of his self-imposed shell and thrilled the Carmichael [Auditorium] crowds with his awesome skills," wrote Al Featherson of the *Durham Sun*. Jordan shot 11 of 15 from the floor for 22 points, and added four steals and a blocked shot. After three games he'd committed just one turnover and was shooting 65 percent from the floor.

His veteran teammates were elated with the rookie's performance. "Michael is everything you see of him," said point guard Jimmy Black. "He can do it all: score, play defense, lead the team, rebound, block shots. What else is there?"

"Honestly, I've never seen anybody pick up the game so fast," Worthy said. "Michael just doesn't repeat mistakes."

"He's thinking all the time on the floor," said Matt Doherty, a sophomore forward on the team. "I tell you, he is going to be something awesome before he leaves this place."

Some writers compared the high-jumping Jordan to David Thompson, others to flashy former Carolina point guard Phil Ford. "I had an edge," Jordan said, explaining why he fit so well into the Carolina scheme. "We ran this system in high school, so I didn't have much to pick up when I got here."

What he had picked up was a deepening sense of self-confidence. "When I got here I thought everybody was a superstar and I would be the low man," he told Featherson after a 20-point performance in mid-January. "After the first game I realized I was as good as everybody else."

"You could see him becoming more sure of himself in everything he did," says James Worthy, reflecting on that season after nine years in the NBA. "Each game he gained a little more respect. He was a significant contributor, the third man to come to behind Sam [Perkins] and me."

Peterson, meanwhile, was spending a good deal of time on the Carolina bench. That hadn't impeded his friendship with Jordan, though. By mid-season the two were so close they were wearing each other's clothes. Sometimes, dressing in a hurry, Michael would swipe the sports coat Peterson was planning to wear, and Buzz would find himself rummaging through Jordan's closet for an alternative. "I have a favorite pair of shoes that have been resoled about three times," Peterson says, "but I have to wear them with a pad because Mike stretched them out so much."

Despite his friendship with Jordan, Peterson was finding the adjustment to college difficult. He felt frustrated on the basketball court and depressed about the failing health of his favorite aunt. Late in the season, he went AWOL.

"I'd had a call from my sister the night before," he says. "My aunt hadn't passed away yet but I had the feeling—we were close—that she was going to and I just, a young guy, just took off and went up there. And Mike was the only one who knew. I left him a note saying she was awfully sick and I thought she might die, 'Don't worry. Love ya, Buzz.'

"I left in a hurry, so my side of the room was a real mess, junk all over the place. And when I came back, my sweaters, everything, my whole side of the room was neat."

In the final two weeks of the regular season, Jordan also began to struggle a bit. He went into a 28-for-62 shooting slump, and came down with a throat problem so severe that doctors considered removing his tonsils. On the eve of the Atlantic Coast Conference tournament, however, they decided against surgery, and allowed Michael to play in the next day's game.

It was a fortunate turn of events for Jordan and the Tar Heels, because if Michael had been hospitalized that day, Carolina might never have won its championship. The following afternoon the would-be patient saved his cold-shooting teammates from elimination, tossing in 18 points as the Heels defeated Georgia Tech, 55–39. Their winning streak continued through the ACC tournament and into the NCAA finals.

More than 61,000 fans filled the Superdome in New Orleans for the showdown between Carolina and Georgetown, a team led by Patrick Ewing, the imposing freshman center. Millions more sat in front of television sets around the country to watch the primetime matchup between Smith and

John Thompson, two of the most respected coaches in the college game. It was a perfect night to make a name for oneself.

Jordan later claimed that he had a premonition before the game, a vague notion that he would take the decisive shot. Yet he played nervously at first and was not a major factor in the opening half. With time winding down, though, Michael evinced for the first time the proclivity for late-game heroics that would soon become his trademark.

Jordan scored three of the Heels' last five baskets. He set up the other two with a steal and a rebound. Twice in the last five minutes, Michael pulled down missed Carolina free throws, allowing his team to maintain possession with the game on the line. His arcing left-hander over Ewing's outstretched fingertips gave the Heels a 61–58 lead with 2:30 to play. Georgetown cut the lead to one, and that is where matters stood when Matt Doherty's free throw rattled off the rim with 1:19 to play.

Ewing grabbed the rebound and the Hoyas broke downcourt. Smith watched from the bench as Georgetown tested his team's defense, working for the shot that would again deny him an NCAA tournament championship. In 24 years of coaching, his Carolina teams had been to the Final Four five times. They'd played for the title twice. They'd never won.

The Hoyas worked the ball to Sleepy Floyd, their All-American guard. He grabbed it near the top of the key, reversed his dribble, spun by Jimmy Black and flashed into the lane. With just under a minute to play, Floyd lofted a soft jump shot that gave Georgetown a 62–61 lead.

The Heels jogged back upcourt and passed the ball deliberately around the perimeter of Georgetown's zone. With 32 seconds remaining, Smith called time-out. He knew that Thompson would gear his defense to stopping James Worthy, who was in the midst of a brilliant 28-point performance. But the Hoyas would also sag back on Sam Perkins. Realizing his best scorers might well be blanketed, Smith decided that Jordan should take the last shot.

Michael was the team's third-highest scorer, but he was also the only freshman in the starting five. The shot, a mid-range jumper from the left wing, would not be an easy one, especially under this kind of pressure. But with the 7-foot-1 Ewing looming in the lane, Smith thought Jordan might be his best bet. "Make it, Michael," he said softly as the team broke its huddle.

Jimmy Black inbounded the ball to Jordan. The two Carolina guards played catch for a few moments, but the Hoyas reacted briskly to each pass and Jordan was too well-guarded to shoot. With the clock ticking down, Black, on the right wing, snapped the ball to Doherty cutting up the middle to the top of the key. Doherty returned it just as quickly. Black dribbled once to his left and heaved a cross-court pass to Jordan.

Michael was open when he caught it. Two defenders rushed toward him, but Jordan knew neither could reach him in time. Seventeen feet from the basket, he launched his shot. It was "a rainbow," he remembers, arcing high above the Superdome floor and snapping through the cords of the net with 16 seconds left to play. Carolina led, 63–62.

Georgetown's last chance to win the game disappeared when Hoya guard Fred Brown mistakenly passed the ball to Worthy. Moments later the game was over and a dozen narratives climaxed at once: Smith and his title; Worthy, the tournament's MVP, was headed for the NBA; Ewing, one of the most dominant collegians in history, had lost in the first of his three championship appearances.

While each of these stories was compelling, the evening, for reasons not then obvious, belonged to Jordan. Michael had scored 16 points and grabbed nine rebounds. His shot not only decided the game, it helped shape his life. "That's when everything started," he said. "That's when Michael Jordan started to get his respect."

Three seasons earlier, an insecure high school kid, he'd been cut from the Laney varsity. Three seasons later, a newly minted folk hero, he would become the NBA's

Rookie of the Year. "After that [the shot] his confidence just shot up and he just grew," Peterson says.

The winning shot put Jordan on the cover of the Chapel Hill phone book. It initiated a new and more public phase in his life. But Michael began this new chapter in an old, familiar way. Two days after he hit The Shot, Jordan was back in Woollen Gym at 3:30 playing in a pickup game.

5

If one could invest in a ballplayer the way one can invest in a corporation, the summer of 1982 would have been the time to get in on the ground floor of Jordan, Inc. That, at least, was the opinion of the inside traders who played against Michael in Woollen Gymnasium in the months after he sank The Shot.

Jordan's teams held the court for hours at a time that summer in pickup games against some of the most illustrious players that Carolina had produced. "He took on everybody," Darryl Summey remembers. "Al Wood, Dudley Bradley. Bradley was supposed to be a defensive ace, but Michael took him outside and then took him inside. He could pretty much do what he wanted in those games. He just about had carte blanche."

"It was always expected that his team would win the game if he had any help at all," Ken Stewart says.

Jordan's leaping ability and his explosive moves to the basket were what awed his peers. But Dean Smith, who knew Jordan could be electrifying, now saw that he could be complete. The difference between the Michael of freshman season and the Michael who emerged from those summer games was, Smith thought, "like night and day."

"Defense, confidence, rebounding, position, passing, ball-handling," the coach said, ticking off the areas in which Jordan had improved. "And growing"—for Michael, who had been almost 6-foot-5 as a freshman, was now nearly 6-foot-6.

Smith, of course, had had a hand in this transformation. He saw that despite an abundance of talent, Michael's game still needed work. Defense was Jordan's principal weakness. While his feet were quick, his concentration was weak and he was frequently caught out of position.

Michael's ball-handling needed a bit of polishing too, Smith thought. Jordan drove to the basket more swiftly than any player in Carolina history. In his freshman season ACC referees often wrongly called him for traveling because they'd never seen a first step so quick. But sometimes Michael took foolish chances with the ball, and he didn't protect it well in the open court.

Finally, for a shooting guard or small forward, Jordan's jump shot was not quite accurate enough.

Michael spent long hours that summer in ball-handling drills. He played the point in pickup games, and fired up countless jumpers, seeking to tame that sometimes uncertain shot. None of this changed the essence of his game. Altitude and agility would always be Michael's trademarks. Turnovers were almost a given at the speed he played. And the jump shot would remain somewhat erratic until his fourth season with the Bulls. But Smith had begun the long process of rounding Jordan into the rare player who could excel at any facet of the game.

The rewards were immediate. Carolina whipped Syracuse in its first test of the season, and Michael used the opportunity to flash his new defensive intensity. He blocked one shot from behind the shooter and caught another blocked shot while still in midair. That second feat came against the

Orangemen's Tony Bruin, whose reputation as a leaper, until that moment, had rivaled Michael's own.

Jordan became so good so fast that Carolina followers, guardians of a long, rich basketball tradition, began to speak of his talents in historical terms. "It's time to give Michael Jordan his due," wrote Al Featherson in the *Durham Sun*. "North Carolina's amazing sophomore swingman can't hide behind Dean Smith's team concept any longer. Quite simply he's become the best all-around player in college basketball. Jordan is the most talented player North Carolina or the ACC has ever seen."

These comments were occasioned by the 32 points and seven rebounds that Jordan amassed in just 23 minutes in the Heels' 103–82 victory over Duke. Each subsequent Carolina triumph seemed engineered to showcase a new facet of Michael's game. A week after the Duke victory, he hit six of seven three-pointers while pouring in 39 points in a 72–65 triumph over Georgia Tech.

Three times that season Jordan saved the Heels from defeat by scoring off last-minute steals. The most meaningful of those came against Ralph Sampson and the Virginia Cavaliers, who were favored to win the ACC championship. Virginia led 63–60 in that late-season matchup when Jordan scored four straight points to give Carolina its biggest victory of the season.

A few nights later the Heels won a share of the regular-season title, beating Duke 105–81 behind 32 points from Jordan. "There are a lot of players on the playgrounds in New York who have the moves and the abilities," said New York native Matt Doherty. "Michael has all those and he has the smarts to go with it."

While Jordan's sophomore heroics made his reputation, they also underscored how frequently the '82–'83 Carolina team teetered on the brink of defeat. Without James Worthy, this squad was not as offensively potent as the one that preceded it. North Carolina State bounced it from the ACC tournament, 91–84. Two weeks later the Heels were upset by Georgia in the third round of the NCAAs. The following day, Jordan was back in Woollen Gym, practicing his shot.

Even in defeat, Michael had to consider the season a success. He'd extended his shooting range, become the team's leader and won 12 of Carolina's coveted defensive player of the game awards, an honor he'd never received as a freshman. His performance was not lost on *The Sporting News,* which named him its College Player of the Year.

That summer Jordan starred on the United States Pan-American team that won a gold medal in Caracas. He says it was this taste of international travel that helped him decide on a major in cultural geography. It seemed an almost useful field of study for a young man who sensed that he might soon be touring the country—or at least its airports, arenas and hotels—as a professional ballplayer.

These were wonderful times for Jordan in Chapel Hill. Popular, confident and relaxed, he moved easily among the diverse groups of students on the Carolina campus. He kept a busy social calendar, but virtually abstained from the carousing and alcoholic initiation that play such a big part in many students' college experience. "He'd have a beer now and then but basically he hated it," Peterson says. "Sometimes what he'd like was a cocktail-type drink, but not that often."

Peterson says Jordan had "a steady girlfriend that he spent a lot of time with." But mostly Michael "stayed free," spending his off-hours at the Pump House playing video games, the student union playing pool, or in his dorm room, *deep* in card and board games—so deep that he once threw Monopoly money at Peterson when it became clear that Buzz was about to win the game.

"He was the most competitive person I'd ever been around," says Kenny Smith, the former Tar Heel point guard who now plays for the Houston Rockets. "Playing pool, playing Ping-Pong, playing video games. He'd put sweat into it. He'd be perspiring and arguing over every point. It made it fun."

The movies were a somewhat less contentious experience. "He'd see any movie," Peterson says. "Unless there was a snake in it. Anything with a snake in it, he's out of the movie theater. We one time talked him into seeing this movie *Venom*. He was out of there in five minutes—even though he must have paid four bucks, or whatever it was back then."

On the basketball court, the leadership of the new Tar Heel team now fell to Jordan and Carolina's other All-American, Sam Perkins. It was not the sort of role toward which either gravitated. Perkins is easygoing, reflective and not much of a rah-rah guy. Jordan, sensitive about all the publicity he received, did not want to set himself above his teammates. Being one of the guys was important to him. It meant people wouldn't take his playful verbal abuse too seriously. Jordan's ideal team, then as now, would consist of five equally intense, equally knowledgeable players who had little need for leadership.

This was an issue that would surface throughout his professional career, as first Doug Collins and then Phil Jackson would urge him to become a more vocal leader, particularly during the postseason. In college Jordan dealt with this challenge in a quiet way. "He became an example and not really a critic," Kenny Smith says. "I think that was his biggest asset as a player."

Always in excellent physical condition, Michael reported to practice both stronger and faster. He had added 12 pounds of muscle to his shoulders on the Heels' weight-training program and had cut half a second from his time in the 40-yard dash, covering the distance in 4.3 seconds. Thus equipped, he proceeded to terrorize his teammates.

"After practice junior year he would write on the board after one-on-one drills, 'Dunked on Buzz twice. Dunked on Kenny twice. Dunked on Joe [Wolfe] twice,'" Peterson says. "He'd let you know about it."

Carolina was tabbed as the top team in the country that fall. Jordan and Perkins graced the cover of *Sports Illustrated*,

Michael proclaiming with a raised index finger that the Heels were number one. "Jordan . . . emerged last season—only his second on the varsity—as merely the finest all-around amateur player in the world," wrote Curry Kirkpatrick.

"The prevailing opinion always has been that Oscar Robertson and Jerry West are the two best all-time guards," former Golden State Warriors guard Jeff Mullins told Kirkpatrick. "But we may have to change that view because of Jordan."

Duly burdened, Michael began the season in a deep shooting slump, the product of trying to meet such great expectations. Fans were quick to wonder what was wrong with Jordan, and Michael says the scrutiny he received then helped prepare him for the media onslaught of his rookie season in Chicago. But Jordan righted himself quickly enough, and the Tar Heels retained their top ranking throughout the first half of the 1983–84 campaign.

The turning point of Carolina's season came on January 29 in an otherwise uneventful game against LSU. Late in the second half, the Tigers' John Tudor hammered Kenny Smith from behind on a breakaway. As Smith crashed to the floor Jordan jumped Tudor, pushing him into the stands before being restrained. Smith, meanwhile, was rushed to the hospital with a facial gash that required six stitches and a broken left wrist that would keep him out of the lineup until the ACC tournament.

His absence was noticed two weeks later, as the Heels suffered their first defeat in 22 games, dropping a 65–64 decision to unranked Arkansas. Carolina recouped quickly, however, rolling impressively through the rest of the regular season. Its most convincing victory came on February 19 against a tough Maryland team, and once again, Jordan nearly came to blows with an opponent.

This time his target was big Ben Coleman, the Terrapin forward. Maryland had forged a 53–52 lead with 11 minutes remaining when Coleman landed a flagrant elbow on Matt

Doherty. Jordan charged across the court to confront him, and the two had to be separated by teammates.

Michael seemed energized by the incident. In the next eight minutes he scored 13 points as the Heels breezed to a 78–63 victory. "You know when the game is on the line, he is going to do something," teammate Brad Daugherty said. "Michael is so competitive it's ridiculous."

A few nights later, Carolina defeated Duke in double overtime to complete a perfect 14–0 conference campaign. The last team to achieve that feat had been the 1973–74 North Carolina State squad that David Thompson led to a national championship. Similar glories were expected from the Tar Heels. "Nobody's road to [the Final Four in] Seattle seems better paved than UNC's," wrote *Durham Sun* columnist Frank Dascenzo.

But the difficulty Carolina had bumping off Duke in the last game was a warning of the collapse to come. The Heels often had trouble scoring in Dean Smith's deliberate offense, and Kenny Smith's return to the lineup only exacerbated the problem. He played a more aggressive, up-tempo game than the guards who had replaced him, and the team seemed badly out of synch. On March 10, the Duke club that had taken the Heels to double overtime finally prevailed, knocking them off in the conference semifinals, 77–75. Upstart Maryland claimed the ACC title that year behind another impressive young talent, sophomore Len Bias.

Carolina's NCAA campaign was similarly brief. In the third round, the heavily favored Heels faced a 21–8 Indiana team at the Omni in Atlanta. Jordan said later that he had a bad feeling about the game. For reasons he was never able to identify, he shot poorly in the Omni throughout his college career. But his vague misgivings were nothing compared to the anxiety that gripped Indiana forward Dan Dakich.

The day before the game, Dakich learned that Hoosiers coach Bobby Knight had assigned him to guard Jordan. "I promptly went to my room and threw up," Dakich said.

Sufficiently steadied, Dakich proceeded to play the game of his life. He harassed Michael into a 6-of-14 shooting performance and forced four turnovers. Jordan fouled out with 1:11 to play and Indiana, shooting 64 percent from the floor, held on for a 72–68 victory.

The powerful Tar Heels had lost two of their last three games, bringing Jordan's magnificent college career to a premature close. The collapse of this Carolina team was a sign to many that Smith's system was too restrictive, that it kept individual stars from leading the team on a postseason tear. That issue would be debated for years on the Carolina campus. Meanwhile, Michael and his family had other things on their minds.

Throughout that spring the Jordans wrestled with a difficult decision. The parents who had once worried about affording Michael's tuition now confronted the issues raised by his stardom. Should he remain at Carolina for his senior year, or should he declare himself eligible for the NBA draft? Perhaps he was on the verge of a professional career that would be lucrative beyond their imagining. Or perhaps he would become another of the many young players who concentrated on athletics to the exclusion of academics and were left unprepared for life after basketball.

Michael's mother wanted him to stay in school. There was something about the suddenness of her son's success that Deloris Jordan did not quite trust. She loved the "family atmosphere" at UNC, was proud of the way other players gravitated to her son and enjoyed having members of the team drive down for the weekend and stay at the house. She also had misgivings about all the time professional athletes spent on the road.

More than that, Mrs. Jordan still believed what she had told Michael when she'd urged him to attend a college where he would be regarded as something more than a basketball machine. "I said, 'No matter where you go and how much money you make, education will always win out,'" she remembers. " 'They can take your clothes, they can take your shoes, but they can't take what is inside your head.' ''

Arrayed against her was the formidable coalition of her son, her husband and coach Dean Smith. "Those three thought he was ready," she says. "They said, 'Will the opportunities that are there now still be there next year?' '' Or would injury or a sudden slump in Michael's performance make him less attractive to professional scouts?

Over the next six weeks, Jordan debated the question with family and friends. The deliberations were draining, and Michael sought refuge in golf, a game for which his close friends did not share his enthusiasm. "At that time," says Adolph Shiver, who would one day accompany his friend onto scores of golf courses, "I thought it was the stupidest thing we had ever tried." But Jordan loved the new challenge and the respite from the uncertainties that were at the center of his life.

In the end, the decision to leave school was Michael's own. "I think he looked at it in terms of his parents having worked hard for him to get an education and now him having the chance to move the next step up the ladder," Shiver says. But Deloris made her son promise that he'd complete his degree during the off-season.

Jordan was scheduled to make his announcement on May 5, 1984, but there were moments, right up to the end, when he wasn't sure what he was going to say. "We went out to dinner the night before he announced and he said, 'Buzz, what am I going to do? What should I do?' '' Peterson remembers. "We went back to the dorm and fell asleep that night talking about it. The alarm went off the next morning and he went out the door.

"I said, 'What are you going to do?' He said, 'I don't know.' Here he is going out the door and I don't know if my roommate is going pro or not.''

Little of this ambivalence was evident at the press conference, where Jordan, casually attired in a yellow polo shirt and sporting the wispiest of goatees, announced in a soft, calm voice that he was ready for the NBA. The decision had been a wrenching one. The years at Carolina had been "the best of my life," Michael said, but he felt it was time for a new challenge.

With one tough task completed, Jordan suddenly found himself faced with another equally important decision. When a ballplayer turns professional, "The wolves are out there," as Deloris Jordan puts it. And it is important for an athlete to find himself a shepherd. Or at least the right kind of wolf.

Selecting an agent is a daunting task for a college kid. The decision is made more difficult by the poor regard in which sports agents are often held. The history of the profession is rich in scandal: dishonest operators who fleeced their clients; reckless investors who pumped an athlete's money into worthless schemes; unscrupulous recruiters whose gifts of cash and cars cost a college kid his eligibility and, sometimes, his professional career.

Young athletes are understandably eager to put their financial affairs in the hands of someone they can trust. Some turn to relatives, others to former coaches. Still others choose an agent based on the factors that had helped them choose a college: Who visited me most often? Who paid the most attention to my family? Who promised that I would be his star?

But a college coach has the absolute authority to fulfill his promises. An agent does not. Every dollar he wins for the player results from a sometimes bitter and protracted negotiation. "The owner of the pro team's job is not to make the player happy, it is to make money," one well-known agent says. "When a player gets drafted, stop the clock. He's done everything he can to make his case. At that point, the only variable in his success is how skilled the person chosen to negotiate his contract is at doing what he does."

At certain schools, and North Carolina is one, the university attempts to aid athletes in making their choice by inviting several agents to campus for interviews with the player, his family, his coach and sometimes a few university administrators. The setting is a congenial one for the new wave of sports agents who are sensitive about the shabby image of their profession. Many of these "player representatives," as they often prefer to be called, have law degrees or MBAs; they have backgrounds in marketing or finance. Some are solo practitioners, but others belong to large, law-firm-like agencies that will cash a player's checks, pay his bills, invest his money, provide him with an allowance and issue him quarterly reports.

These services are essential for all athletes, but the agents for top-name players have to offer their clients something more. Today nationally known sports stars can make more money pitching products than playing their games. "Look at Magic Johnson as an example," this agent says. "His godfather, Charles Tucker, was his agent for years and very little happened. And Tucker probably knew Magic better than anyone in the country except his parents. But the question is: Do you have to know the player and his moves, or do you have to know the people in corporate America? I subscribe to the view that you have to know the people in corporate America.

"So late in his career, Magic divorces himself from this relationship and lets a very young guy named Lon Rosen, who had been one of the Laker public relations people, handle his business. And Lon develops some kind of relationship on Magic's behalf with Michael Ovitz [the high-powered entertainment agent and founder of Creative Artists Agency], who clearly is a mover and shaker in the entertainment world. And—presto chango!—Magic Johnson, who has been a great player for all these years, all of a sudden is on the cover of *Sports Illustrated* with an article, 'Magic Inc.'

"Now why does that happen? Is it because all of a sudden the public has discovered Magic? No. It happens because

Ovitz is a powerful guy, a well-connected guy. He can call up Pepsi [which sold a bottling franchise to Johnson and black publisher and business magnate Earl Graves], can call up whomever, and make things happen for Magic, whereas the people before him were not able to make things happen for Magic.

"If players knew they were always going to get what they deserved then we wouldn't need agents," the agent says. "But if it doesn't happen, *even* for Magic Johnson, who was already a legend when he came into the NBA, who is it going to happen for?"

Athletes have been endorsing products for more than a century, beginning in earnest in the 1920s when Americans first gave themselves over by the millions to spectator sports. The icons of that time, Babe Ruth in particular, endorsed everything from chewing tobacco to automobiles to long underwear. Beginning after World War II, however, two developments altered the dynamics and the economics of athlete endorsements, making the business more lucrative, but also more complicated.

The first of these developments was the popularization of the television. The TV not only expanded the role of advertising and athletics in popular culture, it bound the two inextricably together. In the early days of television, spectator sports were a network's dream. Here was an event the networks did not have to pay to have produced. They could simply buy the rights, broadcast the game and sell advertising to recover their costs. And advertisers, eager to reach a large male audience with commercials for cars, beer and, at that time, cigarettes, were happy to pay top rates. Athletes became more recognizable than ever and, therefore, more attractive as product pitchmen.

The second key development was America's increasing demand for leisure-time activities. A burgeoning middle class, interested in assuming the trappings of prosperity, sought its recreation on the golf course and tennis court. It created, in the process, an unprecedented demand for equipment, apparel, instruction, facilities and, not least, telecasts.

The first sports agent to seize on this trend was Mark McCormack. In 1958 he founded the international Management Group, the first full-service sports agency. The Cleveland-based firm, which now represents entertainers and authors as well as athletes, earned its reputation by bringing together top professional golfers, eager corporate sponsors and willing television networks to help form the PGA tour as we know it today. In the process, McCormack's client Arnold Palmer became a national celebrity. Today, almost 35 years later, he remains one of the two or three highest-earning sports endorsers in the world.

Palmer was the perfect pioneer. He was as laid-back in person as he was hard-charging on the golf course. While his was a country club sport, he'd learned it from his father, who was a greenskeeper. The more audiences got to know Palmer, the more they seemed to like him. He was a regular guy: the hero as next-door neighbor. His breakthrough allowed athletes to enter the nation's living rooms in capacities unrelated to their sports, while his earnings demonstrated that the proper pairing of product and pitchman could make everyone rich, including the agent who arranged the match.

Tennis was slower to abandon the old strictures that kept many of its best players amateurs, thus forestalling the influx of corporate dollars that had enriched and popularized golf. But in the late 1960s, the game finally entered the "open" era. Suddenly players could compete at any time against anyone and keep their earnings. This new state of affairs created an opening for a savvy sports agency to do for tennis what IMG had done for golf. Enter ProServ, the sports agency and management firm now based in Arlington, Virginia.

ProServ was founded in 1969 as the marketing arm of Dell, Craighill, Fentress and Benton, a Washington, D.C. law firm started by former University of Virginia law school classmates. The force behind the new agency was Donald Dell, former captain of the U.S. Davis Cup team and once the second-ranked amateur player in the world. His first two clients were his close friends and former teammates Arthur Ashe and Stan Smith.

Dell, at that time, was what one writer called "the octopus of professional tennis." Following the trail McCormack had blazed, he and his firm paired the players they represented with corporations looking for a way to put their names in front of the affluent tennis audience. IMG plunged into tennis promotions as well, but Dell's reputation within the sport, coupled with his position as general counsel of the Association of Tennis Professionals, the fledgling players' union, gave ProServ the edge. In 1975, veteran tennis journalist Bud Collins called him "perhaps the single most important figure on the international tennis scene."

Overlooked, however, in the early years of the tennis boom were the potential conflicts of interest implicit in the arrangements that had fueled the game's growth. If a single agency represented both the players and the sponsors in a given tournament, it was, in effect, negotiating with itself in dividing the tournament's revenues. Anything the agency did to serve the financial interests of one side had a negative effect on the financial interests of the other, although it was supposed to represent both.

Dell and McCormack claimed that everyone in the relatively cozy tennis community understood the financial workings of these tournaments and trusted the fairness of the agent-impresarios who ran them. Besides, they pointed out, without men such as themselves, many of these lucrative tournaments wouldn't exist, and nobody would be making any money. In the years ahead, these potential conflicts of interest would throw ProServ into internal turmoil and land it in several messy and embarrassing lawsuits. In the meantime, however, business was booming.

The agency, which had a staff of only four or five people in the early 1970s, had 18 executives by 1980 and 50 by

1983. ProServ had also begun to diversify into team sports. The in-house leader in this field was David Falk, a young lawyer who had joined the firm after graduating from law school at George Washington University in 1975. Falk snared his first two big-name clients the following year. John Lucas, the University of Maryland guard who was chosen first in the draft, and Adrian Dantley, the Notre Dame forward who was chosen sixth, both selected Falk to negotiate their contracts. James Worthy, the top pick in 1982, signed with Falk as well.

In 1983, however, at the peak of its influence, ProServ stunned the Washington legal community by splitting in two. Two founding partners, Frank Craighill and A. Lee Fentress, announced that they were breaking away from the firm to begin their own agency, Advantage International. In the legal agreement that finalized the split, both sides said they would not discuss their differences, but many Washington attorneys suggested that Craighill and Fentress were uneasy about the firm's chaotic growth and its lack of long-range planning. Others attributed the split to Dell's autocratic commitment to a future his partners found unsettlingly glitzy.

Whatever the reasons for the rift, Advantage quickly distinguished itself from ProServ, announcing it would not promote tournaments but would concentrate almost exclusively on player representation. The new firm walked off with 22 of ProServ's employees and several of its top clients. Advantage also became an instant rival for the business of top athletes, particularly in basketball. Today the firm represents David Robinson, Sam Perkins, Moses Malone, Brad Daugherty, J.R. Reid and Maurice Cheeks.

ProServ, meanwhile, was battling to right itself. It took a huge and unknowing step in that direction in the spring of 1984, when Dell, Falk and colleague William Strickland traveled to Chapel Hill and made their pitch to the Carolina basketball star who had decided to turn professional one season early.

"We made an hour-and-a-half presentation and that was it," Falk remembers. "After that no more contact was allowed." A few weeks later, Dean Smith called his friend Dell to tell him that Jordan, following the lead of Worthy and former Carolina great Phil Ford, had selected the firm as his representative.

The people at ProServ were pleased, but they didn't really know what they had. "Michael was considered a very flashy player but not a dominating player, not a complete player," Falk says. "No one really had an idea of how good he was, partially because of the system at North Carolina, and partially because he was really a late bloomer. It was obvious that he was going to be marketable, *pretty* marketable, but we didn't really have any glimpse that he would be the most prolific team sports personality of all time."

From the windows that stretch across one wall of David Falk's 18th-story office you can see the Kennedy Center, the Lincoln Memorial, the Washington Monument and much of the rest of this marble city. It is an impressive, if incongruous, sight, because nothing Falk does pertains in the slightest to government or politics. But this view of his is a classic Washington power vista, and Falk knows something about power.

As president of ProServ's team sports division, he is one of the three or four most powerful men in professional basketball. On his walls hang pictures, posters and magazine covers of the clients from whom this power flows: Jordan, Patrick Ewing, Dominique Wilkins, John Stockton, to name only the 1991 NBA All-Stars. He and his colleagues also represent Buck Williams, Jerome Kersey, Mitch Richmond, Xavier McDaniel, Johnny Dawkins, Jeff Malone, Pervis Ellison and Danny Ferry, among others.

Shrewd, relentless, possessed of a great self-regard, Falk is a man not easily diverted by others' attempts at humor. In casual conversation he seems always to be looking elsewhere, searching for someone more important to speak with. In a more structured setting, however, his focus is sharp, his knowledge broad and his opinions incisive. "I feel I can trust David," one NBA beat writer says. "The things he tells me are self-serving, but they are true."

Falk's recitation of his personal statistics falls into that category. His accomplishments as an agent are nearly as impressive as Jordan's statistics as an athlete, and he reels off his achievements with the readiness of Pete Rose. "Of the six highest rookie contracts, I have negotiated four," he said during the 1990–91 season. "Of the 30 highest-paid players, I have negotiated 10 of those contracts. Of the four biggest contracts in the league, I have negotiated three [Jordan, Ewing and Ferry, who earns more than David Robinson]."

This track record has convinced many young ballplayers that Falk is the man they want on their side. From 1985 through 1990, he and his associates at ProServ represented 11 of the 51 players chosen in the NBA lottery, as many as their two closest competitors combined. Other agents admit that Falk generally negotiates the rookie contract that defines the market for that year, and sets the standard against which their own performances are judged. He also represents the top endorsement athlete at most of the major sneaker companies.

All this success, however, has not made him a widely popular fellow. "There are people who don't like me because I am very opinionated, but I think they respect me," Falk says. "I'd like to be liked and respected, but sometimes there are trade-offs. I would rather be respected than liked.

"The nature of what I do—taking money, getting more money—they are not likely to like you."

But Falk's top clients understand that he is intensely loyal and extremely vigilant about whom he allows to approach them. His life has become bound up in many of theirs. Clients Adrian Dantley and Boomer Esiason are the godfathers of his two daughters. He refers to another client, John

Thompson of Georgetown, as his "mentor." It was in marketing Michael Jordan, though, that Falk made his reputation, and the memory is so sweet that it moves him to something approaching modesty.

"We haven't packaged Michael Jordan," he says. "We have done a good job exposing who he is and what he is to corporate decision makers. Once they saw what he was firsthand, the rest flowed from there. Obviously Michael had a lot going for him, but he needed an access to the McDonald'ses, the Coca-Colas, and I think that ProServ provided that bridge."

ProServ's unique contribution to Jordan's fame was its conviction that certain stellar team athletes could be marketed in much the same way as golfers and tennis players. Jordan was the type of athlete they had in mind—explosive, acrobatic and, above all, telegenic. The problem, from a corporate point of view, was that he was black.

"There was a sort of sub-rosa feeling that very few people would openly communicate, but there was a general feeling lurking beneath the surface that black team sport athletes were not marketable, that they would not be accepted by corporate America," Falk says. "Not so much by the people, not so much by the consuming populace, but by the people who were making the decisions to put them on television." As a result the companies were "very, very circumspect about why would Michael, simply because he is a good basketball player, be a useful addition to them in marketing," Falk adds. "And we had to supply the answers. In many cases, early on, it was just simply a question of convincing them to trust us as a company based on other relationships we had had with them."

The marketplace has always reflected white Americans' tentativeness and selectivity in their embrace of black athletes. Superstars like Willie Mays, Wilt Chamberlain and Oscar Robertson never received commercial endorsements commensurate with their professional stature. Rebels like football great Jim Brown were avoided almost entirely. Only

O. J. Simpson (playing Arnold Palmer's goofy sidekick for Hertz), Julius Erving (who pitched Coke and Chap Stick) and Arthur Ashe had enjoyed significant commercial success. Of these three, Erving's success was most relevant to Jordan.

Dr. J. was perhaps the first black basketball player whom advertisers realized did not need to play the fool to be found acceptable by white audiences. A magical presence on court, a man of great gravity off, his appeal, while perhaps stronger in black communities, knew no racial bounds. He had a gift, too, for defusing stereotypes without even seeming to address them. This was most obvious in a Chap Stick commercial during which Erving speaks a few lines and applies a bit of lip balm. Nothing out of the ordinary, but after decades of racial stereotyping the fact that an advertisement based on a black man's lips was not seen as a crude joke indicates how gracefully Erving carried such things off.

To Jordan's great benefit, his personality and style of play were frequently compared to Erving's. He had an example to follow, and Falk, in lobbying corporate decision makers, had a successful precedent to cite. Michael's marketability was further enhanced by Erving's impending retirement. Though the Doctor would play three more seasons, the NBA was already searching for his successor as the game's ambassador at large.

6

The Chicago Bulls were a dreadful team. During the 1983–84 season they had won just 27 of their 82 games, played before an average home crowd of fewer than 7,000 fans and failed to make the playoffs for the sixth time in seven years. There was high-level speculation that another atrocious campaign might well kill the franchise.

Bulls fans were hoping that the team's renaissance would begin with an inspired selection in the June 20th draft. Chicago had the third pick. The three best players available, scouts agreed, were Akeem (now Hakeem) Olajuwon, the big, smooth center from the University of Houston; Sam Bowie, the oft-injured but highly promising pivot man from Kentucky; and Michael Jordan, who might play guard or forward, but might not quite fit at either position.

Olajuwon would be snapped up by the team from his new hometown, the Houston Rockets, who chose first. That put the Bulls' future in the hands of the Portland Trailblazers, who chose second. The Blazers, like the Bulls, were in desperate need of a center.

Chicago's management held out some hope that Portland might balk at the risk Bowie presented. The Kentucky star had been one of the most intensely recruited high school seniors in recent memory, but his occasionally brilliant college career was interrupted by potentially serious leg injuries. There was no guarantee he would hold up under the physical pounding of the NBA.

Still, the Blazers already had Clyde Drexler, a flashy shooting guard with great one-on-one moves, whose game was similar to Jordan's. Their doctors examined Bowie, pronounced him fit, and Portland took its chances. So began the marriage of Michael Jordan and the Chicago Bulls.

The new kid's task was put bluntly by sportswriter Bob Logan in the next day's *Chicago Tribune*: "Can Michael Jordan provide a miracle cure for the terminal boredom afflicting Bulls fans?"

The Bulls' management, wary of overburdening Jordan, began a quick campaign to diminish expectations. "We wish he were seven feet tall, but he isn't," general manager Rod Thorn said. "There just wasn't a center available. What can you do?

"Jordan isn't going to turn this franchise around," he added. "I wouldn't ask him to. I wouldn't put that kind of pressure on him. Olajuwon was the big prize."

Jordan too seemed intent on keeping expectations in check. "I don't think Chicago will go undefeated next year," he said.

Dean Smith was more effusive in his evaluation of the Bulls' choice. "Except for not being a true point guard, he has no real weakness," the coach said. But even he felt the need to dampen runaway expectations. Asked if Jordan could have the kind of impact on the league that Magic Johnson and Julius Erving had exerted, he said: "That's unfair to Michael. He's more a Sidney Moncrief type." Moncrief was one of the league's four or five best guards, but by no means a historical talent.

No matter how they qualified their evaluations, it was

clear that at least some members of the Bulls' front office were proud of their pick. "It's putting too much on Jordan to call him a savior," chief scout Mike Thibault said. "But he is a big-time player."

The first real time David Falk spent with Jordan was at a press conference in this atmosphere of highly charged expectations. "The city had had a lot of success with the Bears at that point and the Cubs were playing well, finally," Falk says. "But the Bulls had just been downtrodden forever and I expected a lot of negativism. So, flying out there on the plane, I wrote down some questions and some suggested things for him to be thinking about to answer them."

He and Jordan met at the airport and went over the notes in the limousine that the Bulls had provided for the occasion. "I started to brief him on what he might be able to expect," Falk says. "He listened very intently for five or six minutes and said, 'Thanks, I think I get the gist of what you are saying and I'm pretty comfortable and I think I'll be able to handle it.'

"I'd barely gotten to my second note.

"Well, he sat down at this round conference table with all the microphones in front of him. There were about 40, 50 people in the room and he was like Johnny Carson. He took the mike off the stand. A guy asked him what it was like to play for Bobby Knight [who was coaching Jordan on the U.S. Olympic team] and he'd wink at him and give him sort of a nondescript answer. You could see in the very beginning this was a made-for-the-media athlete. He had a natural ability to communicate, to provide intelligent answers to questions, to delicately handle the tough questions. He was incredible.

"When we got done I said, 'God, I'm really glad my briefing provided some help.'"

The summer that Michael was drafted, Americans were preparing for the jubilant, jingoistic Summer Olympics, to be held in Los Angeles. The Soviet Union and its allies were boycotting the games because the United States had withdrawn from the 1980 Moscow Olympics after the Soviets invaded Afghanistan. Without Eastern bloc competition, the United States was sure to walk off with medals by the cartful. And each, in the summer before Ronald Reagan's "Morning in America" reelection rout, would be seen as an affirmation of American virtue.

Jordan led an extremely impressive U.S. men's basketball team that included Patrick Ewing and Chris Mullin. Basketball insiders wondered at first if Jordan's proclivity for improvisation might lead him to clash with the domineering Knight, who favors a more tightly controlled offense. But the two got along famously, enjoyed joking with one another and seemed to reach an accommodation of styles almost effortlessly.

In training camp, for instance, Jordan often tried to beat a double team by simply leaping into the air and waiting to see how the defenders would react. "The first few times he did that on the Olympic team, Coach Knight would stop practice and explain to him why it was wrong," said C. M. Newton, the former Vanderbilt coach who was an assistant on the '84 team. "But then we noticed that he could hang in the air for so long and do so many things with the ball that he was almost always successful. So we stopped coaching him after that."

Jordan, for his part, said Knight was a lot like Dean Smith—except for his language.

After impressive victories over a few NBA semi-All-Star teams early in the summer, the U.S. squad drubbed an international field that included fast-improving teams from Spain and West Germany. The Americans claimed the gold medal by going undefeated in eight games, winning by an average of more than 32 points and holding opponents to 38.7 percent shooting.

When the games had ended, Alexander Wolff of *Sports Illustrated* asked Fernando Martin of Spain his impression of Jordan. "Michael Jordan?" Martin said. "Jump, jump, jump. Very quick. Very fast. Jump, jump, jump."

The Olympic medal enhanced Jordan's image as an All-American kid, as did the widely aired press conference at which he draped it around his mother's neck. "It was almost like a power boost to his image," Falk says.

Michael seemed perfectly poised to leap into the national imagination that summer. But the legends of many Olympic champions have bloomed and died in the space of a month. And scores of can't-miss professional prospects go nowhere in the NBA. Others hold their own in Salt Lake City or Sacramento and the national audience never really notices.

Jordan, on the other hand, was headed for the third-largest city in the country, to a leaderless team that was desperate to succeed. And once he got there, he'd be wearing one hot pair of shoes.

"I remember we were getting together one time," Buzz Peterson says. "He said, 'Buzz, better get some Nike stock. They are going to make a shoe for me. They are going to make these Air Jordans and someday it's going to be worth a lot of money.'

"I said, 'Get out of here.' If I had just listened to him there. . . . He's always been a lucky person."

On the outskirts of Portland sits a campus built on air. The buildings are named for Jordan, John McEnroe, Mike Schmidt, Joan Benoit Samuelson, Alberto Salazar, the late Steve Prefontaine, and other athletes who have helped make Nike the most successful sports shoe company in the world. This is the firm's Beaverton headquarters, and if ever a corporation's self-image was captured in its surroundings, this is it.

Nine low, sleek buildings in shades of green glass and graphite rest beside a man-made pond. Around them bloom $1 million worth of imported Japanese cherry trees. The entire facility is surrounded by a well-used running course. The effect, as one approaches from the visitors' parking lot, is cool, stylish, precise, as though one is about to walk into a wonderfully made luxury pencil.

Indoors, the feeling is quite different—light, airy, casual. It is a world of atriums with offices tucked discreetly against the walls. The floors on which shoe designers labor are marked by a loftlike openness. Work spaces pour over eye-high dividers, flowing one into the next as if to represent the collegial development of an excellent idea.

The design of the company's headquarters also captures the quality that is at the heart of Nike's appeal: an ability to have things both ways. The firm portrays itself as corporate, yet casual; intense, yet irreverent; structured, yet spontaneous; fabulously successful, yet unaffected by it all.

"There are no fat cats here," says Tinker Hatfield, director of design. "It is not a typical hierarchy. I am one of the executives, and look at me."

On a mild, rainy, mid-November morning, Hatfield is wearing a tweedy plaid pair of shorts, a vibrant limited edition T-shirt and a blue cardigan sweater, courtesy of CBS Sports. His sleeves are bunched around his elbows. On his head sits a long-brimmed baseball cap. The lenses of his glasses are round and rimless. He looks so much his point that one wonders if he dressed to make it.

Hatfield was a pole vaulter at the University of Oregon, a member of Nike cofounder Bill Bowerman's track team, as was the company's guiding spirit, cofounder Phil Knight. "He [Bowerman] was always designing new shoes," Hatfield says, "and I was one of his test pilots." He placed sixth in the Olympic trials in 1976 before injuring his left ankle.

The ankle hasn't been right since, and Hatfield has recently had it operated on again. That explains the cast wrapped around his left foot and the tweedy shorts.

For the last six years, Michael Jordan has come to the campus to confer with Hatfield about the design of the new Air Jordans that the company unveils each February at the NBA All-Star game. "He really had no input on the first two shoes," says Hatfield, who has designed Air Jordans three through seven. "When I took over, I felt he needed to be involved. He came in and I laid out leathers and textures and different ideas."

If it is difficult to imagine what sort of ideas these might be, or to understand what kind of muse leads a professional architect like Hatfield into sneaker design, listen as he describes his inspiration for Air Jordan number 5, the shoe with Michael's number back near the heel, the one Jordan first wore at the 1990 All-Star game.

"That was the airplane-inspired shoe," Hatfield says. "Michael plays like a fighter pilot. He glides in a certain gear, then all of a sudden he takes off and in the next five minutes he scores 20 points. He's like a plane up there in his own world until he finds his target and strafes the enemy." So Hatfield based his design for Air Jordan number 5 on the P-51 Mustang, a World War II-vintage fighter, because modern jets didn't have "the same romantic image." A drawing of the plane hangs on his office wall.

The Air Jordan number 6 has a more technological lineage. "It's got a dynamic fit system," Hatfield says, meaning that the fit adjusts to the movement of the foot. "Like a water-skiing boot." And, in fact, it looks a bit like a water-skiing boot, with black rubber pull-on tabs attached to the tongue and counter. "Like the spoiler on a sports car," Hatfield says.

But these pull tabs are not the design innovation in Air Jordan number 6. That honor belongs to the shoe's plain toe. That's right—its plain toe, featuring none of the rubber or leather edging that encircles the front of almost every other sneaker in the world.

"One of the things about Michael Jordan is we can take incredible risks in the product area because his wearing them validates it," Hatfield says. "The fact that Michael Jordan is wearing this plain-toed shoe will make it all right for a lot of people. Whereas otherwise the marketing department would as soon shoot me as let something like this out the door."

It would not be easy to keep a straight face through this

discussion—it would not be easy to know whether one was supposed to—were it not for Hatfield's seriousness. It behooves the people at Nike to take the Air Jordan seriously. It is the best-selling basketball shoe in the industry. In a recent survey conducted in suburban high schools, Air Jordan ranked with Nike and Reebok as one of the three best-known "companies" in the business.

The shoe is also symbolic of the forces that helped make Jordan a folk hero. As dazzling a player as Michael would become, his commercial legend was shaped in large part before he took a shot for money. The force behind it was a once-thriving sneaker company that, in the spring of 1984, found itself in a corporate free fall.

It was not possible, ten years ago, to become incredibly wealthy simply by agreeing to wear a particular pair of shoes. In 1982 Kareem Abdul-Jabbar was the only basketball player with a six-figure sneaker endorsement contract; he earned $100,000 that year from Adidas. This was rightly regarded as a regal sum, since Jabbar was going to have to wear something on his feet whether he was paid to do so or not. Within two years, however, a revolution in the way athletes were employed in marketing sneakers made the Laker star's contract look comparatively slight.

For decades, sneaker makers had offered athletes free shoes and sometimes a small stipend to wear their products. The market for basketball shoes, until the late 1960s, was virtually owned by the Converse Rubber Company, which manufactured "Chuck Taylor All-Stars," a canvas shoe with a rubber sole and minimal arch support that was the serious ballplayer's sneaker of choice. "Chucks" developed such a mystique that buying their first pair became a rite of passage for athletically minded adolescents.

In the late '60s two European sneaker companies, Adidas and Puma, made inroads in the American market, with a flashier approach and a more diverse line of shoes. But it was not until the fitness boom of the 1970s that the athletic footwear business became so lucrative and so competitive. Athletes who could testify to the superiority of a manufacturer's product were suddenly in great demand and sneaker companies tripped over one another trying to get their shoes on high-profile feet.

Signing all those athletes to endorsement contracts was costly, however, and sometimes the benefits were not all that tangible. Who cared what sneakers were worn by the backup forwards on the Kansas City Kings? The sneaker companies were not particularly sophisticated in their marketing, either. Their idea of promotions extended no further than furnishing their stars with logo-laden wardrobes of T-shirts and sweatpants. In the early 1980s, Converse shod Julius Erving, Magic Johnson and Larry Bird, yet did little to help them develop recognizable commercial personalities.

By the mid-1980s, the more-is-better approach was being reconsidered by several major sneaker companies. "Nike flew most of the major player representatives out to Portland at its expense and had a meeting to explain to them that they were shifting gears from signing a multitude of players to signing only a few," David Falk recalls. "The theme of this transition was explained to us as 'the best and the brightest.'"

Nike was not the only company considering this new marketing approach. New Balance, Spotbuilt and other sneaker makers were also mulling the idea of building promotional campaigns around a few highly visible stars. The first player to benefit from this rethinking was not Jordan, but his Carolina teammate James Worthy, who graduated in 1982.

Worthy was an All-American. His team had just won the NCAA championship and he had been named the Most Valuable Player in the Final Four. That June the NBA champion Los Angeles Lakers made him the first pick in the entire draft. With so glamorous a client, Falk decided to see how serious footwear manufacturers were about this new strategy. "I told all the companies that we would evaluate offers for James in six figures," he says. "Six figures per year."

At least one sneaker company representative felt Falk was toying with him and said so in strong and profane terms. But the athletic shoe industry was chaotic at this point. It was not entirely unreasonable for a manufacturer to believe that one brilliant pitchman would help his company break from the pack.

New Balance offered James Worthy $1.2 million for eight years to wear a shoe it called the Worthy Express. This marked the first time that an athlete who played a team sport was marketed nationally as though he were a golfer or tennis player. The venture's success, however, was only modest. New Balance did not invest heavily in promoting the shoe. Even if it had, it seems doubtful a mystique could have arisen around a rookie who shared the ball with Kareem and Magic. But marketing Worthy had given David Falk a sense of how much money an eager sneaker manufacturer might commit to an athlete who seemed especially appealing.

By the time the Chicago Bulls drafted Michael Jordan in 1984, the market for athletic shoes was contracting rapidly. The jogging boom had peaked. Fitness buffs were playing racket sports, riding bikes and demanding new specialty shoes. The aerobics craze was in full flourish. To complicate matters, public tastes had also changed. Consumers were tired of the clunky-looking nylon "performance shoes" of the '70s and were looking for more stylish materials and sleeker designs.

Few companies kept pace with these changes; Nike, one of the great corporate success stories of the 1970s, stumbled badly. In 1983, with record sales of nearly $700 million, Nike had displaced Adidas as the world's top athletic footwear company. But by the following spring its earnings had plunged for the first time in 10 years, and the business press was rife with speculation about the firm's demise or, perhaps, its impending sale. Even founder Philip Knight allowed that while he wasn't looking to unload the company, he wouldn't necessarily turn anything down.

Nike's tailspin aroused unusual interest. Knight was regarded by many as the model for a new breed of businessman, the kind of daring chief executive who could lead moribund American industries into a more creative, less bureaucratic and newly productive future. While his predicament drew the attention of the business world, the fate of the shoes he made intrigued more casual onlookers. By the mid-1970s, Nikes had become so much a part of the American wardrobe that Tom Wolfe included them in the official uniform of the Me Generation.

Nike had its start in a term paper. In 1963, while working on his MBA at Stanford, Knight wrote an essay surveying the athletic footwear industry and concluded that because of their low labor costs Japan and other Far Eastern countries would soon surpass Europe as the primary providers of the world's sports shoes. The following year, while on a world tour, he walked into the Tokyo offices of Onitsuka, producers of Tiger track shoes, and walked out with exclusive United States distribution rights. Back in Portland, he and Bowerman founded Blue Ribbon Sports and began marketing the Japanese sneakers.

Business began slowly. Knight worked full-time as an accountant at Coopers & Lybrand and sold the shoes from the back of his station wagon at weekend track meets. In 1972 the company recorded $3 million in sales, but that year Onitsuka revoked Knight's exclusivity clause. After a bitter dispute, he and Bowerman found another Japanese producer, but the split underscored the need for Blue Ribbon to begin developing and manufacturing its own shoes. Here, Bowerman's love of track and field proved essential.

The track shoes of the late '60s seem almost primitive compared to the engineering extravaganzas that runners wear today. Arch support in these shoes was minimal. Cushioning was almost nonexistent. Soles provided little traction in slippery conditions. Bowerman had this last problem in mind when he stuck a piece of rubber into his wife's waffle iron one morning and guaranteed the company's survival. The new "waffle sole" may have reduced Mrs. Bowerman's breakfast repertoire, but it established Nike's reputation as a technological innovator in an ever more competitive industry.

Spurred by this success, the company poured money into now seemingly primitive research. Dick Silverman, editor of *Footwear News*, remembers visiting a Nike research plant in Exeter, New Hampshire, where he found "guys in white coats, people on treadmills, in these little windowless prefab shacks." This research was essential because jogging devotees received unsparingly critical reviews of each new sneaker in *Runner's World*, a magazine that boasted a circulation of 400,000. In 1977 the magazine bestowed five stars, its highest rating, on the Brooks Vantage and, in doing so, began perhaps the emblematic story of how quickly fitness-related fortunes were being made and lost.

When the review appeared, Brooks was a small company with annual sales of only a few million whose entire operation was housed in a warehouse in Hanover, Pennsylvania. In 1978 its revenues rose to $14 million. By 1980 they were nearly triple that figure, making Brooks the third-largest shoe sales company in the United States. Because both firms geared their products to the same sneaker-savvy consumers, competition between Brooks and Nike was intense and often nasty.

In the late '70s, Nike sued Brooks and seven other firms, contending that they had illegally lobbied for increased import duties on foreign-made shoes. Such a tariff would have devastated Nike, which produced nearly 80 percent of its footwear in the Far East. Brooks countered with an unrelated lawsuit, demonstrating that Nike had labeled other makers' shoes with its trademark swoosh to please endorsement athletes who didn't like their Nikes. *Runner's World* also leapt into the litigious fray, suing Nike for libel when the Portland-based firm charged the magazine's ratings were biased in Brooks' favor.

Just when the competition was at its hottest, though, Brooks began to fall apart. The little Pennsylvania firm never really caught up with the flood of orders that resulted from the Vantage's five-star rating. The sudden increase in production led to widespread quality-control problems, and by the early 1980s, 30 percent of Brooks's new shoes were being returned due to manufacturing defects. By 1982, the company was bankrupt and its name had been sold to the firm that makes Hush Puppies. The shoes are still made and are once again highly regarded, but Brooks is no longer a force in the market.

Meanwhile, at Nike earnings were soaring. Between 1978 and 1983, the company's earnings rose at an average annual rate of nearly 100 percent. Its stock, which debuted in 1982 at $22 a share, reached $43 before year's end.

"Phil Knight has nurtured one of the most swinging, entrepreneurial, free-spirited, individualistic organizations that exists today," C. Roland Christensen, dean of the Harvard Business School, wrote in the *New York Times*. "He's built a new type of industrial society. He's sort of a corporate pope and he has lots of apostles and followers."

Christensen was not alone in citing Nike's esprit de corps as an antidote for the stagnation that gripped so many American industries. *Forbes* noted the "almost mystical attachment" of Nike's management—"mostly hale young men with hearty handshakes and the earnest sincerity of the Hardy Boys"—to the products they created.

"Nike has a very distinct corporate culture," Silverman of *Footwear News* says. "Nike people live and die Nike. It's like a religion. They travel together. They run together. They really believe in it in a big way."

Many of the company's executives were former athletes looking for a way to re-create the challenge and camaraderie of competitive sports in their business careers. Yet they were also often children of the Pacific Northwest's counterculture, sensitive to the ethical dilemmas inherent in corporate success. Servicing the fitness boom allowed them to believe that they were building a healthier America while still making a killing in the industry.

But the company's passion for athletics spawned a strange blindness. "The secret to the business," Knight told *Fortune* magazine, "is to build the kind of shoe professional athletes will wear, then put them on the pros. The rest of the market will follow." But athletes were not the only ones who wore the shoes. Many of the people who bought Nikes had only a nodding acquaintance with sweat. The sneakers had simply become a necessary piece of cultural equipment, an outward sign, in the self-obsessed '70s, that one took one's body seriously. A pair of Nikes attested to one's familiarity with questing exertion, even if the only quests one went on were for a matching pair of shorts.

Nike executives knew that perhaps 85 percent of their sneakers were not worn in athletic endeavors. Yet they failed to understand the implications of this fact. Even today, the firm still sometimes seems to deny half its identity, claiming that it is in the business of fitness, not fashion.

That this was not the case became painfully clear in the mid-1980s. The company reacted sluggishly to consumer demand for more stylish and specialized shoes. More damaging was its decision to overlook what Jane Fonda had wrought and ignore the aerobics explosion. In doing so, it created an opening for a then-minuscule firm that is today its principal competitor.

Reebok was an old-line British sneaker company, probably best known in this country for putting shoes on the feet of the 1924 British Olympic team portrayed in *Chariots of Fire*. In 1979, Paul Fireman, a camping and fishing salesman, spotted the firm's footwear at a Chicago trade show and purchased exclusive North American distribution rights. For the next four years the franchise was not a particularly valuable one, and Fireman nearly sold it to Striderite.

Unlike Nike, which prided itself on leading the market by building innovative new shoes, Reebok "followed" the market, asking consumers what they wanted and hurrying to provide. In 1983 female consumers wanted sneakers they could wear while doing aerobics. Almost no one was making them. Reebok decided to fill the vacuum. The shoe they came up with—the Freestyle—was light, not particularly durable and didn't offer much by way of cushioning. Yet its success convulsed the industry.

Part of the Freestyle's appeal was the soft glove leather from which it was made. The shoe had an almost elegant look that made it perfect for casual wear. There is a story, probably apocryphal, that this leather was used by accident, because the designer who assembled it had nothing else on hand.

However it was born, the Freestyle created the immediately burgeoning women's sneaker market. Reebok sales, languishing at around $3.5 million in 1982, rocketed to roughly $200 million in 1985. The stock debuted at $13 a share that year and was selling for $83 a share when it split three for one in June, 1986.

Nike, meanwhile, was in a tailspin. "Nike Loses Its Footing on the Fast Track," wrote *Fortune* in November, 1984. "Earnings are dismal, management is shuffling, and many wonder if founder Philip Knight has run out of breath." As a sign of Knight's blundering, the magazine pointed out that the chairman recently offered a rookie basketball player some $2.5 million to wear Nikes for the next five years.

David Falk wanted for Michael Jordan what he had almost achieved for James Worthy. The demands were not modest: a signature shoe, a line of apparel, a royalty on each item sold and a huge promotional budget to make the whole project work. "Like we do with our tennis clients," Falk says.

The general reaction, he adds, was: "'David, it will

never work. This guy is not a tennis player. He is a team athlete, and while he may be better and more talented than some of his teammates, he is one of five players among starters and 12 players on the team.' ''

Converse passed. Adidas passed. Most firms passed. But, as with Worthy, a few companies seemed mesmerized by the idea that perhaps this player could somehow convince the public that its sneakers were the best. One firm in the early running was Spotbuilt (now Saucony), a small company that couldn't promise Jordan much by way of an advance, but was willing to cut him in for a share of the profits on its proposed "Michael Jordan" collection. The other company considering the situation was Nike.

"They had passed on Worthy," Falk remembers. "[Ralph] Sampson was the catch in '83. He went with Puma. And the year before James, in '81, of the top three players in the draft, [Mark] Aguirre, Isiah [Thomas] and Buck Williams, the first two signed with Converse and Buck signed with Puma.

"So they really hadn't had the major guy in the draft since 1980, which was Darrell Griffith, and Darrell turned out, in Utah, not to have the impact people expected he might have. So Nike was really, I won't say desperate, but they really had a major need for a flagship, for someone to anchor their basketball."

The Oregon firm had a special edge in seeking Jordan's services. Rob Strasser, then its vice president, was Falk's best friend in the industry. Competing shoe companies felt that Falk steered all his best clients Strasser's way, a charge Falk flatly denies. At any rate, a friendship alone could not have led the sneaker company to take the enormous risk it was contemplating.

By all accounts, Nike's presentation to Michael and his parents was extremely impressive. Its centerpiece was a Jordan highlight film set to the music of "Jump!" by the Pointer Sisters. Fred Whitfield says the video gave Michael his first true sense of how exciting he was to watch. "I think that was the first time he was really impressed with himself," Whitfield says.

The Jordans say Michael was so excited by the presentation that he was ready to sign with Nike almost immediately, but Falk still had details to work out. One problem was that Nike wasn't sure what to call the new shoe. The company was leery that simply labeling it "Michael Jordan" would conjure images of the designer jeans craze.

One summer afternoon Falk and Strasser were sitting in the agent's Washington office mulling over Jordan's nicknames—NBC analyst Al McGuire used to call him Prime Time—and trying to come up with a title for the shoe. "Nike was going through a whole program in track and field which wasn't very well-known, certainly wasn't very well promoted, where they developed this air-sole technology," Falk says. "Then all of a sudden, as you get these good ideas sometimes, there it was: instead of 'Michael Jordan,' 'Air Jordan,' because it reflected both the technology they were going to implement down the road . . . and it was the way he played. He was an air player."

Falk had not only coined a name for the shoe, but a nickname for his client that has stuck to this day. That those names are the same is a coincidence for which the people at Nike are extremely grateful.

In the weeks ahead, as Nike developed the first shoe and the attendant ad campaigns, company executives remained concerned that they had committed too much money to Jordan and to promoting his new shoes and sportswear. "So they had a clause in the contract," Falk says, "that said if, in the first three years of the deal, Michael failed to make the All-Star team, the All-NBA team—a couple criteria—they would have the right to discontinue making his own signature shoe. However, even if he did do all those things, but the orders for the shoe going into the third year had not exceeded $3 million, they would still be free to discontinue it.

"It's hard to remember in 1984 just how bold a move

Nike made, and the best way to gauge it is that they wanted an out clause if they couldn't sell $3 million worth of the product.''

The first Air Jordans were airless. Nike had not had time to design an entirely new shoe, so it simply produced new colors—red, black and white—for a sneaker that was already in its line. The shoe was unique otherwise only in that it was heavily promoted and outlandishly unattractive, resembling a clunky mottled boot rather than a sleek new sneaker. On "Late Night with David Letterman," as Jordan tried to explain why the Bulls initially forbade him to wear the shoes, Letterman asked: "Not because they are so ugly?"

Actually the Bulls wanted Jordan to wear a shoe in the team's traditional colors, red and white. Air Jordans were predominantly red and black. The NBA stood by the team. "You've got him looking like a tennis player," one official complained to Falk. "Exactly," Falk said.

The ban was the greatest publicity that the new shoes could have had. The Air Jordan was in the midst of its first six-city test-marketing campaign when Nike hit the air with a new commercial. The camera panned slowly up Jordan's body as he stood pounding a basketball menacingly into his palm. "On October 15, Nike created a revolutionary new basketball shoe," a voice intoned. "On October 18, the NBA threw them out of the game. Fortunately, the NBA can't keep *you* from wearing them. Air Jordans. For Nike.''

It was just the first shot in an extensive promotional barrage. From 1984 through 1986, Nike spent $5 million advertising Air Jordans. The first national commercial aired around Thanksgiving. It opened to a soaring view of Chicago's skyline, the sound of airplane engines and a voice confirming "ready for takeoff." Jordan leapt into the picture in slow motion, clutching a basketball in one hand. As he rose toward the hoop, he extended one arm behind him and splayed his legs, forming the silhouette now known in the industry as "the Jump Man." "Who says man was not meant to fly?" a voice asks as Jordan throws down a dunk.

Howard White, the Nike player liaison who would become one of Jordan's close friends, remembers the day the commercial was shot. "The number of people outside the fence, climbing the fence, was amazing," he says. "We knew we were on to something. We were filming at an all-girls' Catholic school in the suburbs, and the sisters had to hold them back. You could see a fire catching."

Though that first ad never became as popular as Jordan's later commercials with Spike Lee, it helped establish Michael as an inspiring presence, the athlete as artist. The shoe, meanwhile, was an immediate hit. Released nationally in March, 1985, it accounted for $130 million in sales in its inaugural year. Had Air Jordan been its own company, that figure would have made it the fifth-largest sneaker firm in the world. By the following September, 2.3 million pairs had been sold, along with $18 million worth of apparel.

"The shoe is credited with beginning the turnaround of Nike," says Beth Sexer, managing editor of *Sportstyle* magazine. "Nike had the air technology in existence in 1978, but before they came out with the Air Jordan shoe, they had never really capitalized on it."

Some shoe industry experts said Jordan's role was minimal. "I don't think the success of the Air Jordan had so much to do with Jordan as with the distinctive style of the shoe," said Mark Klionsky of *Sporting Goods Dealer* magazine. "The demand has been for very stylish, colored leather."

It is true that market research in the early '80s showed that inner-city kids, the group that sets sneaker fashions, were looking for "matchups"—colored sneakers that could be coordinated with an entire outfit. But in presenting the Air Jordan as a performance breakthrough, Nike was attempting to broaden the sneaker's potential market. In that regard, Jordan's personal appeal was central to the shoe's popularity. Not only was he a captivating player, but he had a multiracial appeal that insured the shoe's success with a wide variety of consumers.

"When he came out of college, everybody knew he would be a premium player," says Gordie Nye, a vice president at Reebok. "What was not predicted was that he would be such a quantum improvement over the spokesmen of the time. No one person had ever been able to drive a business the way he drove it.

"The market for athletic shoes is broad and fractured. It is very difficult to find someone who doesn't alienate part of your market. You put your shoes, say, on Brian Bosworth, teenage boys are going to love it, but their fathers are going to hate it. The thing about Jordan is that he doesn't alienate anybody."

The drawings for Air Jordan number 7 are propped against the wall near Tinker Hatfield's worktable. This is the shoe that Michael will wear in the 1992 All-Star game. He has seen it for the first time just a few days ago, when the Bulls were in town to play the Trail Blazers, and has pronounced himself satisfied.

"It's looser, more passionate, not quite so German techy," Hatfield says of his creation. "I'm trying to bring an exuberance into the design that's rougher. It's this sleek Ferrari-ish approach, combined with a more primitive tribal kind of thing."

This is his way of saying that the sneaker looks like no other you've ever seen. The typical detailing, those raised swatches of leather that intimate the way a sneaker supports your arches and ankles, has been reduced to jagged, laserlike lines that are supposed to give the shoe a futuristic feel. But the leather border that encases the heel resembles the hide of a Technicolor zebra. And the sole is a collage of bright colors and sharp angles reminiscent of the abstract African-influenced art of the early twentieth century.

Hatfield says his influence was the crossover success of "Living Color," the black roots of rock 'n' roll group.

"I've always stayed away from the ethnic tinge before, but my sense is that in '92 it will be okay," he says. By "ethnic," he, like everyone else in the industry, means black. "Before I was a little nervous about offending anybody. But if there is anything special about Michael Jordan that will be of some real long-term benefit to society, it will be the way he has transcended our racial thinking."

Apparently, some people at Nike disagreed because Hatfield's "ethnic" design never found its way to market. While Air Jordan Number 7 retains its multi-colored sole, the rest of Hatfield's adventuresome design was scrapped for a more traditional model.

It is, at any rate, an extravagant claim, that an athlete can change people's racial attitudes, one that in Jordan's case has not quite been borne out. Yet there is no question that he has won a following which knows no class, sex or racial boundaries. And for this, Nike is not the only institution in his debt.

7

The popularity of professional basketball reached its apogee in the late 1960s and early '70s, when the savvy, selfless New York Knicks won two championships. The game was hip, it was cerebral and, as embodied by the Knicks, it was a testament to how whites and blacks could enhance each other's performances and become part of a greater whole.

By the late '70s, however, the game was undergoing an erratic transformation. The athletes were better, yet to many fans the games were less satisfying. Basketball was faster now, its style more personal and confrontational.

Strategy seemed to have vanished, replaced by a run-and-shoot sort of game that many older fans, accustomed to patient, passing-oriented offenses, found off-putting. Many whites associated the seeming chaos on the court with the chaos on the streets of America's inner cities, and they blamed both on newly assertive young black men. The racial reaction that swept America in the late '70s and early '80s hit the NBA early.

These years gave rise to myths that still trouble the

league: the perception that players lacked discipline, played no defense and saved themselves for the playoffs. An NBA game, the joke went, wasn't much different from a track meet, except that every 24 seconds, people jumped up and down. To see a game, another joke had it, you only had to tune in for the last two minutes.

The league's problem was compounded by players' involvement in a succession of drug scandals. In 1980, the *Los Angeles Times* reported that between 40 and 75 percent of NBA players used cocaine. "I don't even read the stories about cocaine and basketball," a former player told Pete Axthelm of *Newsweek*. "The headlines might just as well have said that most players get out of bed in the morning. It's true, but it's not news."

CBS, in the midst of a four-year contract with the NBA, realized the game had lost its grip on the public imagination. That year, despite a dream final—Magic, Kareem and the Lakers versus Dr. J. and the 76ers—the network chose to air the final game on tape delay after the late local news. "The National Basketball Association," wrote *Newsweek*, "has become the sorriest mess in sports."

In 1981–82 NBA franchises lost an average of about $700,000. Thirteen teams were deeply in the red. Six were conspicuously for sale. When things got no better during the following season, the league's owners and its players' association were forced to come together on a pair of emergency measures.

The first of these was a drug policy. The players acceded to a plan that provided treatment for all who requested it, but suspended and would eventually ban repeat offenders. The sanctions were rather lenient and enforcement somewhat erratic at first, but by becoming the first major sport to deal with its drug problem, the NBA recaptured some credibility.

The intent of the second agreement, a cap on team salaries, was to save the owners from themselves. The average player's salary had soared to roughly $250,000 per season. These salaries accounted for 70 percent of most teams' budgets. The cap offered owners a way to stop spending themselves toward extinction. In return they guaranteed the players 53 percent of the league's revenues.

Pro basketball made another breakthrough that year, one much more easily achieved. David Stern succeeded Larry O'Brien as the game's commissioner and taught the NBA how to market itself. In 1980 the league had 25 people on its front office staff. Today it employs 300. "The vast majority of those additional people are in marketing, licensing, sponsorship, publicity, broadcasting, video production, home videos and public relations—all designed to put the players and the game in front of the consciousness in every place and at every level," Stern says.

Putting the game in front of people wasn't enough, though. The NBA had to change the negative stereotypes of the game and its players. To do so, it had to soften the racial prejudices of alienated fans. "We knew somehow we had to dig out from under," Stern says. "We believed if we did everything else well that the American public was more broad-minded than the media attitude trying to shape its opinions."

The league's strategy was similar to Nike's. It planned to highlight the talents of several well-known stars. Fortunately, two such stars had just presented themselves. Magic Johnson and Larry Bird entered the NBA in 1979, fresh from a nationally televised confrontation for the NCAA championship. One was black, the other white. One played for the league's dominant West Coast franchise, the Los Angeles Lakers, the other for its dominant East Coast franchise, the Boston Celtics. The public perceived them, and the league promoted them, as athletic and temperamental opposites.

For marketing purposes, Johnson became the ebullient city kid with the brilliant smile who ran the Lakers' fast-paced "Showtime" offense. Bird, the self-described Hick from French Lick (Indiana), was portrayed as the ungainly but enchanted craftsman whose deadly shooting and unselfish passing powered a more traditional Celtics team. And the league rode them toward prosperity.

In 1980 Bird won Rookie of the Year honors, but Johnson's team won the NBA championship and he was named Most Valuable Player in the finals. The following season their pictures appeared on the cover of the NBA's yearbook, an unusual honor for second-year players. In the decade ahead the two men would all but monopolize the Most Valuable Player award and make the NBA finals a two-team party occasionally crashed by Erving and the 76ers.

Johnson, Bird and Erving came to stand for all that was good in the game; their popularity, along with the success of the drug policy, salary cap and marketing programs, helped saved the league. But this reversal had not fully taken hold when Michael Jordan entered the NBA in 1984. Indeed, some analysts believed the league would never be healthy until the franchises in Chicago and New York experienced a resurgence. Jordan's job was to fill the first half of that bill.

The Bulls bet heavily on him. "Here Comes Mr. Jordan" was the theme of their season ticket drive. Chicago's efforts were augmented by a myriad of Nike promotions as well as Jordan's first commercials for local Chevy dealers. And yet, in sober moments, Michael's friends wondered whether too great a burden had been placed on his shoulders.

"I figured he would do okay," Fred Whitfield says. "Fifteen to 17 points, because he didn't score more than that in college. He's six-five max, and he never handled the ball that much. He was kind of in between being a guard and being a forward."

Michael admits to such doubts himself. "I thought I would come out and be a flop," he said, "because everybody was expecting so much."

Instead, he made those expectations seem meager. "Nobody, I don't care who they are, thought he would develop into a superstar," says Brendan Malone, the Pistons assistant who first scouted Jordan at the Five Star Camp. "Everybody thought he'd be a good player, a very good player in this league, but not to the point where you would say he is the best one-on-one player who ever played the game."

The show opened in Peoria. On a night when most Chicagoans were occupied with the Cubs and their impending collapse in the National League playoffs, Michael Jordan played his first exhibition game with the Bulls, scoring 18 points in 29 minutes in a 102–98 victory over the Indiana Pacers before 2,100 fans at the Peoria Civic Arena. The event was not much remarked upon in the Chicago papers, but the Bulls knew that something special was happening each day in their training camp at Angel Guardian High School on the northern edge of town.

"If I put him with the starters, they win," coach Kevin Loughery said. "If I put him with the second team, they win. If I put him on the offensive team, it seems his team always scores. When I put him on the defensive team, they always stop the offensive team. No matter what I do with Michael, his team wins."

Jordan brought to even the most mundane workouts a zeal that took his older teammates by surprise. "The first couple of weeks in training camp, we'd be running these drills and Michael would be going full-speed, slam dunking forwards, backwards and every which way," said veteran forward Steve Johnson. "With his being here a positive attitude spreads through the team." Orlando Woolridge, the best of the Bulls' veterans, called Jordan's attitude "a good cancer."

Michael, meanwhile, spent much of his time trying to deflect attention from himself. "It won't be the Michael Jordan show," he said on almost a daily basis. "I'll just be part of the team." He was very conscious of "not being a prima donna," of not upstaging his elders. "I wouldn't want that if I were a veteran and I try to put myself in our veterans' shoes," he said.

Try as he might, though, Jordan could do nothing about the publicity he received or the resentment it engendered in some of the Bulls. The problem was exacerbated by the fact that Michael found little common ground with his older teammates. He drank little and refused drugs. They, on the other hand, had earned Chicago a reputation as one of the hardest-partying teams in the NBA.

After that first exhibition game in Peoria, Jordan accepted an invitation to a postgame party, hoping to get to know his teammates better. He knocked on the hotel room door, saw several other Bulls drunk or coked up and quickly excused himself. Whether the incident further distanced Michael from his teammates is not clear, but it presaged the difficulties he would have communicating with older players who were suspicious of the instant hero and his copious press clippings.

While Jordan may have been isolated on the Bulls, he was not without companionship. Throughout training camp he was accompanied by Howard White, a former University of Maryland guard who was Nike's liaison with the players who wore its shoes. "He was a project that Nike was putting tons and tons of money into," White says. "On our part it was a big-time commitment. You had this major part of the company away from the office and you needed to have a little firsthand knowledge, a little hands-on information."

Having what amounted to a company chaperone might have posed real problems for Jordan had the man involved not been as even-tempered and emotionally generous as White. The Nike rep offered Michael a sense of stability and an opinion he could trust. "No reason for me to be the neighborhood good guy," White says.

Nor was Jordan without friends on the team. In training camp he met Rod Higgins, who now plays for the Golden State Warriors and is still Michael's best friend in the league. While other players were put off by Jordan's fame or his straight-arrow lifestyle, Higgins, a devout Christian, had no problems with either.

"It was pretty easy to get past that stuff," he says. "He was down-to-earth and still wearing his Wranglers and stuff. And he was so keyed into playing basketball and taking the next step from college to the professional level that the other stuff didn't really faze him. I'm sure some guys had a tough time dealing with it because of the attention, but as far as I'm concerned it was a blessing. It kept the pressure off the rest of us.''

The two became card-playing buddies, pool-playing buddies, bowling buddies. When Michael decided to put some of his endorsement money into a new home, he bought a town house near Higgins's in suburban Northbrook. Jordan quickly acquired a pool table; Higgins owned one, and Michael did not want to give him any advantage in their long-running rivalry.

James and Deloris Jordan were also on hand much of that first season, helping Michael to find and decorate his home, doing his shopping and attending as many games as they could. "We still tried to bring him the family atmosphere," Mrs. Jordan says. "We wanted him to know, 'If you fall on your nose on the floor there are still people in the stands who are going to care about you. They'll love you anyway.' "

Love, at least its physical component, was not in short supply for the league's newest star. Jordan could hardly leave the house without someone offering to love him. "The NBA?" Howard White says. "You are talking about some of the most beautiful women in the world coming after you."

White tried to protect Michael from gold diggers and thrill seekers. They had to get past him before they could be alone with Jordan. "He would let me ask them all the questions," White says. "They felt like they were on trial. I would find out about their backgrounds and things. You don't want somebody that's in it for all the wrong reasons."

For his part, Michael seemed jubilant within the whirl of his rookie season. His spirits were buoyed, no doubt, by the fact that he was becoming rich.

After Jordan signed his lucrative Nike deal, David Falk's next move was an obvious one: to get him a basketball. "We decided to sign with Wilson because Spalding had

Doc, Larry, Magic and a lot of other people," he says. "At the time Michael came to Wilson, I think they had [Kevin] McHale, Isiah [Thomas], [Mark] Aguirre. And when they signed Michael, they dropped Isiah and Aguirre. I think they felt his profile was sufficient that they didn't need the other two players."

The Wilson contract was worth an estimated $200,000 per year. Like the Nike deal, it did wonders for both parties. Wilson sells a million Jordan-autographed balls each year.

In retrospect it might seem that Michael's commercial success had been assured by his performance in the Olympics. But the sense that black athletes couldn't sell to white America persisted. Even after the tremendous boost of his Nike ads, a great deal of corporate spadework remained to be done.

"McDonald's was a good example," Falk says. "We couldn't even convince McDonald's to use him in Chicago. Not nationally, not regionally, just locally in Chicago. They weren't confident, in 1984, that he could deliver value to them, enough to sign him to a contract for $25,000 to $50,000 a year.

"We said, 'Trust us. We [ProServ] have [Jimmy] Connors with you. We have Gabriela Sabatini. We have a lot of different properties with you that are working well.

"Likewise Coca-Cola. After the initial meeting of the minds that we were going to do some things with Michael it took nine months to get it approved through the various channels.

"To this day, his Chevy contract in Chicago is the only situation he has that's not national. Obviously every advertising survey, every Q score . . . will tell you that if there is anyone in the country who is the heartbeat of America, it's Michael Jordan. Yet we have not been able to convince Chevrolet that they should take the campaign national."

Despite corporate America's initial reluctance, by year's end Jordan had signed endorsement contracts worth roughly $1.2 million, the bulk of that coming from Nike, Coca-Cola and McDonald's. But only Nike marketed Michael aggressively on a nationwide basis. So while he was already the richest commercial endorser in basketball, he was nowhere near the national celebrity he would one day become.

Jordan earned another $125,000 from personal appearances his rookie season, not to mention his $800,000 salary from the Bulls. The question, as the exhibition season progressed, was whether the product would live up to its marketing. The answer, as it turned out, was "No sweat."

In the Bulls' second exhibition game, Jordan gave the team a taste of what lay ahead, scoring 32 points on 10-of-11 shooting as Chicago wiped out the Kansas City Kings, 107–100. "All I can say is he hasn't been in the league a month yet and the refs are treating him like a god," said Larry Drew of Kansas City. Drew was not alone in noticing that NBA referees were not calling Michael for his traveling violations.

As word of Jordan's exhilarating performances spread, the Bulls' exhibition road trip became suddenly chaotic. Fans in almost every city jammed hotel lobbies, massed at arena exits and swamped the team bus trying to get a look at Jordan. "Man, this is like traveling with Michael Jackson," Orlando Woolridge said. "Police escorts, television cameras, sneaking around to avoid crowds. Michael and the Jackson . . . hey, this is Michael and the Bulls. I love it."

For his part, Jordan was both flattered and overwhelmed. "I never thought it would be anything like this," he said. "There are a lot of stars in the NBA: Larry Bird, Dr. J., Magic, Isiah. For a rookie to come in and get this much publicity, whew!"

It was a heady time, but also a difficult one, as Michael acquired his first taste of the isolation that fame would one day force upon him. "People would come out of the woodwork," Howard White remembers. "So you say, 'Well, hold it. On the road we don't go anywhere.'"

Jordan's life in the league began officially on October 26 as the Bulls opened the regular season at the Stadium against the Washington Bullets. Musing on the extravagant air of anticipation that surrounded Jordan, the *Tribune*'s Bernie Lincicome wrote: "One almost expected him to be launched like a new nuclear destroyer by having some patient Bulls season ticket holder crack a bottle of champagne over his head."

When the *Chicago Sun-Times* caught up with Jordan before the game he was immersed in the soon-to-be-ritualistic dispersal of his free tickets. "I've got two women coming tonight," he said, "and I want to put them in different sections."

Michael did not have one of his better games that evening, though one might not have known it from reading the press coverage. The Bulls won easily, 109–93, behind 28 points from Woolridge and 25 from Quintin Dailey. But it was Jordan, who went 5 of 16 from the field for 16 points, pulled down six rebounds and committed five turnovers, who received all the attention.

"They should have hung a halo atop Chicago Stadium Friday night because this was no basketball game," wrote Jim O'Donnell in the *Arlington Heights* (Illinois) *Herald*. "It was a revival meeting. Step aside Elmer Gantry. Shut down Billy Sunday. The Bulls have been saved."

"No one," he wrote, "was denying that the celestial Mr. Jordan had alleviated the spiritual malaise plaguing the team for much of the past three seasons." High praise for such a mediocre performance, but as Bob Sakamoto of the *Chicago Tribune* pointed out, while Jordan "forgot to bring along his jump shot . . . [he] did something else instead. He brought back fun to the stadium."

Jordan did that as much through his abandon as his acrobatics, diving for loose balls and sailing into thickets of thicker bodies to pull away rebounds. In the second quarter he collided with the Bullets' burly Jeff Ruland and crashed to the floor, where he remained for 30 Stadium-silencing seconds. After a single game Jordan was the recipient of accolades usually bestowed in the midst of a long career.

"In every sport there is the athlete who has the capacity for making everything around him better," wrote Steve Daly in the *Tribune*. "One game into his career as a professional basketball player Michael Jordan has shown one more time, that he is such an athlete."

Perhaps the most remarkable aspect of Jordan's rookie season is how quickly he established himself not only as an exciting player, but as a dominant one. In the Bulls' second game of the season he tossed up an airball at the buzzer in their 108–106 loss to Milwaukee. Not an auspicious moment, but evidence of how willing the rookie was to take the shot that would decide the game.

"He looks for the opportunity to be the hero or the goat," Higgins says. "He's not afraid to have that pressure." In a rematch with the Bucks two nights later, Jordan scored 37 points, including 20 of his team's last 26, as Chicago triumphed 116–110.

Even on off nights he drew respectful praise from the opponents who had stymied him. "He is similar to David Thompson in his prime," said T. R. Dunn of Denver, one of the league's defensive stalwarts, who held Jordan to 17 points in a 129–113 Nuggets victory. "He can shoot, penetrate, pass, handle the ball and whew, everybody knows how he can jump. The key is to try and stop him from getting the ball."

Michael's renown brought an almost carnival atmosphere to the Bulls' first trips to New York and Los Angeles. After Jordan pumped in 33 points during a November 8 victory over the Knicks, the mob of media people around his dressing cubicle grew so deep that teammates had trouble getting dressed. "Michael Jordan, get your own building!" yelled reserve guard Wes Matthews.

The scene in Los Angeles was even more frantic when the Bulls arrived on November 30 to take on the Clippers. The Clippers play second violin, if that, in the hearts of most Los Angeles basketball fans. But on that night, even Jack Nicholson deserted the Lakers to get a look at Jordan.

Michael did not play one of his better games, scoring just 20 points, but he made the evening memorable nonetheless.

With 1:26 to play and the Clippers leading 100–98, Jordan nailed an 18-foot jump shot to knot the score. On defense he smothered Clippers point guard Norm Nixon, who forced up an airball. The Bulls' Caldwell Jones gathered in the errant shot as Jordan bolted for the other basket.

Jones heaved an outlet pass that Michael ran down beyond mid-court. As Jordan swooped in for the tie-breaking layup, the Clippers' Derek Smith wrapped him in a flying bear hug. Somehow, Michael got the shot off.

Somehow, it went in.

Jordan sank his free throw, and the Bulls hung on to win 104–100. After the game Michael had to be driven to the Bulls' bus in a truck to avoid the horde of fans who jammed the bowels of the Los Angeles Memorial Sports Arena. "I enjoy the challenge," Jordan said. "People come out ready to play against me because they like to find out if the ink is really true about Michael Jordan."

A week later he sank a 20-footer with five seconds to play as the Bulls beat the Knicks 95–93. At the season's quarter-mark, Chicago, with perhaps the worst roster in the league, was 12–9 and tied for the Central Division lead with Milwaukee. The following evening the Bulls chalked up their fifth straight victory, a 99–97 decision over the Dallas Mavericks.

But that was as good as it got for the humble Bulls. After winning five straight, they lost five straight. Game after game, they would play well for three quarters, even three and a half, then falter in the stretch. On December 18, they led the Houston Rockets 96–93 with the clock running down, but Houston scored the last 11 points to win, 104–96.

While Jordan continued to pack arenas on the road, Chicago fans showed fitful interest in the Bulls. Only 7,516 had been on hand on November 19 to see Jordan score 34 points against the Indiana Pacers. Just 8,022 saw his last-second heroics on December 7 against the Knicks. In

Jordan's rookie season, the Bulls sold out the Stadium just seven times, six of those against the league's top attractions: Bird and the Celtics; Dr. J. and the 76ers; Magic, Kareem and the Lakers; and the Twin Towers of Houston, Olajuwon and Sampson.

Meanwhile, in the midst of a roller-coaster season, Jordan was slowly adjusting to life in the NBA. He was not then the savvy traveler, stylish dresser and seasoned businessman that he is today. Instead, friends say, he seemed more like a fugitive college senior—which, in fact, is what he was. Jordan still dressed in sweats, watched the soap operas he'd once planned courses around, and ate at McDonald's whenever crowd control was not an issue. "Right now," he told Sam Smith of the *Tribune*, "is the best time of my life."

Jordan was already the most popular, and perhaps the most extravagantly praised, rookie in the history of the league. "Michael Jordan is not only a great scorer, he is a great passer," said New Jersey Nets coach Stan Albeck after his team had taken a 100–94 decision from the Bulls on January 16. "He has unbelievable hang time. He can stay up there, jump over the double team and then have the innate ability to get the ball to the open man no matter where he is on the floor. That part of him isn't talked about enough."

The notion that some part of Jordan's game had escaped their appreciation must have struck basketball fans as peculiar. They had elected Michael to the starting lineup of the Eastern Conference All-Star team, placing him in the company of Bird, Erving, Thomas and Moses Malone. It was, at the time, the thrill of Jordan's career.

"Remember when I said one of my goals was to play in *one* All-Star game?" he asked reporters. "God, I just know I'll be so happy playing in that game. I'll be playing with four Hall of Famers who have already proven themselves and earned the people's respect. I'm in the process of trying to get where they are.

"I'm going to be so nervous I probably won't remember

how to play. I may not score a point. I may not do anything and be back on the bench after two minutes I'll be so nervous.''

''Nervous'' is not a word the other Bulls would have used to describe Jordan. The team was increasingly his to lead, and on occasion he accepted that burden. In mid-January, Michael, who was leading the club in scoring, assists and steals, found that he was also among the Bulls' top rebounders. After scoring 45 points and grabbing eight boards in a 117–104 victory over the Atlanta Hawks, he issued a friendly challenge to the team's big men. He told them that he intended to lead the Bulls in rebounding too. ''I'm going for it,'' he said. ''By me challenging them it will force them to work harder and will be good for competition.''

Not everyone on the Bulls was comfortable with Jordan's increasing command of the team. The first one to betray his anger was Quintin Dailey, who had led the Bulls in scoring in 1983–84, and whom Jordan had displaced at the shooting guard spot. Dailey's outburst was published in late January by a suburban newspaper, the *Daily Herald*. It was aimed not directly at Jordan, but at Bulls coach Kevin Loughery and assistant Fred Carter.

''Michael didn't ask for it, but he was their boy,'' Dailey said. ''And I was at the other end, the one who could do nothing right. Jordan's got great natural talent, but he's still learning the NBA game. But even when he'd take a messed-up shot or throw a bad pass during the preseason, Loughery and Carter would be clapping their hands and giving him encouragement and everything.''

Dailey was, he admitted, ''a player who likes to shine a little bit himself.'' He was also an extremely troubled young man. In 1978 both his parents had died within a month and Dailey's life started downhill, taking others with it.

In 1981, while among the nation's leading collegiate scorers, Dailey pleaded guilty to aggravated assault on a student nurse. The incident led the University of San Francisco to drop its basketball program. The Bulls, nonetheless, made him their top draft pick in 1982, and he responded by making the All-Rookie team. But by 1983, Dailey, still averaging more than 18 points a game, was mired in a drug-related depression and at one point attempted suicide. He was still struggling with his drug problem when he lashed out at the coaching staff and, by implication, his rookie teammate.

Jordan tried to minimize the damage done by Dailey's remarks. "We get along fine," he said. "As far as being a teammate and a friend, he's been straight with me. He's been a friend." Considering Dailey's personal problems, his criticism might have been easily dismissed, except that it captured a growing resentment toward Jordan that surfaced on All-Star weekend, February 8 through 10 in Indianapolis.

Michael cruised into that weekend fresh from a 41-point outburst against the Celtics, a performance marred only by an airball at 0:13 that left the Bulls 107–106 losers. "Never seen anyone like him," said Larry Bird, who was in the midst of a three-year reign as the league's Most Valuable Player. "He's the best ever. Yep. At this stage, he's doing more than I ever did."

But the accomplishments hardly guaranteed Jordan a warm welcome in Indianapolis. The two players challenged most directly by Michael's popularity were Magic Johnson and Isiah Thomas, the league's other premier guards. Each was a bona fide star, each a fan favorite, but neither had reaped remotely the endorsements or the adulation that Jordan received. Johnson and Thomas are close friends who had other close friends among that seasons' All-Stars. Those included George Gervin, the former scoring champion who played for San Antonio, and Mark Aguirre of the Dallas Mavericks. Aguirre, along with Thomas, had lost his Wilson endorsement after the sporting goods firm signed Jordan.

Michael was circumspect in his approach to the weekend. He did not want to be perceived as bigheaded. Instead he behaved with such uncharacteristic diffidence that veteran All-Stars found him aloof.

"I'm not the type of person to go and see Isiah or see George Gervin and hold a 30-minute conversation," Jordan said later. "I don't know them personally and they don't know me personally. You know, I speak and hold a brief conversation and get to know them slowly."

Jordan made matters worse for himself during the slam dunk competition, in which he finished second to Dominique Wilkins. The slam dunk was then only a year old and was still taken seriously by the league's most artful jammers. Contestants competed in their uniforms. Not Jordan, though. He showed up wearing gold chains and a new paratrooper-style sweat suit emblazoned with the Nike logo.

"We had a lengthy meeting the day before with the Nike people and they wanted to display the new line of Air Jordan clothes," Falk said. "We thought the slam dunk contest would be the best time to display it." But the other All-Stars disagreed. They felt Jordan was boasting about his endorsements and belittling the competition.

The following day Michael's teammates had a chance to express their disapproval. Jordan suffered through a difficult game, shooting just 2 of 9 from the floor and finishing with 7 points. On defense Gervin burned him repeatedly and none of Michael's teammates seemed interested in helping out. Jordan managed six rebounds and three steals and blocked a shot by the 7-foot-4 Ralph Sampson, but he wasn't himself.

"Usually your nerves leave you on your first trip up the court," Jordan said. "Today, I didn't feel like myself until the second half. I've never had that feeling before, never been as nervous. After all, this is the highlight of my career."

Much of the weekend's luster faded for Michael the following day as stories began to appear suggesting that Thomas, point guard for the East squad, had engineered an effort to freeze Jordan out. Thomas has always denied this, but several sources say they saw Johnson, his godfather Charles Tucker and Gervin at the airport laughing about the lesson Jordan had been taught. One Detroit columnist wrote: "The attitude of the players was Michael Jordan will get star treatment when he learns how to act like a gentleman."

"That makes me feel very small," Jordan said when he heard the charge. "I want to crawl inside a hole and not come out. I'll go home and mope the rest of the day."

In a television interview more than a year later, Jordan sounded as though the incident still stung. "I was very hurt when the articles came out," he said. "I didn't know anything about it. The cameras came up and they told me about it. I was very shocked and I couldn't even do an interview. . . .

"I just think a lot of people misinterpreted my reactions. . . . From that point on and up to now, I've been kind of introverted a little bit. I was very cautious with my outgoing personality."

Two days after the freeze-out the Bulls faced Thomas and the Pistons in the Stadium. Out on the court before the game, Thomas and Jordan spoke briefly. "To iron things out," Jordan told one interviewer. "For show," he said to another. Whatever resentment Jordan bore was channeled into the finest performance of his early career, 49 points and 15 rebounds, as the Bulls defeated the Pistons in overtime, 139–126.

As the season wore on some observers felt that Michael was beginning to wear down. He'd been playing almost nonstop for nearly 18 months straight, first for Carolina, then for the Olympic team and now for the Bulls. "When I look at him I think of all the responsibility I had with the Clippers in my rookie season," former DePaul star Terry Cummings said. "It seemed like so much fun in the beginning, but after a while it's like a horse carrying too much. There's too much on the wagon."

Jordan claimed that he wasn't tired. He blamed his ragged mood on "the frustration of losing." Michael was, by this point, the odds-on favorite to become Rookie of the Year; Akeem Olajuwon of Houston was his only real competition.

But despite Jordan's individual efforts, the Bulls sank further below the .500 mark.

Only 6,965 fans turned out on February 26 to see Michael rack up 28 points and nine rebounds in a 123–118 loss to Cleveland. The following night in Detroit, the Bulls set a dubious club record, dropping their 12th straight road game. On March 3, Quintin Dailey was suspended for failing a drug test. In that night's 117–113 loss to the Nets, Jordan had 14 rebounds, five more than Chicago's starting frontcourt combined. The Bulls were 27–32.

For the first time in his life, Michael was playing for a losing team, a team jeered and hooted at by its own fans. His best efforts could do little to change that. Frustrated and impatient, Jordan began to doubt that even his coach wanted to win.

On March 11, in a 119–112 loss to the Washington Bullets, Loughery rested Jordan for the last 10 minutes of the fourth quarter. It was the team's 13th game in 20 days and the coach thought his star looked "very fatigued." But Jordan was livid.

"That's his decision and I don't question that, but I don't quit," he said. "From where I come from and the way I've been taught, you try to win every game you play. I wanted to go back in the whole time. I was unhappy sitting there."

The outburst said more about Jordan's difficulty in adjusting to life on a losing team than it did about Loughery's will to win. But it was also a sign of Michael's growing confidence in himself and his own judgment. He was showing greater independence than he had at UNC. By the following season, he would be willing to take his disagreements with the Bulls' management public in the most contentious sort of way. And just in time, as it turned out.

Back on the road Michaelmania reached a new height. On March 23, the Bulls made their only appearance in Dallas. For 129 nights leading up to the game, a Texas sportscaster had featured Jordan highlights on every broadcast. That night at Reunion Arena scalpers who got $100 a ticket when

Bird, Magic and Dr. J. came to town were moving their merchandise at $225 a pop. Jordan had an off night, shooting only 5 of 17 from the field, but he handed out 10 assists and grabbed nine rebounds in Chicago's 107–97 victory.

At 38–44, the Bulls made the playoffs in spite of themselves. A 100–91 victory over the Bullets on April 3 made matters official. After the game Jordan's teammates pushed him into the shower and doused him with beer. "It was a toast to Michael for all he has done for us and the organization," said forward David Greenwood. "This man has brought the Bulls national attention and it is the least we could do for him."

The Milwaukee Bucks bounced Chicago quickly from the playoffs, taking the best-of-five series, three games to one. Jordan was disappointed that his team had not acquitted itself better after splitting a six-game regular season series with the Bucks, but he couldn't be downcast about his own success. He led his team in scoring (28.2), rebounding (6.5) and assists (5.9). Only Larry Bird and Dave Cowens had ever done the same. Jordan also led the club in steals (2.39). He was the easy winner of the NBA's Rookie of the Year award, and seemed to be on the threshold of greatness.

Near season's end, someone asked Celtics coach K. C. Jones what Jordan had to accomplish to be considered in the same class as Johnson and Bird. "He's there," Jones replied. "How many games does he have to play to show he belongs in that class? He was there from the time the first ball was thrown up in the first Bulls game."

Others were more cautious. "I think to be compared in that category you have to turn your team into a championship-caliber club," Julius Erving said. "Bird and Magic have led their teams to championships. That's something we don't know if Michael can do or not."

But there could be no argument that he had helped reverse the financial fortunes of his team. Bulls attendance increased from an average of 6,365 to almost 12,000. The team took in an extra $10 million in ticket revenues.

Ragged as it was, the 1984–85 Bulls campaign inspired hope for a new season in which the team would be operating under new ownership, a new general manager and a new coach. A group led by Jerry Reinsdorf, majority owner of the Chicago White Sox, had purchased the Bulls late in the season. On March 25, Reinsdorf had fired Rod Thorn and replaced him with former basketball and baseball scout Jerry Krause. Krause, in turn, had fired Kevin Loughery and replaced him with Stan Albeck of the New Jersey Nets. Together they looked forward to a new season with Jordan. But it was a season that would offer them less to savor than to dread.

8

All smart sports fans are at least a little bit cynical. It is almost impossible not to be. The reason is that we nurture two contradictory visions of professional sports. On the one hand it is a dream world, a land of games that thrill and instruct us, a realm whose currencies are strength, grace, craft and bravery. On the other hand it is our economy in microcosm, a free-wheeling marketplace in which players all owners are driven, not surprisingly, by financial self-interest rather than sporting success, a country whose currency is—currency.

It is essential to hold these two visions simultaneously in our minds. Without the first, sports is simply competition, no more rewarding an experience than hanging out at the supermarket to see whether Coke is outselling Pepsi. Without the second, we lose our ability to make intelligent moral distinctions, believing too easily that sports is a world apart, that all athletes are knights and all owners King Arthur.

But the second vision undeniably diminishes the power of the first. The more we understand about the economics of professional sports, the harder it becomes to believe in the authenticity of the games we love. We see athletes play splendidly right before they become free agents and indifferently afterwards. We see general managers trading talented veterans for unproven rookies to avoid paying the veterans what they are worth. We read of owners threatening to leave their government-financed arenas and head to another town unless the city makes further concessions. Cynicism is the only intelligent response.

Being cynical, in this case, is preferable to being angry because it allows us to keep watching. We can put a little distance between ourselves and our sports and laugh at our passion for such a compromised endeavor. All the while we are watching for a player who loves the game for the same reasons as those of us who cannot earn a nickel from our devotion.

In the 1985–86 season Michael Jordan proved he was that kind of player. He put his career on the line to come back early from a serious foot injury and lead the Bulls into a postseason series that became his personal showcase. The decision Jordan made was risky, even foolish, yet in a single stroke it dispelled any suspicions that he was a creation of Nike, ProServ or the NBA and established him firmly as his own man.

As coach Stan Albeck put it: "There aren't many times that a superstar is told to sit out by the medical profession, the ownership and his agent and still tells them all to go to hell and that he wants to play."

The season began badly for the Bulls. They were in the midst of an 0–8 exhibition campaign when Quintin Dailey asked to be sent to a drug treatment facility. His request caught the team by surprise. They thought Dailey's off-season marriage and his work with local young people were signs that he had regained control of his life. His mid-October departure left Chicago with a vacancy in its backcourt, and in filling it Jerry Krause first ran afoul of Michael Jordan.

Krause sent David Greenwood to the San Antonio Spurs

for George Gervin, the aging gunner who was one of the key figures in Jordan's All-Star humiliation. "Right now we have the best-shooting backcourt in basketball," the general manager exulted. But Jordan was somewhat less enthusiastic. "I have no comment on the trade," he commented. "Just say that I am unhappy about it."

That same day, Rod Higgins, Michael's only confidant on the team, was placed on waivers. Chicago suddenly seemed a chillier place for Jordan. Despite his funk, though, Michael was near top form in the Bulls' home opener against Cleveland on October 25. He scored 29 points, seven of those in overtime, and his final free throw gave Chicago a 116–115 victory. It was the sole high point of his early season.

The following night the Detroit Pistons came to town and Michael was introduced rather rudely to Bill Laimbeer. In the fourth quarter, with the Bulls leading 103–98, Jordan drove the lane. Laimbeer hurtled after him, less interested it seemed in blocking Jordan's shot than in smashing him to the floor. Michael hit the deck hard and both benches emptied. The melee that followed was so chaotic even coaches Stan Albeck and Chuck Daly found themselves flailing at one another.

"I went to the hole and he didn't try to block the shot, he just slammed me down," Jordan said after the game. "Then he just walked away. He didn't try to help me up or say he was sorry. I think he did it intentionally. That's when I got mad."

Michael's anger, fueled by three years of postseason frustration against Detroit, has only intensified over the years. It has turned him, at least against the Pistons, into a colder, more businesslike and, at times, meaner ballplayer. The only punch he has thrown on the court was aimed at Laimbeer. The only opponents he publicly baits are the Pistons. Hostilities between the two teams became so overheated during the final game of the 1990–91 season that NBC's Bob Costas kept some tongue-in-cheek statistics on Cheap Shots, Heated Moments and Fights. On the evening he first tangled with Laimbeer, Jordan took out his anger on the not-yet-fabled Detroit defense, scoring 33 points as Chicago held on to win 121–118.

The Bulls' season, their exhibition schedule included, was only three weeks old, but already Jordan had begun two of the feuds that would flare up repeatedly throughout his career. He wouldn't see any more of Bill Laimbeer until the following season, but the friction between himself and Jerry Krause was about to increase exponentially.

On October 29 against the Golden State Warriors, the Bulls' season all but fell apart. Late in the second quarter, streaking cross-court, Jordan suddenly crumpled to the floor of the Oakland Coliseum. Michael's fans had seen this happen before. He played with such abandon that such spills were inevitable. All they could do was wait for him to regain his feet.

On this night, that took some time. Jordan was helped from the court by teammates and taken to the locker room. Word circulated during the game that the injury was a minor one, probably a recurrence of the jammed ankle he'd suffered in the last game of the exhibition season. The following day's papers focused on the Bulls' 111–105 victory and on their signing of guard John Paxson.

Jordan showed up for practice that day on crutches. He was hobbled, but only slightly concerned. Word was that he would miss two games. "It isn't a serious injury," said trainer Mark Pfiel.

Then, suddenly, it was. "Jordan will miss six weeks," read the *Tribune*'s November 5 headline.

Michael had broken the navicular tarsal bone in his left foot. The break was so small that X rays had shown nothing. It took a CAT scan to diagnose the damage. Because the break was tiny, however, did not mean it would heal quickly. The navicular tarsal gets as little blood as any bone in the body and is therefore slow to mend.

Michael's charmed life had led him to the conviction that everything happens for the best, and he was deeply shaken by the news. "I've never gone through anything like this before,'' he said. "I don't know how to deal with it. Right now I can cry all night and wake up tomorrow and find out what it's all about.

"Somehow," he said, "there has to be a good reason for why this is happening to me. Something good has to come out of this. I just can't see it right now."

After Jordan's injury the Bulls lost four straight. In Michael's absence Quintin Dailey returned to the club, seemingly hustled out of his rehabilitation program to bolster Chicago's backcourt scoring. He tossed in 23 points in a 116–101 loss to Atlanta on November 20, but his grip on recovery was tenuous and did not last long.

Jordan, discouraged and confused, left Chicago just before the Bulls went on a two-week western road trip. He returned to his parents' home in Wilmington, and later stayed with Adolph Shiver in Chapel Hill. He spent most of the time trying to shake a slowly growing sense of despair.

The Bulls, 5–9 by the time he left, were not happy about his absence. On November 24, while his teammates were being roughed up by the Washington Bullets—John Paxson got slammed into the basket stand—Michael sat smiling beside Dean Smith on the bench during a University of North Carolina contest. Both games were broadcast on cable television in Chicago and Jordan's "desertion" was a hot topic on the sports pages.

The following week, Jerry Krause called Michael and asked him to join his teammates in Phoenix for the last three games of their trip. Jordan refused. He was working out in Chapel Hill and coming to terms with his injury. Also, he said, he couldn't stand to watch his teammates play so poorly night after night.

The Bulls, sporting an 8–17 record by early December, resented his absence but were circumspect about saying so. "Who's going to admit that it does bother us?" center Dave Corzine asked rhetorically. Jordan returned to Chicago just after the road trip. Smarting over the criticism he had taken from teammates and the media, Michael took a swipe at Jerry Krause.

"I know Krause didn't think I was keeping up with my conditioning while I was home," he said. "He's wrong." In fact, Jordan had begun a weight-lifting regimen that would add 10 pounds of muscle to his slender upper body. But that was not the part of his anatomy in which people were interested. Even his jab at the general manager went largely unnoticed in the anticipation that surrounded Michael's December 12 physical.

The report from Bulls team physician Dr. John Hefferon was expected to be a positive one. The papers speculated that Jordan might return by January 1, and general managers around the league spoke hopefully about how his comeback would boost the Bulls' road attendance. Pat Williams, general manager of the Philadelphia 76ers, said a healthy Jordan was worth 5,000 tickets a game in the Spectrum.

But Michael wasn't coming back. "Air Jordan remains grounded," read the *Tribune*'s December 13 headline. The bone had not healed. Jordan would be out for another four weeks, Hefferon said. Maybe more.

The waiting made Michael profoundly uneasy. "I'm a spontaneous type of person," he said. "I want to do things, *bam*, just like that. I was seeing myself come back too soon. . . . I had to learn how to be a patient."

The lesson never really took. By late December a hint of desperation surfaced when a *Tribune* reporter asked whether the injury might force him to be less acrobatic. "Don't even think like that," Jordan said. "I have to be the same way. I just have to."

For Michael, the winter that followed was a bleak one, punctuated by moments of false hope. After his Christmas time physical the Bulls announced that he would be back in the lineup on February 1. But it was January 28 before Jordan traded his cast for a splint, and his return was postponed until February 14 at the earliest. The Bulls, meanwhile, took a 17–33 record to the All-Star break, and were all but forgotten in the excitement that surrounded the Bears' march toward the Super Bowl.

"It's not like we are sitting around waiting for him to come back," Dave Corzine said after one loss. "But he is such a great player he makes up for a lot of the things we're doing wrong. . . . Whatever shortcomings we have, Michael is such a great player he can compensate for all of them. I truly believe that."

NBA fans held Jordan in equally high regard. Though he was unable to play, they once again selected him to the Eastern Conference's starting All-Star team. The league was intent on having him attend and offered to fly Jordan and a friend along for free.

After Higgins's departure, Michael didn't really have a close friend on the team, but he was just getting to know rookie forward Charles Oakley. Oakley had joined the club on draft day in a four-player deal with the Cleveland Cavaliers. At 6-foot-9 and 243 pounds, he had the size and, occasionally, the temperament of an enforcer. He was an inspired rebounder, an area in which the Bulls were conspicuously weak, and he set very sturdy picks. These attributes were not lost on Jordan, who had spent more time than he thought desirable pulling himself off arena floors.

"Guys were always trying to aggravate him, especially Detroit; cheap fouls," Oakley remembers. "You can't have guys bouncing around your best player. I said I would stand in front of him for anything. Except a bullet."

The rookie forward also enjoyed the verbal roughhousing that Jordan loved. Michael decided to take Oakley along to the game and whet his appetite for All-Star competition. "I told him to come with me and that he wouldn't have to pay for anything," Jordan said. "That's my bodyguard. I am going to be like a big brother to him."

The weekend was an uneventful one for Michael, with none of the bitterness of his rookie season. His spirits were high and he was already looking forward to returning to practice. "I'll bring some laughter to the team," he said. "Many days I would come in and get them going—have fun and still compete in practice. You don't see much of that this year.''

In reality, though, Jordan's relationship with his teammates had been strained by his sojourns in North Carolina and by the comments he made upon his return. Just before the All-Star break Quintin Dailey was suspended from the team for his continued use of drugs. The Bulls' decision to allow the troubled guard to rejoin the club back in November now looked particularly shortsighted, even cruel. But Jordan expressed little sympathy for his teammate. "You never know when Quintin will be with us," he said. "He has let the team down. At a time when we really need him, he hasn't been there."

Michael's relationship with the other Bulls frayed a bit further after a mid-February team meeting at which he asserted that some of his teammates just weren't playing hard enough. "I'm not a quitter and I wouldn't classify my teammates as quitters," said forward Sidney Green. "When one of your teammates says things like that it really hurts."

Publicly Jordan was coy about the charge. "I'm not trying to create a controversy, but I also believe a hurt dog will holler," he said. "I didn't say the whole team wasn't trying, just certain players."

The remark not only infuriated some of Jordan's teammates, it indicated how frustration had warped his judgment. These, after all, were the people who would be setting him picks and getting him rebounds. There was no reason to alienate them.

"I am a little depressed," Jordan admitted. "I still believe that things are meant to be and that something good comes out of everything. But right now, I just don't know what it is."

He would remain in the dark for another two months. The foot just didn't seem to be getting any better. Jordan met with his agent David Falk, who pointed out the financial risks of returning too quickly and recommended that he sit out the season. He met with foot specialists in Eugene, Oregon, and in Cleveland. They also recommended a further delay.

"Jordan lost for season?" asked the *Tribune* headline on February 13.

Michael seemed on the verge of admitting he was through for the year. "I listened to the advice of three doctors I consulted and in what was an emotional decision, I have decided the best course is not to play until I go through another examination in four weeks," he told the press.

Jordan's decision had the full support of the Bulls' management. "We believe Michael has made the correct decision," Jerry Reinsdorf said. "His future is more important to us than winning games now."

In fact, it seemed that winning games served little purpose. On February 17, Jordan's 23rd birthday, the Bulls dropped a 124–110 decision to Indiana and fell 21 games below .500. Their chances of making the playoffs seemed slimmer than those of making the NBA draft lottery. The lottery seemed like a good idea to a lot of people. A top draft pick, teamed with a healthy Michael Jordan, would make for a much more impressive Chicago roster the following season.

Jordan didn't see it that way. For him, recovery was an even mixture of dedication and desperation. It seemed impossible that the life he had just begun to build could crumble so quickly. After the All-Star break he returned to North Carolina, splitting his time between Wilmington and Chapel Hill.

Deloris Jordan remembers her son sitting around the house, staring at his X rays and CAT scans, trying to convince himself that they said what he wanted them to. "It was so funny," she says, "how he'd look at them and say, 'See the X ray; I know it's healed.' I told him, 'You know your body better than anyone else. You know if this is a risk you want to take. You'll have to live with this the rest of your life, so if you want to take that risk, take it.'"

It was a difficult winter for the Jordan family, and Michael's injury was not the only reason. A criminal investigation begun the previous summer at General Electric's Wilmington plant had revealed that James Jordan received $7,000 for his part in an embezzlement scheme. According to papers filed in New Hartford County Superior Court, Jordan, in March of 1983, submitted an $11,560 purchase order and receipt for equipment that the company neither needed nor received. The money was paid to local contractor Dale Gierszewski who wrote Jordan a $7,000 check the following month.

Early in 1986 Mr. Jordan prepared the guilty plea he would file later that winter. The best he could hope for was the suspended sentence and supervised probation that he ultimately received. The family knew that the plea would be the talk of Wilmington and that people would speculate about whether the Jordans had spent beyond their means in following the North Carolina basketball team to games in Europe and Hawaii. It was a nervous time, but the family refrained—and still refrains—from making any public comments on the incident.

Michael, meanwhile, was spending much of his week in Chapel Hill, where he applied himself to a grueling regimen of physical therapy, followed by the course work he needed to complete his degree.

For all the Bulls knew, this was how he spent his days. But once again the guys at Woollen Gym had inside information. Late on those winter afternoons, in public, yet somehow in secret, Michael Jordan took the brazen step of playing basketball.

"I started gradually," he later told the *Tribune*. "First I took some free throws, then some shots. We got up a couple of two-on-two games. Then three-on-three. Finally, one of the guys in the gym started a good five-on-five game and I just got into it.

"I went through the mental thing: Should I be doing this? This was going through my mind. But as I came down the court I couldn't feel anything wrong. As I continued to play

I could tell parts of my game were beginning to come back. When I finally dunked it felt wonderful.''

On March 10 he returned to Chicago, secretly convinced he was ready to play. The test he took that day indicated he had regained all of the strength in his left foot. It was the first truly encouraging news he had received since October 29.

''He has worked so hard rehabilitating the injury that in some motions his left foot is stronger than his right one,'' said Judy Joffe, the occupational therapist who worked with Jordan. ''At first I thought, 'No way should he go back.' Then I started working with him and I saw the power, the determination, the enthusiasm. It makes you wonder.''

That day, for the first time in five months, Jordan practiced with his teammates. That night he was scheduled to meet with Reinsdorf, Krause and others to discuss his return. ''Maybe I should just buy them off,'' Jordan joked.

Once again, good news was followed by bad. A CAT scan showed a tiny crack in the bone. His doctors estimated that if Jordan returned to action, he had a 10 to 20 percent chance of reinjuring himself. If he waited until the next season, the chance of reinjury would drop to 1 in 100. But Michael still wanted to play.

On March 13, in an 11:30 P.M. conference call, he stated his position to Reinsdorf, Krause and his three doctors. Each advised him to sit out the season. Jordan was adamant. Reinsdorf compared Michael's return to a game of Russian roulette. Jordan asked for the gun.

What emerged after long hours of dickering was a bizarre compromise. Jordan was allowed to return, but only on the condition he play no more than seven minutes each half. Krause and Reinsdorf would increase his time only when they saw fit.

''We were trying to hedge our bets,'' Jerry Krause says now. ''I wasn't going to be the guy who let Michael Jordan break his foot again.''

''In retrospect,'' says Reinsdorf, ''I probably should have told him, 'I talked to the doctor and he says you shouldn't play.' What we had was a ridiculous compromise. I think he should not have played for the rest of the year. I think if you ask Michael now he'd probably tell you I was right."

He did not think so then, however. Jordan's will to play was so strong, his sense of himself so dependent upon basketball, that even limited action seemed a moral victory. "I made the decision best suited for Michael Jordan and I'm happy and willing to live with it," he said. "I'm not going to make any flashy moves. If all that comes within the course of how I'm playing, I'll be pleased."

But, while he tried to sound sober, Jordan was clearly enjoying his rebellion. "Krause and Reinsdorf won't be there," he said of the first game. "They thought they were going to die if they watched me play." To *Tribune* columnist Bob Verdi he quipped: "And if they'd have told me I wasn't going to play tonight we'd still be in that meeting. I packed a lunch."

Michael returned to action on March 15 before a crowd of 15,208 who had come to see the Bulls take on the Milwaukee Bucks. He played just under six minutes in the second quarter and just under seven in the fourth. When the game went into overtime, he asked Albeck if he could break his seven-minute pledge. Albeck's job rested on his management of Michael's minutes. He refused.

Jordan finished with 12 points, including a soaring dunk over 7-foot-3 Randy Breuer. Oakley added 35 points and a mammoth 26 rebounds. Still, the Bulls lost 125–116. The next day, Michael began lobbying for 10-minute halves.

Jordan's peculiar new status made for some equally peculiar performances by the Bulls. On March 17, in one six-minute fourth-quarter surge, Michael led his once-trailing teammates to a 96–88 lead over the Atlanta Hawks. But Jordan's clock struck with 1:47 remaining, and the other Bulls promptly turned into pumpkins. Atlanta scored the last 18 points of the game for a 106–98 victory.

"I think I am going to have to fight Krause," he said afterward. "I'm out there worrying about my time rather than just playing the game. . . . I think I'm ready for more time, but the organization doesn't have the heart to see me play.''

The Atlanta scenario repeated itself on March 19 against the 76ers, when the Bulls once again blew a fourth-quarter lead after Michael's exit, losing 118–112. These collapses were not entirely the fault of Jordan's teammates. The Bulls had won seven of their last 12 games before Michael's return and were playing their best ball of the season. They still trailed the Cleveland Cavaliers in the "After you; no, please, after you" race for the last Eastern Conference playoff spot, but they had finally begun to gel as a team.

Unfortunately, they had begun to gel in a deliberate, half-court offense that took little advantage of Jordan's breakaway skills. When he returned, they developed a severe case of split personality. The Bulls played like Clydesdales for much of the ballgame, revved up to race-horse speed when Jordan entered, then turned back into Clydesdales when he left.

Losses to Boston and Cleveland dropped the Bulls two and a half games behind the Cavaliers, and a frustrated Jordan took out his anger in the press. "After the Cleveland game I realized I was disrupting the chemistry of the team,'' he said. "What else can I think? They had won three in a row and since I've been back we haven't won a game. I'm hurting the team with my spurts of minutes. Either let me go back to playing a full game or forbid me from playing at all.''

It was true that Jordan's comeback, while flashy, had been wildly inconsistent. He'd hit just 23 of 66 from the field and had thrown up a welter of poorly chosen shots. "I don't know if I can contribute coming off the bench,'' he said. "By the time I get into the game, tempo is already established. I know my teammates don't want to say it, but if I feel my presence is hurting the team, I am not afraid to speak out.''

Nor, as it turned out, were his teammates. "Jordan's return to Bulls brings confusion, jealousy,'' read the *Tribune* headline of March 25. "Have you noticed,'' asked Kyle Macy, ''we're caught halfway between slowing things down like we had been doing and speeding them up for Michael?'' That day, too, owner Jerry Reinsdorf called Jordan's play-me-or-bench-me bluff, refusing to expand Michael's minutes.

The Bulls split their next four games, but remained two and a half games behind the Cavs with just six games to play. Jordan played 11 minutes a half, then 14. His shooting touch began to return, and he twice led the team in scoring. Still, he wasn't satisfied. He wanted to play the entire game, and with the season waning, he thought the Bulls were holding him out on purpose in hopes of qualifying for the lottery. To Michael, his conflict with management had become a simple question of integrity.

"Losing games on purpose reflects what kind of person you really are," he said. "No one should ever try to lose to get something better. You should always try to make the best with what you have. If they really wanted to make the playoffs, I'd be in there whenever we had a chance to win a game."

But the club's management did not respond to Michael's prodding and so, on April 2, he forced them into a public confrontation. "I talked to Dr. Hefferon today and he told me that the X ray showed enough improvement that I could play a whole game," Jordan said. "If Krause said anything else he was lying. It's not a medical decision anymore. It's all business."

But Krause *did* say something else. He said Hefferon and his consultants continued to advise Jordan against playing. In fact, Jordan's most recent CAT scan had shown no worsening in the break, but also no improvement. Willfully or otherwise, Michael had misinterpreted the doctor's comments in labeling the general manager a liar.

"Michael is missing the point," said Jerry Reinsdorf. "The fact that he is playing hard and not feeling any pain has nothing to do with the chances of reinjuring himself. The doctors told him not to be misled by the fact that there was no pain. In his case there will be no warning."

The following evening, against the Indiana Pacers, the Jordan Compromise finally fell apart. After two first-half appearances, Michael reentered the game with just under 10 minutes to play and the Bulls trailing 96–86. He scored 15 of his team-high 26 points in the next nine minutes as Chicago rallied to claim a 107–106 lead. But the Pacers responded with a basket that put them in front with 31 seconds remaining.

Once again, Jordan's clock ran out. When the Bulls returned to the court after a time-out, Michael was not among them. Jerry Krause says he believes Stan Albeck was trying to prove a point that night, to show how absurd the restrictions on Jordan were. Krause did not appreciate it. "If he turned around—I was right behind him—I would have said, 'Play him,'" he says.

Albeck never turned around, and the move may have cost him his job. What it did not cost him was a ballgame. John Paxson's jumper with seven seconds remaining gave Chicago a 109–108 victory. That didn't seem to matter much the next day, though, as a furious Jordan told the media that this was just the most recent evidence that the men who ran his team were giving away their season.

Michael's tirade led to another lengthy meeting with Reinsdorf and Krause. The two older men were in a difficult position. Jordan was their best player, their biggest drawing card, the future of their franchise. They could not treat him too severely. On the other hand, neither man appreciated Michael's assault on the club's integrity.

Jerry Krause still sounds anguished when he recalls the meeting. Getting a lottery pick was "the farthest thing from my mind," he says. "What I wanted was a healthy Michael Jordan. I think there is a legitimate chance that he is playing now because of what we did then."

But all that mattered to Michael was the moment. "It's a risk for me, but it's not a financial decision," he said after the meeting. "Basketball is my dream, my love. I'm not worried about the financial part." He said the two-hour session had done nothing to restore his respect for the club's management. "I'm not a piece of property," Jordan said. "I don't care what they pay me; I'm still a human being."

In the next week, Jordan's erratic but inspired comeback continued. He shot poorly in the first half, but wonderfully in the second, scoring 30 points and leading the Bulls by Atlanta, 102–97, before a Stadium crowd of 17,769. That victory, coupled with a Cleveland defeat, left Chicago in a tie for the final playoff berth.

On April 7, Jordan got his first start and scored 10 of his 26 points in the first quarter. His three-point play in the closing moments helped seal a 107–101 victory over the coasting, playoff-bound Milwaukee Bucks. The Cavs, meanwhile, had lost again.

Chicago had a chance to clinch the final postseason spot on April 11 in the Stadium against the Washington Bullets, but trailed at halftime, 56–48. That is when Jerry Reinsdorf decided to revoke Jordan's time limit. "This is something I have to do for all these people," he said. All 18,869 of them, the biggest crowd of the season.

The game was emblematic of Jordan's comeback. He shot badly, making just 12 of 36 from the field, but he scored 31 points and spearheaded the Chicago comeback as the Bulls edged the Bullets 105–103. "He took the risk and gave me a chance to play," Jordan said of Reinsdorf. "So he is a kind man. He does have a heart." Michael still wasn't very fond of Jerry Krause.

By winning four of their last six games, the Bulls had earned the right to be crushed by the Boston Celtics. That Boston, the eventual NBA champions, would win the best-of-five series was a foregone conclusion. What no one could have anticipated was the manner in which Jordan would make this brief series his own.

Michael so dominated the first two games of this three-game set that they are remembered more for his performances than for the Celtics' victories. Julius Erving once said that basketball was just a game but that a man with a basketball can be so much more. For one weekend in April, Michael gave people a sense of what the Doctor meant.

Watching these games on tape, one gets the sense that Jordan's performance has been technologically enhanced. He seems to move in "fast forward" while all those around him labor in "play." In the first half of game one, Jordan poured in 30 points and the plucky Bulls trailed only 61–59. But in the second half, Larry Bird, who finished with 30 points, and Dennis Johnson, who had 26, triggered a Celtic surge that left Chicago a loser, 123–104.

Jordan, who played with a virus, finished with 49 points and a host of admirers. "He's by far the best guard in the league," Dennis Johnson said. "I read a little program insert that said he would have been a great athlete in any sport he chose to play. Well, I believe it, and I wish he chose some other sport."

"You can't stop him," added the Celtics' Jerry Sichting. "He runs too fast and jumps too high. What we were eventually able to do was clog the middle and make it difficult for him to drive."

But game one was just a warm-up. In game two Jordan recorded probably the greatest individual performance in playoff history, almost single-handedly pushing the Celtics to the brink of defeat. This game was perhaps the most inspired of Michael's career, and there is no real tactical explanation for why it occurred. Time after time, he went one-on-whoever-thinks-he's-up-to-it, outrunning, outjumping, outtwisting-and-turning several Celtics at a time. And when that didn't work, he'd step back and stick the jump shot.

Jordan hit 22 of 41 from the field, 19 of 21 from the foul line, had six assists, five rebounds, three steals and two blocked shots. It wasn't enough though. The Celtics downed the Bulls 135–131 in double overtime to take a 2–0 lead in the best-of-five series.

"I was watching and all I could see is this giant Jordan and everyone else is sort of in the background," K. C.

Jones said. "He was awesome last time. I don't have a word for today."

"I think he's God disguised as Michael Jordan," said Bird, who had been more quietly magnificent with 36 points, 12 rebounds and 8 assists. "He is the most awesome player in the NBA."

After the game though, a dejected Jordan said that what would stick with him was not the 63 points he'd scored and not the steal and free throws he'd made to send the game into overtime. What mattered, he said, was the one clutch shot he'd missed, a 15-footer that glanced off the rim at the end of the first extra period. "I can't believe I missed that last shot," he said.

Two days later, the Celtics held an exhausted and foul-hampered Jordan to just 19 points and completed their series sweep, 122–104. Michael had ten assists and nine rebounds, but fouled out at 5:24 of the final period to a roaring ovation from nearly 19,000 fans.

When it was over, Jordan did not mind pointing out that he had proved something. "I feel I showed the Bulls management that I am a very competent young man and that I can make my own decisions," he said.

The Bulls management was not complaining. After years of playing to empty seats, the Bulls were on the verge of becoming one of the league's most popular franchises. They had the most exciting player in the game. He was healthy and ready to tear up the league. Whatever tribulations Jordan had subjected them to were quickly forgiven.

"In the first year you could see he was going to be a superstar," Jerry Reinsdorf said. "But it wasn't until the third year that I began to realize he was going to be the greatest player who ever played.

"Somewhere in that third season I probably realized we had Babe Ruth on our hands."

9

Chicago Stadium is an imposing old pile of bricks that looks across West Madison Street to the desolation of the Henry Horner Homes, one of the city's worst housing projects. From the street the old building, completed in 1929, resembles a turn-of-the-century train station. Inside, its tiny lobbies, with their crown-topped ticket booths, seem to fade to black and white before the eyes, giving the place the feel of a Depression era photograph.

Step into the arena proper, though, and all that changes. The vista is of a vibrant, cavernous barn with a gleaming yellow court and vast, sweeping balconies. An ocean of red seats fills every cranny and mercifully precludes the building of luxury boxes. The Stadium is one of only two arenas in the league built before 1960. With its narrow hallways, tiny locker rooms and lack of office space, its days as a basketball facility are numbered. But it is a gloriously cantankerous and splendidly noisy place to see a ballgame, not least for the atmosphere the Bulls create here.

Before each game the building goes dark and spotlights

chase one another across the crowd. One by one the Bulls' starters are introduced to a manufactured exuberance that was once well out of proportion to their achievements. When Michael Jordan takes the court, the tumult grows somehow louder. The noise takes on texture. It quivers between clapping palms.

Until the 1990–91 season, when his teammates assumed their share of the load, it was Jordan's job to justify this buildup, to keep its promise. Beginning in the 1986–87 season, he did so in almost every game.

Sometimes it seemed the point of that season was to convince students of basketball that everything they knew about the game was wrong. Here was a player who had mastered most of the sports fundamentals, but played as though he were out to destroy its conventional wisdom. What was a coach to make of a magnificent leaper who took to the air with nothing in mind and simply waited for his creativity to kick in? What did he say to a ball-handler so talented that he made hitting the open man irrelevant because he could beat the double team all by himself? How should he build a team around a scorer capable of offensive binges that would render his teammates superfluous for five minutes at a time?

"He borders on being too good, and by that I mean he's causing a lot of things that have always been taught in basketball, particularly relating to the team concept, to be reevaluated," Tex Winter, then in his second season as an assistant coach with the Bulls, told *Chicago Magazine*. "I'm questioning these things myself, and I've been coaching for 40 years."

No guard has ever been as dominating and pervasive an offensive force as Jordan was in '86–'87. Not since Wilt Chamberlain had any player poured in so many points. Michael's scoring saga was so compelling that on many nights, it overshadowed whether his Bulls won or lost. He was becoming bigger than the game he played.

In the way that an exciting political candidate brings new

voters into the electoral process, Jordan was drawing new
fans into NBA arenas and telecasts. The Bulls played before
316,000 more fans (with attendance increases of 181,000 at
home and 135,000 on the road) than they had in the
previous season when Michael was injured. Central Division titles and playoff pairings meant little to many of these
fans when compared with Michael's personal exploits. For
them the game was less a contest than a dramatic tour de
force. No matter who had the ball, no matter who won the
game, Jordan was always the protagonist in a season-long
epic.

In his third season, Michael felt he was making up for the
time he'd lost in his second. Always lean, he'd returned to
Chicago even trimmer than he'd been at the end of the
season. A training camp physical put his body fat at just 3.3
percent. That fall he ran a 5:22 mile. "I'm hungrier and
more anxious than I was my first year in the league," he
said.

Jordan found out quickly that few of his teammates could
score. In an effort to rid the club of dissenters and tailor the
team to Michael's talents, Jerry Krause had gotten rid of
Orlando Woolridge, Quintin Dailey, George Gervin, Sidney
Green and Kyle Macy. Jawann Oldham would also soon be
gone. Of Jordan's other teammates, only John Paxson and
Charles Oakley still start for NBA teams. In the exhibition
season, Michael averaged 33 points in 33 minutes, but the
club went 3–5.

Jordan attacked every game with the passion of a man
perhaps too eager to prove he was his old self again. This
sense of urgency was fueled by Doug Collins, the Bulls'
new coach. Collins—collegiate All-American at Illinois State,
member of the 1972 Olympic team, number one pick in that
year's NBA draft, four-time All-Star and standout on the
Philadelphia 76er teams of the mid-1970s—was, in some
ways, the perfect coach for Jordan. He believed in the
supremacy of speed and talent. As a teammate of Julius

Erving and George McGinnis, he had seen how one creative player could take over a game and transform a team.

Michael was his kind of star emotionally as well. Both men had overcome adolescent athletic disappointments through hard work and sometimes harsh self-discipline. Each had succeeded where others expected they would fail. As a result they shared a bottomless confidence in their own judgments. Each needed athletic hobbies—golf for Jordan, golf and tennis for Collins—to absorb the excess energy that drove him. "I think he's drawn to high-pressure situations," Kathy Collins said of her husband. "I think he is motivated by them."

At times during his three-year tenure with the Bulls, Collins set the perfect tone and provided the ideal stage on which Jordan could display his unprecedented talent. At other times the coach, whose career had been shortened by a knee injury, seemed to identify too closely with his star. Any disagreement seemed a personal slight, a rejection of big-brotherly love.

In his first season as coach, Collins realized that Jordan was his only real offensive resource, and simply decided to turn him loose. Michael took a tremendous number of shots, launched himself on scores of seemingly hopeless drives and tore up and down the court with a frightening and, some feared, destructive abandon. The 1986–87 Bulls campaign became a season-long shooting of the Michael Jordan highlight film.

Reel one. Clip one. November 1: In the Bulls' opening game, Jordan shoots just 3 of 12 in the first half, but blitzes the New York Knicks for 50 points, 21 of them in the fourth quarter. Chicago wins 108–103.

"When you have a superstar like him, all you need is for the four other guys to work hard and the opportunities will come for him to win the game," says Knicks coach Hubie Brown.

Clip two, November 2: Jordan tallies 41 points against the Cavaliers, 16 in the final period. Chicago wins 94–89.

Clip three, November 11: Jordan tosses in 34, two of which come on what Collins calls "your routine, twisting, 360-degree, double-pump layup." That shot, with 19 seconds to play, gives Chicago a 112–110 victory over the Atlanta Hawks.

Clip four, November 14: Jordan pours in 48, but the Bulls lose at home to the Celtics, 110–98. "You get numbed to the spectacular in this league, and I practice with Larry Bird every day," Celtic Bill Walton says, "but Jordan, he is unbelievable."

Clip five, November 21: Jordan notches another 40, including his team's final 18. His drive through three Knickerbockers knots the score at 97 with 13 seconds to play. After Gerald Wilkins answers for the Knicks, the ball comes to Michael with eight seconds left. He speeds past Wilkins, cuts inside Darrell Walker and launches a 22-foot jump shot. Chicago wins 101–99.

"He just played infallible ball the last five minutes," Hubie Brown says. "Eighteen points in a row during crunch time with two guys on him. What else has to be said?"

The Bulls downed the Bullets on the following evening to run their record to 7–3. "For pure excitement," wrote Bob Sakamoto in the *Tribune*, "the Bulls right now are the hottest ticket in town." Collins's team was outrebounding, outstealing and outhustling its opponents. But mostly, it was out-Michaeling them. "We know Michael is the star and the rest of us know our role, which is to win ballgames," reserve forward Earl Cureton said.

Jordan was averaging 36.3 points per game. He led the team in scoring every night. His leaping ability had become the object of cultish fascination. "Someday an up draft will catch him in mid glide, or Tinkerbell herself will sprinkle him with fairy dust and he will waft on over the basket and up into the wires and lights of an NBA arena like a raptor soaring into the clouds," wrote Rick Telander in a mid-

November *Sports Illustrated* cover story. "And no one will be surprised."

The rampage of November was just a hint of what lay ahead. Beginning with a 41-point performance against the Lakers at the Forum on November 28, Jordan scored 40 or more points in each of the next nine games and in 11 of the next 12. In doing so, he established himself not simply as one of the best basketball players in the world, but as that rarest of performers, the one who pushes back the limits of human possibility.

Jordan's ability to inspire rested only partially on his mastery of the game. At that point in Michael's career, he may not yet have been as complete a player as Magic Johnson or Larry Bird. Yet neither of these men, wondrous as they often were, inspired the sort of excitement that Jordan did.

As the Bulls took the court each night that season, the pregame din subsided and a hum filled the old building. It was the sound of people who were fully prepared—and who firmly expected to be delighted, people who knew that with Jordan on the court the game would be replete with opportunities for the miraculous. They had seen it happen before— in slow motion and from several angles. But that particular night, when he soared down the lane for a dunk or snaked through the defense for a layup, they would be there. And the following day, when the talk in the car pool, at the water cooler or around the school lunch table turned to what Michael had done, they could speak of what they'd seen and share in the community that Jordan had created.

The late and revered columnist Red Smith used to warn against "godding up the ballplayers," but there is no use in denying the religious component of Jordan's popularity. This is not to say that Michael's fans regard him as divine, but rather that his performance transports them, puts them in touch with something larger than themselves. They feel elevated by the furious grace of his surge to the basket and the unearthly altitude of his ascent for a rebound, by the breathtaking quickness of his passes and the slashing confrontation of his defense. They rise when he rises to release the often perfect trajectory of his jump shot. But what they feel most keenly is Jordan's joy.

"There is a genuine sense of playfulness, a sense of wonder about the way he plays the game, and his sense of joy transmits a feeling of ecstasy," says Joseph Price, professor of religious studies at Whittier College. "They can celebrate because he celebrates." The sense that one is in the presence of something magical is augmented by the feeling that Jordan's adversary as he swoops to the basket is not another player, but gravity itself. "There is the sense that somehow he transcends," Price says. "That he succeeds in doing that which all of us aspire to do. That he is capable of flight and that this is as near a thing to human transcendence as we are likely to see."

The season as highlight film. Reel two. Clip one.

December 27: Jordan racks up 44 points despite playing with a temperature of 101 degrees as the Bulls thump the Indiana Pacers 105–93. "When I'm sick I always play better," he says. "Your concentration is much better. You know you have to fight off a sickness."

Clip two, January 2: In the years before the Jordan Rules were instituted Michael owned the Pistons. He scores 47 as the Bulls win 124–119.

Clip three, January 8: With the Bulls leading 104–102 in the final period, Michael takes a pass in the post against Portland's Clyde Drexler. As Jim Paxson (brother of Jordan teammate John) drops back to double-team Jordan, Michael blows between the two defenders, bolts across the lane, leaps by Caldwell Jones, turns his back to Jerome Kersey and flips in an over-the-shoulder layup. "I just felt that any shot, because of the way things were flowing, was going in," says Jordan, who hits 20 of 34 from the field and finishes with 53 points. The Bulls win 121–117.

"I'm a little embarrassed about scoring so many points,"

he adds diplomatically. "It's like stealing something from the team, and this was a whole team effort."

Clip four, January 17: Despite Charles Barkley's pledge to break him into pieces before allowing him to go on a scoring binge, Jordan puts up 47 points, pulls down 10 rebounds and hands out six assists as the Bulls coast by Philadelphia, 105–89.

Clip five, February 7: At the Kingdome in Seattle, on the eve of the All-Star game, Michael wins his first slam dunk title with his Kiss the Rim jam. He leaps into the air, holds the ball tightly against his body and leans in to the basket until his face is almost intimate with the hoop. Then, hurtling by the rim, he turns and slams the ball down through the basket. His performance earns him $12,000, which he splits with his 11 Chicago teammates. "They worked so hard this half [of the season]," he says. "And I got all the publicity and credit."

The following day he scores a quiet 11 points as the West wins 154–149.

The slam dunk championship confirmed Jordan's status as the most electrifying player in the game. But his fame had begun to spread beyond the bounds of basketball. People who paid little attention to sports suddenly found themselves interested in the young phenomenon. Their curiosity was whetted by the first of the Spike and Mike commercials that appeared late in 1986, and by the endless flow of newspaper, magazine and television profiles that began in earnest that season.

On All-Star weekend, NBC profiled Jordan on its "Nightly News." "That he is one of the greatest players ever is indisputable," Tom Brokaw said. "He is also a very nice man." Diane Sawyer checked in for "60 Minutes" with a piece so wide-eyed the people at ProServ called it "our 10-minute Michael Jordan commercial." Even cynical sportswriters seeking to get below Jordan's friendly image found another friendly fellow waiting for them. When he asked how your trip was, said *Sports Illustrated*'s Curry Kirkpatrick, it actually seemed like he wanted to know.

This good nature seemed so rare because Americans had become justifiably skeptical of their sports heroes. The NBA had been ravaged by drugs. Two seasons earlier some of the brightest stars in major league baseball had paraded to a witness box in Pittsburgh to confess their cocaine addictions. The sports pages were studded with stories of athletes' alcoholism, gambling, wife beating and prodigious infidelities. Michael Jordan seemed an antidote to all that, a throwback to a time when athletes might not have been any more innocent, but fans certainly were.

Jordan emerged also at a time of crisis for black men in America's underclass. One of every four young black men was incarcerated, on probation or on parole. Nearly 40 percent were functionally illiterate. Roughly 50 percent of black families were headed by single women and one in every three black children was growing up in poverty. The reality behind these statistics generated profound unease among blacks and whites alike, for the nation was in the midst of an economic recovery in which many of its poorest citizens seemed not to be sharing.

In such an atmosphere there was a hunger for strong upper-middle-class black role models. Whites wanted to be reassured that the country's economy was not built on racist foundations, that the rising tide of Ronald Reagan's recovery really would lift all boats. The black middle class wanted to see some reflection of its own hard-won successes in the popular culture. And in the inner city there was, as always, the hunger for a hero who had succeeded against the long odds that ghetto-dwellers faced.

Jordan and Cliff Huxtable of "The Cosby Show"—both of whom arrived on the national scene in the year of Reagan's reelection—were able, somehow, to appeal to all of these constituencies. By the middle of the 1986–87 season, Michael was becoming what no black man before him had ever been: America's favorite athlete. His resume was perfect for the job: strong, loving family, college diploma from a prestigious school, straight-arrow lifestyle, easygoing manner and a sincere fondness for the people to whom athletes matter most—kids.

"The way I look at it now, every kid I meet is my kid," Jordan said. "I treat them as my kid. I love kids and I love to see them smile." Michael also possessed a nascent social conscience, an understanding that he was "obligated to give something back to the community." He concentrated his efforts on children's charities, the safe, worthy sort that demonstrate a hero's concern without drawing him into public controversies.

"There's something very American about him," sociologist Shelby Steele says in assessing Jordan's appeal. "He seems to have a good business sense. He's very refined. He's the kind of figure who goes down easy with most of America."

But other black performers who went down easy with white America were often charged with selling out, a fate that Jordan so far has avoided. The reason, Steele says, is that for many blacks Jordan is their representative in an inaccessible world. "He comes out of an area where blacks traditionally excel, and because he is probably the best basketball player alive, he has legendary status among blacks, who prize that game more than any other," Steele says. "I think they are proud of the way he conducts himself in the mainstream of American society."

It sometimes escaped people's attention that the man hauling this symbolic freight had not yet turned 24, and that many of the most difficult decisions he would make still lay ahead. Choosing a wife, for instance.

Michael was a shy kid who had matured into a ladies' man in college. At the 1984 Olympics he struck up a relationship with Kim Gallagher, the silver medalist in the women's 800-meter, who, according to *Sports Illustrated*, had to be spirited into a closet by Michael and his suitemates one night when coach Bobby Knight came by for a bed check. When Jordan hit Chicago and his marketing campaign kicked into gear, he found himself one of America's most eligible bachelors. Women would lie beneath the tires of his limousine until he stepped out and spoke with them. Models and actresses would wander into practice to meet him for lunch dates.

Michael had a strong sense of what he was looking for in a mate. "I like an independent woman, very positive-minded, not too possessive, very understanding of the sports game, what I have to do, and the position I am in," he confided to an audience of several million on "Oprah Winfrey."

It wasn't easy to find a woman like that. "You date a lot of girls and it gives you a lot to think about," his mother said of Michael's situation. " 'Is it me they are liking or what I represent?' Any individual would go through that. 'Do they see *me* for me?' "

Michael had met someone whom he thought understood. He and Juanita Vanoy were introduced one night at a Bennigan's restaurant, not long after Michael moved to Chicago. "She was one of the first ones he liked and respected," friend Kevin Jones says.

It made him happy that after all the women who had offered themselves, he had noticed her first. They dated steadily, and became increasingly committed to one another. But Michael seemed to be of two minds about settling down.

During the 1987 season he told one interviewer he was planning to marry and another that there was "no downside" to being single. Donald Dell mentioned that ProServ was advising Michael on a prenuptial agreement, but no wedding plans were announced. "My first few years in the league were an opportunity for me to experience life as a single person," Jordan says now.

Not long after Howard White was married, he remembers Michael saying to him, half-jokingly: You can't possibly be happy. "Or he'd say, 'You can't tell me nothing. When I come down, I'll see how it is.'" White recalls. "He started seeing things weren't all bad." But he still wasn't ready to get married.

Reel three. Clip one.

February 13. Jordan pours in 45 as the Bulls drop the SuperSonics 106–98. "We tried everyone but the bus driver on him," says Seattle coach Bernie Bickerstaff.

Clip two, February 26: Jordan shoots 16 of 25 from the field and 26 of 27 from the line, for a club regular-season record 58 points—this despite sitting out the last three minutes of an easy 128–113 victory over the New Jersey Nets.

Clip three, March 4: He breaks that record, notching 61 points, 26 of those in the fourth quarter, as the Bulls beat the Pistons in overtime, 125–120. Jordan shoots 22 of 39 while grabbing seven rebounds and coming up with three blocks. In the last several minutes Jordan defends the Pistons' leading scorer Adrien Dantley and comes up with three steals.

Clip four, March 24: In Dr. J.'s last appearance in Chicago, Michael leads the Bulls to a 93–91 victory over the Sixers. He hits 22 of 32 from the field for 56 points, to go along with eight steals and seven rebounds. But he also commits five fourth-quarter turnovers and looks, as one observer put it, "too intense for his own good."

That intensity may have had something to do with the fact that this was the last time Jordan would face Erving. Michael revered the man who had once said that watching Jordan play was like "looking in a mirror." He knew Erving's was the one example he could look to in dealing with the challenges presented by his own fame.

Erving, for his part, felt Jordan was a messenger of sorts, the man who would succeed him as the game's great ambassador and make it possible for him to move on. "I viewed him as coming in and taking up where I left off, and then exceeding that," Erving says. "It made it easier for me to make the decision I had to make of leaving the game behind and going on to operate outside the arena.

"I was in a position, at that point, of looking at what I had accomplished and asking myself, 'What does this make me responsible to do as an American, as a human being?' It [Jordan's emergence] helped in ridding me of some of the shackles that one has when one has to operate from within the role of being a professional athlete."

Jordan also succeeded Erving as the game's greatest artist, the one who took fullest advantage of his opportunities for audacity, for creativity, for inspiring awe. These traits were not much valued even 30 years ago. But since the 1960s the sport has been transformed by generations of young black men who learned the game on urban playgrounds.

Basketball in its early years knew as much of rugby as it did of ballet. For more than half a century after Dr. James Naismith hung the first peach baskets in 1891, most players' offensive arsenals consisted entirely of the layup. Even the set shot, now gone the way of the pterodactyl, awaited its inventor. Leaping, other than to rebound, was considered bad strategy—dangerous too. "In those days you couldn't leave your feet," said Slater Martin, a Hall of Fame guard who played for the Minneapolis Lakers in the 1940s and '50s. "They'd just knock you into a wall."

But a few unorthodox stylists were breathing new life into the moribund game. In the 1940s, Joe Fulks, a high-scoring guard from Kentucky, popularized the jump shot. A decade later Bill Russell revolutionized pivot play with his shot-blocking skills. But legendary college coaches like Hank Iba still taught that the only good shot was an absolutely sure one. He and others like Adolph Rupp at Kentucky exercised iron control over their teams. The men on the floor were just the outward manifestation of the inner geometry in their coach's mind. It was a view that held sway as recently as 1972, when the talented American Olympic team, slowed to a crawl by Iba's coaching dictates, lost the gold medal to the Soviets.

Cut at one point from his high school squad, Jordan eventually served notice that he was in basketball to stay. *Wilmington Star-News.*

As a college freshman, Michael helped lead the North
Carolina Tarheels to the NCAA Championship.
The Charlotte Observer.

Michael is frequently compared to LA Laker Magic Johnson, shown here defending.
Copyright © 1991, Andrew D. Bernstein, NBA Photos.

Among the many weapons in Jordan's offensive arsenal: his fantastic leaping ability, which has inspired the name "Air."
Andy Hayt, *Sports Illustrated*.

Cradling the 1991 NBA Championship Trophy. Copyright © 1991, Andrew D. Bernstein, NBA Photos.

Jordan's high-altitude moves make him one of the league's top defenders. Copyright © 1990, Bill Smith, NBA Photos.

ordan shows off his golfing skills.
Walter Yooss, *Sports Illustrated*.

Working with Special Olympians. Gene Hickmott.

Making a promotional appearance for McDonalds. ProServ.

NO BRAIN NO GAIN

STAY IN SCHOOL

Coke

...ssuing a public service message on behalf of Coca-Cola. ProServ.

Trading stories with David Letterman. ProServ.

Hitting it off with TV anchorwoman Diane Sawyer.
ProServ.

Basketball's counterculture grew up outdoors on the nation's playgrounds. Young black athletes didn't have access to college coaching gurus, who plied their trade at segregated schools. Instead, they learned their craft in neighborhoods where the game was looked on, in Bill Russell's words, as a combination of art and war. Sinking a jump shot was fine, but if it had the arc of a rainbow, so much the better. Protecting the ball was useful, but dribbling through the other team was thrilling. Rebounds were essential, but snatching coins from atop the backboard is what made your name.

The Harlem Globetrotters played this quicker, more free-flowing brand of basketball, and in 1948 they took two of three games from George Mikan and the Minneapolis Lakers, champions of the National Basketball League. Many white strategists looked down their noses at the Globies, and considered them nothing more than a minstrel show, but "scientific" basketball was about to be overwhelmed by the talented black athletes who began flooding into the NBA in the late 1950s. Elgin Baylor, the Lakers' marvelous forward, was the harbinger of this new style. He could jump over defenses and around opponents who had boxed him off the boards. What really popularized this acrobatic style, however, was white fans' discovery of the black playground.

It happened in the late 1960s when Pete Axthelm wrote *The City Game*. A student of the Harlem summer leagues, Axthelm captured the great gifts and grim lives of men like Earl Manigault and Herman "The Helicopter" Knowings for a mainstream audience. David Wolf, who wrote *Foul: The Connie Hawkins Story*, took the tale one step deeper, showing how black playground stars were denied the educations they needed to attend college and, hence, the experience they needed to earn a shot at the NBA. The ghetto heroes who emerge from these books are something more than basketball players. Like the great blues singers, they turned their rage into art and became symbols of flickering transcendence.

Julius Erving grew up on the playgrounds of western Long Island. He began his career in the more freewheeling American Basketball Association, and for years he kept it afloat almost single-handedly. No one, with the possible exception of Earl Monroe, had as many offensive moves. And absolutely no one could execute them two feet above the rim. Erving was so spectacular that he won the hearts of even the stodgiest basketball fans and legitimized the playground game once and for all.

"I remember one night playing the Kentucky Colonels in Rupp Arena, and Adolph Rupp came to the game," he says. "He was a basketball purist. His teams would always work the ball around, try to get an open set shot. I don't think he cared for the fast break. He came to me after the game. He shook my hand and said, 'I saw you do things I've never seen other players do. I didn't think I would enjoy seeing them, but I did.'

"He was talking about things like taking a pass above the rim and throwing it down or coming up off the dribble with the ball in one hand. These were things that were not fundamentals, but this was my style of play."

It is also Michael Jordan's style of play. By this point, actually, it is the style of any player, black or white, who can successfully effect it. Yet its roots remain in the playground. It is a uniquely black contribution to American sports. And much of Jordan's resonance with black Americans is rooted in an art form that, according to trumpeter Wynton Marsalis, is not very different from jazz.

"Basketball is like jazz in terms of improvisation," Marsalis says, seated at a piano. "Say you are playing 'Embraceable You.'" He breezes through the first few bars of the Gershwin song, playing it cleanly but without much feeling. "Now," he breaks in, "when you are improvising in music the obstacles are the chord changes. So you can do this"—he begins a quirky skittering riff—"as long as you do this," and suddenly melody and digression are woven into a seamless new sound.

"In basketball," he says, "the obstacles are the defenders, and with the most skillful players, you can see them working their way through the obstacles to a successful resolution."

Jordan is the improvisor he likes best. "The only person in the NBA who can be compared to him is Magic Johnson. But Magic is like Duke Ellington. He is an orchestrator, and an orchestrator never captures the public's fancy like the soloist. You can come to see Louis Armstrong and understand what he does, but you couldn't do that with Duke Ellington."

Marsalis's metaphor comes closer than most to capturing the rigorous abandon of Jordan's style, a subject about which Michael himself seems reluctant to become analytical. "It's all spur-of-the-moment," Jordan says of his most outrageous acrobatics. "If I'm in a situation where I have to do something spectacular to get out of trouble, I do it.

"I never practice the fancy stuff. If I thought about a move, I'd probably turn the ball over. I just look at a situation in the air, adjust, create and let instinct take over.

"Those are times when I do things other people can't do and wish they could," he told Dave Kindred of *The National*. "My intention always is to score, but in *that* fashion, with *that* creativity. . . . I see a move and I say 'How'd I do that?' It just happens. You don't really think about it and you can't work on it. You've just got to have it."

For several seasons, skeptics questioned whether Jordan had too much of it. They acknowledged his brilliance, but said he "didn't make anybody better." Showmen didn't win championships, these purists said.

After a late March loss to Portland, in which Jordan scored 46 points, Trail Blazers general manager Bucky Buckwalter said Blazers guard Clyde Drexler was a better player than Michael. "The thing that Drexler does that Jordan doesn't is help out his teammates," Buckwalter said. Doug Collins fired back. "I would like to ask Bucky if he would trade Jordan for Drexler and if not whether he has a brain tumor or what."

Jordan regarded the remark as sour grapes from the team that could have had him but chose the oft-injured Sam Bowie instead. But the Blazers were not the only team expressing this sentiment. Even Larry Bird, who had generally spoken well of Jordan, said it was boring to watch the same player put the ball up time after time. In fact, Jordan was taking about one-third of Chicago's shots, about the same percentage Bird took on the 1979 Indiana State team he led to the NCAA finals.

"People say Michael scores too much, shoots too much," Doug Collins said. "It's an unfair evaluation. Look at what Larry did to carry Indiana State in college, and look at what he does now. He doesn't have to score 45 now because he's got other people around him. Michael will do the same, when the time comes."

But the time wasn't coming soon, and in the last weeks of the season, Jordan went on one last rampage.

Reel four. Clip one.

April 7: The Bulls and the Pistons get nasty again. Early in the first period, Bill Laimbeer knocks a driving Jordan into the basket support. Jordan leaps to his feet and shoves the Piston center. He's nailed with a technical.

"I felt I had to take a stand," Jordan says later. "This is the third year he has done that to me on a fast break. . . . I had to let him know, let a lot of people know, I'm not going to take that anymore, especially when I think he did it on purpose.

"I don't know what it is going to take to stop it. Maybe somebody will get more frustrated than I got tonight and just clobber the guy. That's the only way he'll learn."

The proceedings do not get any more orderly. Later in the game, Dave Corzine shrugs Isiah Thomas off his back and takes a swing at Rick Mahorn. Adrian Dantley clotheslines Jordan. In the intermittent outbreaks of basketball, Michael tosses in 39 and the Bulls romp 116–86.

Clip two, April 12: At home against the Pacers, Jordan

begins a streak of three spectacular performances, scoring 53 points, dishing out eight assists and notching four steals while shooting almost 70 percent from the floor. He scores 13 straight Chicago points in the fourth quarter. In one three-minute span, no other Bull touches the ball as he takes it upcourt and either scores or is fouled. Chicago wins 116–95.

Clip three, April 13: In Milwaukee, Jordan scores 50 points to go with nine rebounds, four steals and three blocked shots. Chicago wins 114–107. "It was a case of too much Michael Jordan," says Warriors coach Don Nelson. "He got 50 points, he found the open man and he played good defense. Michael Jordan has it all. He has a brain, he knows the game, he can pass, he can shoot, he has strength and he has quickness."

But Michael is only warming up.

Clip four, April 16: In a home loss to the Atlanta Hawks, Jordan scores 61 points and grabs 10 rebounds, becoming the only player other than Wilt Chamberlain to total 3,000 points in a season and to score more than 50 points in three consecutive games. From 6:33 of the second quarter to 2:12 of the third, he scores 23 consecutive Chicago points, breaking his own NBA record.

The reel runs out as the Bulls end their season losing four straight games to the Boston Celtics, one to close out the regular season at 40–42, and three more to exit the playoffs. Jordan finished the season with 3,041 points, the most ever by a guard. He led the league in scoring with 37.1 points per game, and became the first player in NBA history to record more than 100 blocked shots (125) and 200 steals (236) in the same season. It was one of the most statistically impressive seasons in recent memory, but it earned Jordan exactly nothing by way of postseason honors. Magic Johnson won the MVP, and Michael was denied a spot on the league's All-Defense team.

It was the second omission that really hurt. "Look at [All-Defense team member] Michael Cooper," he said.

"Michael Cooper is great at ball denial. But look at his other numbers." Cooper had 43 blocks and 72 steals. "They give awards in this league based on reputation. It really tees me off.

"Next year, I'd like to score less and let other parts of my game shine. I don't want to have any more .500 seasons. Whatever it takes, I'm all for it. I don't want to lead the league in scoring. I don't want to average 37 points a game."

Jordan had made similar remarks at the beginning and the end of almost every one of his professional seasons. It was always important to him to stress that he was a team player, that he scored so many points because the Bulls needed him to. He would be happy, he had often repeated, to make more diversified offensive contributions to a better-rounded team. It is difficult to know whether Jordan was completely sincere about this, because no matter how shiny the rest of his game, he has always found a way to pour in points, capture imaginations and sustain the lucrative commercial network that has sprung up around him.

10

He is the kind of man at whom one looks twice: cascading black pompadour and thin mustache, bulging eyes and pancake makeup, fringed leather pants and a jacket so bedecked with pins that one is convinced a convention of costume jewelers has reenacted the stabbing of Julius Caesar. All these register at first glance. The double take is for asking: "Hey, isn't that Little Richard?"

And, of course, it is. "There is no way in the world anybody is going to mistake me," the rock 'n' roll legend says. "I been sparkling and shining and there ain't nobody who looks like me."

This last assertion cannot be contested. There is the matter of all those pins—silver stars, glass-ruby crowns, gold-plated antelopes, rhinestone roaches—not to mention Richard's taste in footwear. Among the 22,000 people who have filled the Charlotte Coliseum for the 1991 NBA All-Star game, he alone is wearing gold-lamé slippers with elaborately curling toes. Little Richard calls them his "Genie shoes." His Aladdin must know Nike, because the slippers bear the company's trademark swoosh—in purple, no less.

The shoes are part of the ensemble Richard wears in Nike's latest commercial for its new line of Air Jordans, a commercial that will be broadcast for the first time on All-Star afternoon. In the new spot, Richard plays a genie who offers to grant a single wish to Mars Blackmon, the fast-talking Brooklyn bicycle messenger played by filmmaker Spike Lee.

Mars is stumped. He doesn't want money. He can't drive a car. What to wish for?

Anyone who has seen the previous installments of this long-running series knows the answer. Mars, who made his first appearance in Lee's breakthrough film *She's Gotta Have It*, is Michael Jordan's greatest fan, a guy who won't even take off the aforementioned sneakers when he's making love. After a sudden brainstorm Mars snaps his fingers, the genie roars a rock 'n' roll incantation and the screen fills with smoke. Suddenly, there stands Michael wearing Mars's clothing. "Look, Mom," says the messenger's voice, "I can fly."

The people from Nike have flown Little Richard and his brother to Charlotte, put them up in a nice hotel, paid for their meals and given them the best seats in the house—front row, center court. All this was done in the hope that he would do for them what he's done so well for himself—generate attention, create a scene, make people look twice.

Nike is in need of a public relations coup. From a free-publicity standpoint the weekend has belonged to its arch rival, Reebok. A brief network ban on Reebok's new commercials ("Pump up! And Air—out") has been the talk of hotel lobbies and cocktail parties all over town. To make matters worse, Dee Brown, the slam dunk champion, stooped before almost every round of that competition to "pump up" the tongues of his Reeboks. The gesture was duly reported in newspapers and on sportscasts around the country.

Nike was banking heavily on Little Richard and the new Air Jordan commercials to recoup its promotional advantage.

And he didn't let them down. No sooner had Richard found his seat than the aisles around him were clogged with admirers.

From the rear came fans for whom he autographed copies of his brother's born-again pamphlet, "Finding the Peace Within." From the front came sports columnists and television crews wanting to know what brought Richard to the ballgame, what he thought of Michael Jordan and where he got those wild shoes. Tape rolled, shutters clicked and Richard kept his slippers conspicuously within the frame. Even Bob Costas, broadcasting the game on NBC, popped from his seat during a time-out and bounded up the stairs to shake Richard's hand.

Mark Thomashow, the Nike executive who had coaxed his superiors into shelling out the money for Richard's trip, watched the proceedings with a sense of relief and vindication. Now, he said, even the most obstinate corporate bean counter would realize that the investment was worth it. "I don't know about that," said a colleague, gesturing at Richard's footwear. "They'll probably say it's not an in-line shoe."

When he first entered the NBA, Michael Jordan said he wanted to be the best-marketed player in the game. That was achieved within his first two seasons. For six years, he has been expanding his own portfolio and setting a precedent for other basketball stars who will do the same. Today, Michael pitches Gatorade for Quaker Oats, fast food for McDonald's, cereal for Wheaties, cars for the Chicagoland Chevy dealers, basketballs for Wilson, lottery tickets for the state of Illinois, calendars, school supplies and greeting cards for the Cleo company and underwear for Hanes. Guy Laroche makes the Time Jordan watch. CBS-Fox markets Michael Jordan videos. The Bulls star has a chain of sneaker and sportswear stores in North Carolina, a restaurant opening soon in Chicago and three lines of clothing marketed through Bigsby & Kruthers.

There is little question about his ability to move merchandise. The Air Jordan is the best-selling basketball shoe in the country. Wilson has sold more than six million basketballs bearing Jordan's signature. His first Cleo calendar was not even in the company's catalog, yet it was the firm's top seller.

What is remarkable about Jordan's commercial success, however, is not simply its breadth, but its durability. Sports fads Jim McMahon, Refrigerator Perry and Brian Bosworth have come and gone during Michael's extensive commercial career. "Athletes today are clearly aware of the business opportunities out there," David Falk says. "But they become fads. They pick one fad and they ride it through. Michael is not looking to invest all his energies in a very small niche. He wants to have a broad-based impact and a well-rounded growth pattern."

Neither Jordan nor Falk will say what Michael earns each year, but his salary from the Bulls is $3.25 million and the Nike deal alone is worth roughly $2.5 million. In 1990, *Forbes* magazine estimated Jordan's income that year at about $8.1 million, but a source close to Michael said that figure was low by at least half. In 1991, the source said, Jordan earned roughly $17 million from endorsements. Michael's precise earnings are difficult to calculate because several of his endorsement contracts provide for royalties and stock options.

Jordan is not the only one who benefits from his success. He has proved that white America can respond well to black athletes as commercial spokesmen. During the past five years basketball stars, as a group, have placed higher than any other athletes in the advertising industry's "Q" scores, a mysterious ranking that ostensibly measures how well a celebrity is known and liked. In the overall 1991 ratings, Michael was tied for first place with Bill Cosby.

No basketball player, no matter how talented, no matter how personable, has ever found himself in such a position. But talent and personality are not all that Jordan has at his disposal. Behind him stands a sophisticated network of men and women who make a sizeable portion of their living interpreting him—warmly, humorously, ironically, heroically—

and packaging him for an American public eager to believe in Michael Jordan, the commercial legend. A staff of eight people—divided between ProServ, Nike, JUMP Inc. and the Michael Jordan Foundation—screens his offers, negotiates his contracts, handles his finances, draws up his schedule, answers his mail and organizes his charitable activities.

Jordan is in such demand today that his agent has the luxury of simply screening offers for him, most of which he rejects or attempts to steer toward other clients. Because Michael, now married and the father of two children, can't make as many promotional appearances as he did when he was single, Falk has explored other endorsement options. "One of the vehicles that I've pursued over the last three years is to become more aggressive on the licensing side," he says, "passively using his name to sell sleeping bags, trading cards, golf equipment, back-to-school notebooks, lunch pails, whatever, as opposed to making eight or ten appearances a year for Coca-Cola bottlers or McDonald's franchise operators.

"Just last week we presented him with two opportunities in the same industry, one that was a licensing deal and one that was an endorsement deal. The endorsement deal was about double the money and it required *one* day a year in appearances. He said, 'No, let's do the licensing one.'

"His time is his most precious commodity."

And Jordan is Falk's. ProServ, which had billings of over $150 million in 1990, takes 4 percent for negotiating a player's contract, and anywhere from 15 to 25 percent on endorsement deals. The estimates of what Jordan will pay the agency in 1991 range from $2.5 million to $4 million.

"I think Michael is in a position, if he wanted to, he could leverage us, he could leverage our company and me to do almost anything that he wanted," Falk says. "And you ask yourself, would you risk losing a client of his importance? How high would you jump if he cracked the whip? And to his credit, he has never cracked the whip."

Until he does, Falk will perform the lucrative function of

deciding who enters Jordan's commercial world and who doesn't. "I enjoy being in the flow," he says. "You want to feel a little bit like a power broker."

The flow is particularly thick on All-Star weekend. Designers unveil new lines of sneakers and sportswear. Commercials and highlight videos receive their premieres. There are few better illustrations of how gleefully commercial the NBA and its athletes have become.

Here is Mr. (David) Robinson, the Nike pitchman, preparing to go one-on-one with Minute Maid soda salesman Patrick Ewing. There is Magic Johnson, who wears Converse sneakers and gets his fried chicken from KFC, talking about his injured friend, Detroit's Isiah Thomas, emissary for a Japanese car company—Toyota—and a Japanese sneaker firm—Asics.

Here are the corporate executives and middle managers, men and women who enlist these athletes to help them sell things to children—or, as they would have it, "to service the youth-oriented market."

Here, too, is a more irreverent contingent composed of men and women like Jim Riswold, the creative director at Weiden and Kennedy. Riswold is the man who matched Spike and Mike, built Mr. Robinson's neighborhood and gave Bo Jackson the chance to tell everyone how much he knew.

He and his counterparts at other agencies are entrusted with turning the athlete into an asset, creating for each endorser a new commercial persona. Sometimes the results are trashy, like the Converse spots that waste Magic Johnson in an MTV fantasy world where all the cars have big fenders and all the women have big breasts. Sometimes they are classy, like Bernard King explaining his comeback for Converse. And sometimes they're cute, like the Minute Maid commercial that features Dominique Wilkins leaping out of the picture and landing beside a can of orange soda.

At all times, they are endeavors in modern mythmaking, efforts to create for the athlete an image as friend, warrior, hipster, whatever will sell the product. Many athletes are defined and limited by a single successful commercial the way a musician can be limited by a hit song. Others control their image, use it to transcend the product they are endorsing and become celebrities in their own right; Michael Jordan is the best example.

Jordan's first sneaker commercials, produced by the Chiat/Day agency, established him as a hot property, but it was his appearance with Lee, the innovative black director, that helped him cross into the culture at large. Jim Riswold got the idea to pair the two while he and a colleague at Weiden and Kennedy were watching *She's Gotta Have It*, Lee's film about Nola Darling and her three lovers. One of those lovers was a slightly dorky, obnoxiously witty bicycle messenger.

"We liked the character of Mars," Riswold says. "He was the ultimate Michael Jordan fan. But what was interesting was when he wouldn't take his Air Jordans off when he went to bed with Nola. My friend and I looked at each other and said, 'Aha!' And the next day we called Spike."

Since 1986 Lee, Jordan and Riswold have collaborated on the popular series of commercials known in the industry as the Spike and Mike show. The spirit of the campaign was inspired by a remark former Celtics star Bill Russell made to Jordan's parents. "He said: 'Your son is a better person than he is a basketball player,'" Riswold says. "And that was great coming from somebody who is not known to give compliments.

"So I had that in mind when we were developing the Spike and Mike campaign. I looked at it as a way of showing him as more than a magnificent basketball player, but as a human being, and as a way to have some fun with him. And that campaign, to me, was our turning point with Nike, because it allowed us to have more fun with the athletes and make them seem more accessible."

In the first Spike and Mike commercials, Mars was Michael's comic foil. In one spot Mars lost Nola to Jordan. In another, Michael left him stranded atop a backboard. But as the campaign matured Jordan came in for a little lampooning himself as the distance between basketball star and bicycle messenger was narrowed.

In one 1990 commercial, Mars, bent on learning the secret of Michael's leaping abilities, creeps around Jordan's body asking whether Michael's strength flows from personal idiosyncracies like his haircut, his baggy shorts, or his almost invisible socks. In a 1991 spot, Mars hypes "The Michael Jordan Flight School," where other NBA players can learn how to appear in television commercials, stick out their tongues, play a lot of golf, sign autographs and increase their hang time.

"The point is here's a guy who is Michael's number one fan, but he's also a good friend of his," Riswold says. "And I think that is the way people feel about Michael."

These Nike spots established Jordan as hip with that segment of the population to whom hipness mattered. But if that were his only image, Jordan would have remained what Falk calls a "niche player." Instead, a succession of large, conservative American corporations helped craft him an alternate persona, one that won the hearts of parents and children around the country.

For Coca-Cola, with whom his contract expired after the 1990–91 season, Michael played the boy next door, leaping so high that he could hand a six-pack to his young friends in their tree house. For McDonald's he was the big man on campus spotted by kids at the local hamburger stand. For CBS-Fox he played the big brother of "Michael Jordan's Playground." For Wheaties he was the dutiful son talking nutrition with his mom, or the funny friend eager for a rematch in tabletop basketball. His 1991 Gatorade commercials made their point succinctly, urging kids to "Be like Mike."

This wholesome Jordan is the one who broke new ground. Black athletes had been doing endorsements for decades, but none had the breadth of Jordan's appeal. And none were marketed as the embodiment of American virtue.

Michael, in many ways, was perfect for the part. He was

handsome, but not overtly sexual; accomplished yet unthreatening; intelligent but unsullied by controversial political opinions. Jordan was a hero to the rebellious young and
a symbol of cultural pride for many blacks; yet nothing in
his dress, hairstyle or demeanor alienated conservative whites.
He had even stopped wearing gold chains in his rookie
season, not long after one advertising director suggested he
"lose the Mr. T starter set."

"We seem to have so few Jack Armstrong types any-
more," says Glenn Rupp, chairman of Wilson Sporting
Goods, invoking the name of radio's All-American boy.
"Michael fits into that."

Jordan seemed so safe that even a company which had
confined its marketing primarily to cartoon characters felt
comfortable with him. "We know Walt Disney will never
allow Mickey Mouse to have a marital problem," explains
Robert Sgarlata, vice president of marketing and development of the Cleo company. "We know Donald Duck is
never going to beat Daisy. Yogi Bear is probably not going
to develop a drug problem. But now we have a human
being. You worry about human beings. But with Michael it
is different. Michael is such a wholesome kid."

Yet, this wholesomeness has not proved confining—at
least not in commercials. In one series of Chicagoland
Chevy spots, Jordan plays the young man of the world
discussing his values and contemplating the future. For
Hanes, he's been a Jim Palmer-type sex symbol. ("When
I'm not slammin', I'm jammin', in my Bill Blass underwear
from Hanes.") And for his friends at Bigsby & Kruthers, he
is the opportunity to develop a new, distinctly American line
of clothing.

"Ease, comfort and elegance," says Joe Silverberg. "I
think that's what America feels about him in general. He's
like Fred Astaire."

Jack Armstrong. Mickey Mouse. Fred Astaire. It is almost as though Jordan has ceased to be a human being and
has gone to live in a world of commercial fantasy, a place

where Americans create and consume visions of what it means to be innocent and playful, or talented and modest, or strong and courageous, or graceful and sophisticated. Or all of these things.

The Michael Jordan who inhabits this world is a projection of the national imagination, an adman's fiction in the flesh. Everyone who interprets him seems able to find in Jordan a reflection of their own values and those of the consumers they are trying to reach. Yet these images never seem to collide. Jordan is like the politician who portrays himself as all things to all people. And so far he has had the luxury of seldom having to please one constituency at the expense of another.

Michael's success, and the success it has helped make possible for other black athletes, has helped to balance the negative portrayals of young black men that flood the nation's media. His commercial ascension, at a time of increasing racial polarization, highlights the values that blacks and whites hold in common and suggests the circumstances in which reconciliation is possible. For all that, though, Jordan's breakthrough is an ambiguous one, underscoring the problems as well as the promise of consumer culture as a tool for black advancement and improved racial understanding.

He might never have become so popular had he not played a sport in which whites had become comfortable with black domination, or had he used his prominence to challenge the economic status quo, rather than cutting himself in for a piece. Michael's wealth sends a mixed message to young black men already disproportionately drawn toward nonexistent careers in professional sports. They know that Jordan has a college diploma, but understand that it was not his grasp of cultural geography—Michael's major—that made him rich.

And earning these riches has embroiled Jordan in the larger moral questions of the American economy. Michael's personal appeal helps sell a wide range of products that are of dubious impact, particularly in the inner city. Should he be encouraging ghetto children to eat hamburgers and french fries when bad nutrition plagues so many of America's poor? Should an affluent athlete push the false hope of lottery tickets on the less fortunate? Does Jordan bear any responsibility for the mayhem young men commit to obtain a pair of his sneakers? (This last question will be examined at greater length in another chapter.)

Jordan, though he does not endorse cigarettes, alcohol or other lucrative American vices, is still compromised by the products he pushes. Yet the wealth and visibility that these endorsements provide have put him in the position to act as a role model. They have given him the potential to emerge one day as an important businessman or philanthropist. At the beginning of the 1987–88 season, these moral responsibilities were being urged on him with a greater vigor than ever.

"He is carrying the torch and he will be perceived as a leader," says Erving, who pioneered the territory Jordan now rules. "In his religious views, social views, political views, he will be expected to lead. When I get a chance to spend time with him I try to make sure he is aware of that."

Ironically, even as Michael was being cast as an example for American children, he was being castigated for his style of play and its purportedly deleterious effect on the game.

Jordan began the 1987–88 season with a chip on his shoulder. Some sportswriters had begun referring to him as Team Jordan, a joke on the Bulls, but on their star as well. Basketball purists compared his game unfavorably with Magic Johnson's and Larry Bird's. These criticisms might not have stung Jordan had they concerned his technical mastery of the game, but their subtext was quite personal: either Michael wasn't as selfless as Bird and Johnson, or he wasn't as smart.

"I don't think they have the facts right," Jordan said. "One thing they see in me that they don't see in Larry and Magic is the athletic ability. I have a little bit more than those guys. They. . . have great talents, but in terms of raw athletic talent I think I have a little more.

"So it's hard for some people to believe someone can put raw athletic talent together with fundamentals and become a complete player. But that's what I did at North Carolina. Because of my dunking and jumping they see the athletic part, so they don't believe I can think the game too.

"But I do think the game. Just because I can jump doesn't mean I can't box out."

There was also, he pointed out to Curry Kirkpatrick, the matter of supporting casts. The people he was trying to "make better" were basketball immortals like Brad Sellers and Granville Waiters. "Are you telling me that Kareem and James [Worthy] wouldn't be All-Stars without Magic? That [Kevin] McHale or DJ [Dennis Johnson] wouldn't make it without Bird? Anybody who thinks that is a damn fool."

In the heat of an intrasquad scrimmage during the first week of practice, Michael became convinced that Doug Collins had cheated his team out of a point. Suddenly incensed, Jordan stormed out of the gym.

"I know after a long, tough practice the losing team has to run," he said later. "If he wants me to run, fine. Stop practice and I'll run all he wants. But why make me kill myself in the scrimmage and then run? People may think this to be so trivial. But when you are a competitor and want to win, nothing is trivial."

Jordan was right that arguing over a single point in a meaningless scrimmage seemed trivial, but the incident was evidence of how deeply Michael felt that he had something to prove in the upcoming season. So was the range he'd added to his jumper. Jordan had spent the summer laboring on this sometimes erratic shot, and it was now deadly from inside 20 feet.

Two days after Michael stormed out of practice, he and Collins literally kissed and made up on the evening news and the Bulls' camp was quiet again. This was a watershed year for the young team. Oakley, an offensive liability, reigned as one of the league's leading rebounders. Rookie forward Scottie Pippen could run the floor and handle the ball, while Horace Grant, his fellow first-round draft pick, had the makings of an excellent power forward. With Jordan dunking less, passing more and surprising the league with long-range jumpers, Chicago bolted to an impressive 7–1 start.

Michael's biggest offensive outburst of the early season was the 49 points he put up in an overtime loss to the Pistons in late November, but his most satisfying all-around performance came in the Bulls' nationally televised victory over Houston a week later. Jordan scored 44 points, but his defense was equally electrifying. He grabbed five steals and blocked five shots, one by each of Houston's twin towers, Ralph Sampson and Akeem Olajuwon. "I wanted to show the difference between this year and last year," he said after the Bulls' 98–86 victory. "I wanted to show that I can play defense and that I don't shoot as much as Larry Bird would say."

The talk around the league was that Michael had mellowed a bit, that he wasn't quite as explosive as the season before. On December 2 in Salt Lake City, however, Jordan was his flashy self in a 111–105 victory over the Utah Jazz. But it wasn't his 47 points that stuck in people's minds so much as the exchange between Jordan and a spectator sitting courtside.

It began after Michael swiped a Utah pass and soared in to slam over 6-foot John Stockton. "Pick on somebody your own size," screamed a fellow sitting near the basket. Moments later Jordan went sailing down the lane once again, jamming this time over hulking 7-footer Mel Turpin.

"Is he big enough?" Michael shouted as he headed upcourt. The fan was Jazz owner Larry Miller.

Its victory in Utah improved Chicago's record to 12–3 and marked the crest of the Bulls' early season. They were a deceptively shallow team, lacking an established point guard to direct the offense, as well as a low-post scorer who could lighten Jordan's scoring responsibilities. After their break-neck beginning, the Bulls suddenly floundered, losing nine of their next 12. Erratic and immature, they were capable of blowing big fourth-quarter leads on their home court, as they did in a December 22 loss to the Dallas Mavericks.

But when the Bulls were hot, or when Michael was, they were among the league's elite. After dropping to 15–12, Chicago won 11 of its next 15. Foremost among those games was their most memorable out-and-out brawl with the Pistons, a grudge match that took place on January 16 at the Stadium.

Detroit was shooting poorly, and Chicago was leading 57–52 with 9:09 to play in the third period when Bulls forward Brad Sellers lofted an errant jump shot from the left corner. Jordan and Joe Dumars leapt into one another pursuing the rebound. Dumars hit the floor.

As Jordan grabbed the ball and darted to the hoop, a pair of huge arms encircled his chest. Rick Mahorn, the Pistons' 6-foot-10, 255-pound forward, wrapped him up and threw him to the floor, Charles Oakley grabbed Mahorn and the two engaged in a heated shoving match that drifted toward the Chicago bench. The Pistons' forward had his back to the sidelines and never saw Doug Collins leap up and lasso his neck.

The coach didn't keep his hold very long. Mahorn swayed backwards, smashing Collins down on the scorer's table and into the lap of Bulls announcer Red Kerr. Collins leapt up and Mahorn struck him in the face.

After order had been reestablished, Oakley and Mahorn were ejected and the Bulls were on fire. Paced by Michael's 36 points, 10 rebounds, 10 assists, four blocks and four steals, they raced away with a 115–99 victory. "I understand he [Mahorn] had to stop me," Jordan said when it was over, "but not to the point where he had to throw me to the floor, not knowing if I'd get hurt or not."

The Pistons intimated that Jordan was a favored child, protected by the officials and unwilling to absorb his share of the punishment that came with driving the lane. "Michael Jordan is a great player and all that, but he is going to get fouled," Adrian Dantley said. "You mean you can't touch the guy? When I led the league in scoring I got fouled harder than that every night.''

Dantley's memory on this subject is questionable. A prodigious post scorer, he was never the high-flying and therefore hard-falling sort of player that Jordan is. But the concern he expressed was shared around the league. Short of tough physical play, how did you stop a guy who was averaging 33.3 points and seven assists per game? And if you didn't stop Michael, how did you beat a team that was a surprising 27–18 at the All-Star break?

In the course of just half a season, Jordan had all but silenced his critics. He was playing the best basketball of his life, leading the league not only in scoring but in steals as well. ''The biggest improvement in Michael Jordan over the last two years is how he is penetrating and finding the open man now,'' said Jay Humphries of Phoenix. Although the Bulls were still occasionally a one-man team, the difference was that this season, they were a much better one-man team than they had been a year earlier.

Jordan was once again the leading vote-getter for the NBA All-Star game, an honor all the more meaningful because the festivities were to be held in Chicago Stadium. If his first All-Star game underscored the tension between Michael and his peers, this one illustrated the respect. For the first time, Jordan, who was literally at home, felt that way emotionally too.

''We were all backstage before the All-Star show Saturday night laughing and joking and talking about the season and the game on Sunday,'' he said. ''For the first time I really felt accepted by everyone.''

The other All-Stars clearly sensed that the weekend belonged to Jordan and did what they could to make it special for him. In the slam dunk competition, Dominique Wilkins's whirling dervish finale was a shade more spectacular than Michael's take-off-from-the-foul-line homage to Dr. J., but

Jordan won the title on a hometown decision, and Wilkins had the good grace not to complain too loudly.

Even Isiah Thomas, the engineer of Jordan's rookie disillusionment, got into the act on Sunday, running an offense geared toward pleasing the Chicago fans. Late in the game Jordan had 36 points, and the All-Star scoring record of 42 seemed within his grasp. Twice Thomas hit the barely defended Bulls star for sure shots, but on the East's final possession, despite Isiah's theatrical pleadings, Jordan declined to cut toward the basket.

Michael hit 17 of 23 shots, scored 40 points, pulled down eight rebounds, picked off four steals and blocked four shots, all of which earned him the game's Most Valuable Player award. The East won, 138–133.

"Everyone came to see the Michael Jordan show," said Thomas, a Chicago native. "I was glad I could help."

"I was embarrassed," a joyful Jordan said. "I didn't want things handed to me. The first 36 points were earned. The last four were respectfully given to me."

Asked if it felt good to be one of the guys, Jordan said: "I never thought about it like that before, but if that's how they feel then I'm glad to be in the fraternity." And the fraternity was glad to have him. "A lot of older guys think you have to pay your dues, and I think Michael Jordan has done the job," Larry Bird said.

Even the old controversy over who was the league's best player—Bird, Johnson or Jordan—was defused for the weekend. "No one is the best player," Michael said. "If I had a choice of naming the best player or dying, I think I'd die right here."

That might have been overdoing it a bit, but for Jordan a long nap was certainly in order. He resumed the season a drained and exhausted player, and the Bulls dropped three of their first four games after the break. Two of those losses came to the Pistons and helped begin a tailspin that lasted nearly a month.

After a March 7 loss to the Knicks, the club's record

stood at 33–26. The Bulls were 6–8 since the All-Star break, and the season seemed to be slipping from their grasp. But at this ebb, Collins named Sam Vincent his starting point guard. Vincent had joined the team just 11 days earlier in a trade with Seattle. He was quick, a decent ball-handler, a solid shooter, and he made the Bulls a faster and more offensively potent team. With Vincent directing the offense and Jordan putting up the points, Chicago roared through the final quarter of the season, winning 17 of its last 23.

On March 18 Michael tossed in 50 as the Bulls beat the Celtics 113–103. Five nights later he scored 49 as Chicago beat the 76ers 118–112. Even the Pistons fell to the resurgent Bulls. On April 3, Jordan blitzed Detroit for 59 points on 21-of-27 shooting. When that wasn't enough, he snuffed Isiah Thomas with 24 seconds remaining and started the fast break that gave Chicago a 112–110 victory.

"He hit a few shots that I know even he had to be impressed with himself," Detroit's Vinnie Johnson said.

In the midst of his most dominant season Michael was perhaps the most underpaid player in all of sports. The $4 million, five-year deal Jordan had signed four seasons earlier had been the highest ever for a rookie guard. But both profits and salaries had soared in the resurgence that Michael had helped fuel. The Bulls were drawing 18,000 fans per game, a 284 percent increase since Jordan joined the club.

Jerry Reinsdorf knew what a bargain Michael had been and realized how much he owed him. Late in the 1987–88 season he contacted David Falk and the two came to terms that were announced on April 8, just hours before Jordan scored 40 points in Chicago's 131–122 victory over the Knicks. The new eight-year contract would pay Michael an average of $3.25 million per season. It was, if briefly, the biggest contract in team sports and is still among the three highest in the league.

Chicago's regular season wound down in a celebratory atmosphere. Jerry Krause was named Executive of the Year.

The Bulls won 50 games for only the second time in franchise history. And for the first time in Michael's tenure, they seemed to have a chance of surviving the first round of the playoffs.

Chicago had split its six-game season series with Cleveland, but somehow the Bulls lost sight of that. It wasn't so much the Cavaliers who confounded them as the pressure of the postseason itself. In this frenetic series a pattern emerged that would last for three years. Jordan's teammates, after a season of building their own identities, would collapse, only to have Michael hoist them on his shoulders and carry them farther than they deserved to go.

In game one Jordan ripped the Cavaliers for 50 points, and personally outscored them 20–19 in the pivotal second period. Chicago won, 104–93. In game two he carried his club to a 106–101 victory on the crest of a 55-point rampage. "Before he's through," wrote the *Tribune*'s Bernie Lincicome, "maybe the only way he'll be able to astonish anyone is to do the laundry and heal the lame on the way to the basket."

But the Cavs held Michael to just 15 shots in game three. He made 12 of them, but managed only 28 points as Cleveland staved off elimination, 110–102. Jordan scored 40 in game four, but the rest of his mates barely bothered to dress as the Cavaliers tied the series with a 97–91 victory.

The Bulls had once again become Team Jordan. Going into the deciding game, Michael was shooting 56 percent from the floor, his teammates 37 percent. He was also scoring 46.8 of the Bulls' 100.8 points. "It's Jordan against Cavaliers one last time," read the headline in the May 8 *Chicago Tribune*.

But this seemingly bankable prophecy did not come to pass. When it mattered most, the rest of the Bulls suddenly materialized. Jordan scored 39 points and Scottie Pippen had 24, along with three decisive third-quarter steals, as the Bulls won 108–101. The Jordan-Pippen collaboration was an omen of things to come—but not too quickly. The Bulls' victory ended their long postseason drought, but an even more frustrating dry spell was about to begin.

The Detroit Pistons commenced their postseason mastery of the Bulls in the second round of the 1988 Eastern Conference playoffs, but the seeds of their domination had been sown on Easter Sunday, after Jordan scorched them for 59 points. Not long afterward Chuck Daly and his assistants, Dick Versace and Ron Rothstein, developed a set of defenses that would break the Bulls' hearts for three straight seasons. They called them the Jordan Rules.

Opponents had been wondering how to stop Jordan for two full seasons. Everyone had a theory, or was working on one. Some teams, notably the Pistons and Celtics, tried to force Jordan to the middle. This strategy was based on the notion that by creating a clog of bigger bodies one could prevent Jordan from driving so frequently to the basket.

But Michael had enjoyed some of his greatest games against these teams, and Sidney Moncrief of Milwaukee, then one of the league's top defensive guards, thought the strategy flawed. "Generally," he said, "there will be more passing options, more ways for him to break your defense down in the middle."

Some teams, like Moncrief's Bucks, attempted to force Jordan as wide as possible on the wings and as deep as possible on the baseline. This minimized Jordan's passing opportunities, but Michael's one-on-one moves were so effective that he could often shake free from his defender even when seemingly forced out of bounds.

Double-teaming Jordan became almost a necessity, but this alone was no guarantee of success. If the double team developed too slowly, he could scoot between the two defenders. Or, as Jordan himself once explained, he could use the extra defender's body as a screen against his original guard and dribble around them both. Of course there was always the option of doing something simple, like passing to an open teammate.

One thing players around the league had come to agree on was the importance of challenging Michael when he was on defense, running him through picks, making him cover the fast break, anything to wear him out. In fact, John Bach, the Bulls' defensive coordinator, thinks that talented, athletic offensive guards like Dumars, Ron Harper of the Clippers, Reggie Miller of Indiana and Jeff Malone of Utah generally give Michael the most trouble. Of course Jordan gives them a great deal of trouble too, and going into a playoff series, the Pistons couldn't afford that.

"You are talking about the ultimate scorer in basketball," Chuck Daly says. "You have to have some kind of defensive plan. One person can't do it. You've got to use three or four."

None of the coaches involved will discuss the specifics of the Jordan Rules, but Versace remembers how they were formulated. "It was the brainchild of the three of us," he says. "What we were doing was sitting around trying to come up with a way to play this guy.

"We came up with one way with everybody chipping in their ideas and then we came up with another way and another way. And Chuck said, 'Let me go home and think about this and make a decision in the morning.' Then when he was leaving he said, 'You know that first way we came up with—if I was to make just a gut decision, I'd kind of like that.' And he still liked it the next day.

"The percentage is that you can make these shots go elsewhere," Versace says. "It didn't take him out of their offense, but it does direct the offense elsewhere."

The problem for Chicago was that "elsewhere" in 1987–88 was not a very impressive place. Yet, going into the series the Bulls believed they had a chance to win. Detroit had taken four of the teams' six meetings that season, but two of those victories had come in overtime and two others during Jordan's post-All-Star slump.

Their illusions lasted through two games.

The Pistons won the opener 93–82 as Dumars held Jordan

to just 29 points, with Michael hitting only six of his first 16 shots. But the Bulls rallied in game two, as Jordan scored 36 points and the streaky Sam Vincent added 31. Detroit pitched in, missing 19 of 41 free throws, more than enough to give Chicago a 105–95 victory.

That was the Bulls' one impressive interlude. Two minutes into the third game, Pistons center Bill Laimbeer set an illegal pick, blindsiding Jordan and skewering him with an elbow that Michael said hit him "where it hurts." Jordan threw a right cross at Laimbeer and missed, picking up a technical in the process. That was only the beginning of his frustration, however, as Detroit's defense hounded him all over the court. Jordan went scoreless the game's first 17 minutes, and by the time he shook free, a rout was already in progress. Though Michael scored 31 points, the Pistons won handily, 101–79.

Detroit cruised through the remainder of the series, winning the two final games easily. On the afternoon of its last victory, a pair of diagrams, purported to be the Pistons' new anti-Jordan defenses, appeared on the sports page of the *Detroit News*. It took another season before these defenses acquired their nickname, and a little longer before anybody could make sense of them for the general public. But the tactics that won the '87–'88 playoff series were basically the same ones described by Jack McCallum in the August 14, 1989 issue of *Sports Illustrated*.

One: The Pistons clogged the middle with big bodies—Laimbeer, James Edwards and Rick Mahorn—to stop Jordan from whirling and weaving down the lane.

Two: They played a shot-blocker—Dennis Rodman or John Salley—on the weak side of their defense so he could knife across the lane to contest any shot should Jordan drive by his man.

Three: They seldom left Jordan in man-to-man coverage, either running a second man at him as soon as he touched the ball or playing "help and recover," a sort of part-time double team where the second defender bounced between Jordan and his own man.

The Rules would have been less than successful were it not for the Pistons' personnel, and Chuck Daly was the first to say so. "You at least have to have somebody who can stand in front of him," he says. "And Joe can do that on most nights."

In fact, Dumars' ability to stick with Jordan much of the time was the key to these defenses. "I basically know I am going to have to expend more energy in a game against Michael Jordan than against anybody else," Dumars says. "Not to slight anybody else, it's just that it is almost mandatory. I think it is mental energy. You tell yourself that you can't get tired, because if you do, he senses any kind of a letup and then there will be an explosion from him."

Dumars couldn't do the job alone for a full 48 minutes, though. Dennis Rodman's ability to spell Dumars was critical, as was Isiah Thomas's skill at darting around the perimeter between Jordan and the Bulls' point guard. Salley's shot-blocking completed an intimidating defensive package.

But at least one former coach feels that a strictly tactical analysis overlooks the key element in the Pistons' special defense. "The Jordan Rules?" says Frank Layden, who coached the Utah Jazz. "You know what the Jordan Rule is, don't you? Knock him on his ass. They can talk all they want, but the one thing they did—when he got in midair—they knocked him down.

"The only way to stop him is with a cannon."

The 1987–88 season had been a personal triumph for Michael. He'd scored 35 points per game while his shooting percentage soared from .482 to an astonishing .535. He'd also notched six assists and 5.5 rebounds per game, and led the league in steals with 259. The writers who cover the NBA voted Jordan the Most Valuable Player as well as the Defensive Player of the Year. It was the first time anyone had claimed both honors in a single season.

Michael was gratified but not overly impressed. In his

own eyes his performance had not been very different from his performance the preceding year. The key, he said, was that his team had won 50 games. "That's the way society is. Winning has a lot to do with it," he said. "You have a winning season and people try to find out the reason behind it."

While there is something to Jordan's criticism of the way the league distributes its awards, it is also more than slightly disingenuous. In 1987–88 Michael played with greater control, showed greater leadership and demonstrated, with his new jump-shooting prowess, that there was no longer a weakness in his offensive game.

After four seasons in the NBA Jordan had established himself as the league's most exciting player, and perhaps its best. But something was happening to him that was based only in part on his basketball abilities. He toured Europe for Nike in the summer of 1988 and found that even there he could not always move unmolested down city streets. He was becoming not simply a celebrity, but a standard-bearer, one of those individuals whom a nation thrusts forward and says, "Here, this is what is best about us."

In Michael's image contradictions were somehow reconciled. He was a sublimely gifted overachiever—glamorous, yet wholesome; avant-garde, yet traditional; anarchic, yet bourgeois. In Jordan the corporate and counter cultures found common ground. He made more inclusive the "All" in All-American.

That the young man who embodied these virtues was black gave his accomplishment special historical resonance.

11

Six years ago, Nicholas Oxley saw Michael Jordan swoop across his television screen. "He seemed like a pretty good role model," says Nicholas, who is now 14. "He didn't do drugs, he didn't smoke and he had the ability to fly."

The Oxley household has not been the same since. Nicholas's room is papered with Jordan posters. So is the room of Trevor, his eight-year-old brother. William Oxley, now two and a half, was taught, before his first birthday, how to "do like Michael Jordan"—sticking out his tongue the way Jordan does as he drives to the basket.

The Oxleys' devotion to Michael spread quickly to friends like Trevor's buddy Matthew Lilly. When he had to make a mask in art class of someone he wanted to be, Matthew drew Jordan's face. "With a big red tongue hanging out," he says.

The Oxleys and Lillys live in a West Virginia county that has virtually no black residents. The boys' only exposure to black people is through popular culture, particularly televised sports. Jordan plays a role in their lives similar to the role black athletes have played in this country for almost a century.

Until the civil rights movement of the late 1950s, athletes and entertainers were the only black Americans written about in mainstream newspapers. Many whites learned what little they knew about black people not from the examples of intellectuals like W.E.B. Du Bois, labor pioneers like A. Philip Randolph or educators like Mary McLeod Bethune, but from Joe Louis, Jesse Owens or Jackie Robinson.

Today, despite increasing black visibility in politics and other fields, the impact of black athletes on white racial attitudes remains strong. It is a burden of influence no white athlete has borne since Hank Greenberg and the DiMaggio brothers made baseball safe for Jewish and Italian immigrants in the 1930s.

With its emphasis on the physical rather than the intellectual, on the symbolic rather than the practically political, sports was never the ideal battleground on which to wage the struggle for racial equality. But for decades athletics remained one of the few battlegrounds available—the largest public arena in which racist assumptions could be tested and put to rout. After baseball, football and basketball were desegregated in the mid-1940s, sports was also the profession in which blacks and whites worked most conspicuously together.

Black athletes, consequently, acquired a significance in American life that they would never have achieved in a less divided society. Some, such as Jack Johnson, the first black heavyweight champion, and the young Muhammad Ali, chose to attack racism directly and lived in constant confrontation with white society. Others, like Joe Louis and the young Jackie Robinson, met animosity with forbearance, and risked the appearance of servility to prove that they and other blacks deserved a fair chance. Jordan has been spared this excruciating choice. While he has allowed advertisers to craft him a wholesome and unthreatening commercial persona, he has never had to swallow his pride to succeed. His stature in American culture marks a new high point in black athletes' long struggle to be accepted on something approaching their own terms.

But progress has not come without its pitfalls. Young black men seek and are shepherded toward careers in athletics in numbers that far exceed the opportunities. The image of African-Americans as naturally superior athletes has fueled the pernicious corollary that European-Americans have naturally superior intellects. Colleges use talented young black men to bolster their sports programs but do little to prepare them for life after their athletic eligibility has expired.

These drawbacks notwithstanding, sports has traditionally been a lever that black men have used to move the world. As the nation's best-loved African-American athlete, Michael Jordan inherits that legacy, and that lever.

On the day after Christmas in 1908, Jack Johnson knocked out Tommy Burns in the 14th round of their heavyweight championship fight in Sydney, Australia. The victory made Johnson the first black man to hold the title. It also initiated one of the uglier chapters in American race relations.

For the next seven years Johnson was the target of white outrage. His success in the ring and his liaisons with white prostitutes threatened a race-obsessed society that feared black social and sexual domination. Johnson understood these fears and took pleasure in exploiting them. Before sparring in public, he occasionally wrapped his penis in gauze to make it seem larger than it was.

''The White Man must be saved,'' wrote Jack London in 1909 after the champion returned to the United States and dispatched five white challengers in a year. Boxing promoters began searching for a Great White Hope, but the best they could do was a retired former champion. Jim Jeffries hadn't boxed in five years, but he was subjected to such intense public pressure that he could hardly refuse the fight.

At issue, wrote one sportswriter, was whether Jeffries

could "beat down the wonderful black and restore Caucasians the crown of elemental greatness as measured by strength of brow, power of heart and lung, and withal, the cunning or keenness that denotes mental as well as physical superiority."

On the day the bout took place in Reno, some 30,000 people massed in Times Square to await results as they came across the ticker. When Jeffries paraded to the ring, the crowd serenaded him with a popular ditty called "All Coons Look Alike to Me." But once the match began, Johnson's superiority was evident. He toyed with the former champion for 14 rounds, taunting him all the while. In the 15th round he knocked him out.

Reaction to the champion's victory was swift and hysterical. The Reno newspaper headlined its story "Jeff Mastered by Grinning, Jeering Negro." An editorial cartoon of the day showed Johnson wrapping enormous lips around a slice of watermelon in which the seeds spelled out "Jeff."

Racial violence broke out around the country. In Uvalda, Georgia, three blacks were killed and five wounded when a white gang fired on blacks celebrating Johnson's triumph. In Houston a black fan had his throat slashed from ear to ear. Another black man was beaten to death in New York City. Thirty people were hurt in a Pueblo, Colorado race riot. Two whites were fatally knifed by black assailants in Washington, D.C.

Nine governors banned screenings of the fight film. But white paranoia only escalated. In Baltimore, a minister claimed that Johnson's victory made it unsafe for white women and children to walk the streets. Congressman Sealon A. Roddenberry of Georgia sponsored a constitutional amendment banning intermarriage. A popular comic book captured the tone of the times: "Black Ape Splitting the White Princess."

Johnson's own behavior exacerbated these tensions. Back home in Chicago he opened a raucous integrated nightclub and cavorted openly with white prostitutes—two of whom he married. His liaisons with white women so outraged federal prosecutors that they twice tried him on trumped-up morals charges, the second of which stuck. On May 12, 1913, Johnson was convicted by an all-white jury of having transported a woman across state lines for purposes of debauchery and was sentenced to a year in prison.

He chose exile over incarceration, fleeing to Europe and entering a steady decline in which he lost his money and his title before returning to the United States in 1920 to serve his prison term. Near the end of his life he put on vaudeville exhibitions and worked in circus sideshows.

Johnson was killed in an automobile accident in 1946 at the age of 68, but his legend survived. He was revered by black activists and white liberals of the late 1960s. In *The Great White Hope*, Howard Sackler's famous play, the former champion is portrayed as a tragic hero undone by his refusal to accept racial conventions. Many saw him as a spiritual ancestor of Muhammad Ali, including Ali himself.

Johnson's penchant for confrontation was considered foolish by many of his black contemporaries, however, and when a promising black heavyweight came along in the mid-1930s, his managers presented him as everything the former champion was not.

Joe Louis Barrow fought his first professional bout on Independence Day in 1934 at the age of 20. Within a year, as a contender for the heavyweight championship, the barely educated boxer was the most famous black person in America.

Louis was especially fortunate in having two managers, John Roxborough and Julian Black, who understood that a black man who beat up white men in public needed to appear otherwise unthreatening. And so they sold their fighter to the press as a model citizen. He neither smoked nor drank. He did not denigrate his opponents, and never smiled after knocking down a foe. Above all, Louis avoided having his picture taken with white women.

Although he privately indulged his sexual appetite without regard to race, Louis took pains to reinforce his public image. He married a pretty black schoolteacher from a solidly middle-class family, bought his mother a new home, extolled the virtues of capitalism and had his picture taken holding the Bible. He seemed to be telling middle Americans, "My values are yours; accept me." Many did, but Louis encountered more prejudice than admiration as he fought his way to the heavyweight title.

In his illuminating study *Champion: Joe Louis, Black Hero in White America*, Chris Mead shows how the fighter's image passed through distinct, if occasionally overlapping, phases, each of which demonstrated white America's discomfort in coming to terms with a black hero. Even in the first and most benign of these phases, race was paramount. Louis's nickname—the Brown Bomber—was just one of the press's alliterative appellations. He was also referred to as the Dark Destroyer, the heavy-fisted Harlemite, the Mahogany Maimer, the Mocha Mauler, the Sepia Slugger, the Sable Cyclone, the Saffron Sphinx, the Tan Tarzan of Thump and the Coffee-Colored Kayo King.

After the 21-year-old fighter knocked out Primo Carnera on June 25, 1935, his "jungle-killer" phase began in earnest. It was epitomized in a column by Paul Gallico. Though he was one of the more cultured sportswriters of his generation, Gallico wrote of Louis in crude and stereotypically racist terms, finding his subject "a mean man, a truly savage person on whom civilization rested no more securely than a shawl thrown over one's shoulders." He referred to Louis's managers as "his keepers" and added: "I had the feeling that I was in the room with a wild animal."

These jungle analogies abated as the press got to know Louis better. But even writers who attempted a more fully human portrayal of the young fighter were undermined by ingrained racial prejudices. "There isn't an ounce of killer in him," wrote Bill Corum in the *New York Journal*. "Not the slightest zest for fighting. He's a big, superbly built Negro youth who was born to listen to jazz music, eat a lot of fried chicken, play ball with the gang on the corner, and never do a lick of heavy work he could escape. The chances are he came by all those inclinations quite naturally."

This was written during what Mead calls Louis's "darkie" period when the press was full of details about how much the fighter liked to eat and sleep. Writers decided that he was lazy and didn't like to train, though he had done little else from early 1934 through the middle of 1936. Photographers, meanwhile, often shot the fighter eyeing a plate of fried chicken and tried, unsuccessfully, to get him to pose eating watermelon.

What ultimately won the press to Louis's side and made him a national hero were his two bouts with German boxer Max Schmeling. The two first met in June of 1936, just a month before the Berlin Olympics, for which Adolf Hitler's racial theories had set the symbolic agenda. When Schmeling scored his memorable upset, knocking Louis out in the 12th round, Nazi propaganda chief Joseph Goebbels proclaimed a genetically ordained victory.

By the time Louis and Schmeling met again two years later, much had changed. The Nazi threat had grown stronger and the prospect of war more likely. In this tense period, black athletes had emerged as America's symbolic warriors. Jesse Owens had embarrassed Hitler at the Berlin Olympics, winning four gold medals. Louis, who had won the heavyweight championship since his loss to Schmeling, hoped to do the same.

"Tonight," said his ghostwriter in a syndicated column that bore Louis's byline, "I not only fight . . . to revenge the lone blot on my record, but I fight for America against the challenge of a foreign invader. This isn't just one man against another . . . it is the good old U.S.A. versus Germany."

The good old U.S.A. scored a stunning first-round knockout and Joe Louis became a hero of American nationalism. His stature as a patriot grew rapidly in the years ahead. Just a month after the bombing of Pearl Harbor, he knocked out Buddy Baer in a charity fight that raised more than $80,000 for the Navy relief fund. The following day he enlisted in the Army.

Even Paul Gallico liked Joe Louis now:

"Years ago I wrote that Joe Louis was 'mean.' Then he was a primitive puncher just emerging from the pit. Somewhere on his long, hard climb Joe found his soul. It was this, almost more than the physical person, that he handed over to his country."

Louis appeared in posters, fought exhibitions, made goodwill tours and rallied black support for the war effort, all of which made him increasingly popular with white Americans. "Joe's accomplishments in causing good feeling between the white and Negro races are established facts," wrote Margery Miller in her 1945 biography *Joe Louis: American*. "It is these, more than his accomplishments in the ring, that Joe would have people remember."

This, by and large, *is* the Joe Louis whom people remember. Despite revelations about his abusive relationships with women, his slide into bankruptcy and the mental illness that overtook him late in his life, Louis remains one of the most admired Americans of this century. When the former champion died in 1981, Pope John Paul I wrote: "He had opened sports to blacks and made athletics a cutting edge of the civil rights movement."

Jackie Robinson took Louis's breakthrough one step further. A black boxer might beat a white opponent senseless, but nothing in his victory argued that the races should live and work together. Many who cheered Louis's triumphs believed in the doctrine of separate equality. Robinson took that luxury away from them. Where the boxer struggled against prejudiced attitudes, the ballplayer struggled against prejudiced institutions.

African-Americans had been excluded, though not formally banned, from white professional baseball leagues since the late nineteenth century. In the early 1940s, only the American Communist Party and a few black sportswriters pressed the issue of desegregating the game. That situation changed dramatically in October, 1945, when the Brooklyn Dodgers' top farm club announced that it had signed Robinson.

The Dodgers' general manager was Branch Rickey, a blustering, speechifying moralist whom the New York press had nicknamed the Mahatma. Rickey was an often pompous and unnecessarily controversial man, but one whose knowledge of the game was unquestioned. In the 1930s, while general manager of the St. Louis Cardinals, he had founded the first modern farm system. Many of the best young players *and* executives in baseball had matured under his tutelage.

Still, when he signed Robinson, Rickey's motives came under fire from whites and blacks alike. Some charged that this risky venture was a publicity stunt. Others saw it as a ploy to draw black fans.

The Sporting News, the so-called Bible of Baseball, checked in with what might have been the first anti-affirmative-action dispatch in the game's history. Robinson, the paper said, "is reported to possess baseball abilities which, were he white, would make him eligible for a trial with, let us say, the Brooklyn Dodgers Class C farm team . . . if he were six years younger." Blacks, on the other hand, feared that Robinson was being set up to fail and that his failure would be cited as proof that blacks were not good enough to play in the major leagues.

To make his plan work, Rickey developed and Robinson executed a strategy whose principal components—nonviolent resistance, broad publicity and economic pressure—were identical to those that would be employed by the Rev. Dr. Martin Luther King, Jr. and his allies a decade later. Nonresistance did not come easily to Robinson. Just two years earlier, as a second lieutenant at Fort Hood, Texas, he had risked court-martial rather than obey a driver's directive to move to the rear of a supposedly desegregated bus.

But Robinson understood the historic role for which he

had been chosen and throughout his rookie season he was nonresistance made flesh. He ignored hecklers, downplayed death threats, avoided confrontations when spiked or beaned and swallowed his rage when opponents "aimed" their bats and mimicked the sound of machine gun fire. When the Dodger second baseman finally exploded in a September argument with Joe Garagiola of the Cardinals, many observers took it as an important and encouraging milestone. The only black man in the game had won the right to beef.

By the end of a brilliant season in which he hit nearly .300 and ran the bases with unprecedented panache, Robinson had persuaded even *The Sporting News* that he belonged. The publication named him its Rookie of the Year. In a popularity poll held that winter, Robinson finished second behind Bing Crosby. The popular recounting of Robinson's story generally ends on this positive note. But—as Jules Tygiel writes in his wonderful social history *Baseball's Great Experiment: Jackie Robinson and His Legacy*—the desegregation of baseball illustrates not only the successes, but the limitations of Rickey's strategy.

Perhaps the greatest of these successes were the realizations that black athletes and black consumers could exert tremendous economic influence on white businesses. Robinson was the hottest attraction in baseball. Many Southern towns, realizing that the Dodgers could take their financially lucrative exhibition games elsewhere, dropped their bans on interracial competition.

Had the game's owners been of a mind, Robinson would later argue, they could have demanded the integration of all public facilities in spring-training towns. But they were not of such a mind. Even Rickey ducked this confrontation, building the Dodgertown campus in Vero Beach, as a refuge from segregation.

If baseball executives were reluctant to exercise the power of their purse, black fans were not. Beginning in the early 1950s they effectively boycotted teams in the Southern Association, Texas League and Cotton States League to protest discriminatory league policies or the unjust treatment of black players. "The acceptance of blacks in interracial competition," Tygiel writes, "dented Jim Crow's armor and, in many instances, caused people, particularly business leaders to reevaluate the efficacy and wisdom of southern racial policies."

But not everyone in baseball was vulnerable to such economic pressure. By 1953, only six clubs had blacks on their rosters. The Boston Red Sox were not desegregated until 1959. By that time some sportswriters were wondering whether certain teams might have too *many* blacks.

When Robinson criticized the baseball establishment for its persistent racism, his popularity plunged. "You owe a great deal to the game," *The Sporting News* instructed him. "Put down your hammer Jackie and pick up a horn." Repay baseball, he was told, with "glad tidings, not bitterness."

Years later, Robinson wrote in his autobiography, "I learned that as long as I appeared to ignore insult and injury, I was a martyred hero to a lot of people who had sympathy for the underdog. But the minute I began to sound off I became a swell-headed, wise guy, an 'uppity nigger.' "

After his retirement in 1957, Robinson came to inhabit an ideological no-man's-land. Opponents on one side thought him an ungrateful troublemaker for his continued criticism of the game. Opponents on the other regarded him as an Uncle Tom for his pro-business views and his friendship with New York's Republican governor, Nelson Rockefeller. He had fought to win blacks a place in baseball's power structure, but by the late '60s, for many black athletes, to be on the inside was to be the enemy.

Muhammad Ali was one of those athletes. He and the young athletes who took him as their model represented a new, more radical stage in the evolution of black athletic consciousness. By the time Ali won the heavyweight title in 1964, many blacks felt that American society was irredeemably racist and that their only moral alternative was full-fledged opposition. Ali, the born provocateur, willing to suffer rather than seek accommodation, became a hero to these people. His eventual triumphs in court, as well as in the ring, broadened his legend. By the mid-1970s, when he recaptured his heavyweight crown, white Americans not only acknowledged his right to dissent, but many admired him for having exercised it.

The young Cassius Clay began his rebellion on February 26, 1964, the day after he stopped Sonny Liston after six rounds to win the heavyweight championship. At a well-attended press conference he announced that he had become a member of the Nation of Islam. From then on, he said, his name was Muhammad Ali. "I don't have to be who you want me to be," he told one antagonistic reporter. "I'm free to be who I want."

The announcement created an immediate furor. Much of this outrage was provoked by the radical tenets of Ali's new faith. Black Muslims, as they were branded by the white media, argued that the nation owed blacks land reparations, the release of prisoners and exemption from taxation and military service. Further, their appeals were often cast in vitriolic racial terms in which whites were the enemy, at best, and disciples of the devil at worst.

What many blacks found attractive about the Nation of Islam was its advocacy of separatism. Muslims, for the most part, rejected the nonviolent integrationist program of Dr. Martin Luther King and his allies. They argued instead that only through stringent self-discipline and rejection of "evil" white ways could blacks develop the resources to better their lot.

Ali's new faith made him profoundly unpopular with white Americans, but this animosity did not lead to persecution until 1966, after the selective service mysteriously revoked the champion's draft deferment. (He had been classified as 1-Y after scoring in double digits on an IQ test at age 18, possibly because he was a slow reader.)

Ali applied for a ministerial deferment, but was rejected. He applied for exemption as a conscientious objector, saying his Muslim beliefs made it impossible for him to go to war. He was rejected once again. "I have no quarrel with the Vietcong," Ali said. "They never called me nigger."

Reaction to this statement was swift and strident. Sen. Kenneth Keating (R-N.Y.) called for the champion to be stripped of his title. Rep. L. Mendel Rivers (D-S.C.), chairman of the House Armed Services Committee, threatened to investigate Ali's draft board if the fighter were not inducted. In Kentucky, Ali's home state, the legislature unanimously passed a resolution calling for his induction.

On April 18, 1967, the champion officially refused induction into the U.S. Army. Within 24 hours he was stripped of his title. Two months later an all-white jury in Houston convicted him of violating the selective service laws. The average sentence for such a violation was 18 months but, despite his prosecutor's request for leniency, Ali was sentenced to five years in prison.

In retrospect, it is clear that the conviction made Ali's legend. Suddenly he was a hero to people who cared nothing about boxing. In the peace movement, the counterculture and urban ghettos, he became a symbol of resistance to unjust authority. Free pending appeal, he traveled widely and soon built an international constituency. As the war continued to go sour, public antipathy toward Ali diminished, and he began a triumphant comeback.

On June 20, 1970, the U.S. Supreme Court reversed his conviction, 8–0. Four months later he made a successful return to the ring. Ali recaptured the heavyweight title four years later in one of the most brilliantly plotted strategies in boxing history, knocking out the heavily favored George Foreman in the eighth round after using his now-famous rope-a-dope tactics.

Suddenly the 32-year-old champion found himself invited to visit Gerald Ford in the White House. That same year he was named *Sports Illustrated*'s Sportsman of the Year. In 1976 he campaigned for Jimmy Carter who, as president, used him as a goodwill ambassador to Africa.

In some ways, Ali had won the last major symbolic battle in the black athlete's long campaign for public acceptance. He had not acted the part of a supplicant, had not shaped a persona he hoped would appeal to white prejudices. Where Johnson had futilely provoked the white establishment, Ali had triumphed over it.

Racism, of course, did not disappear from American sports. Henry Aaron still got "Dear Nigger" letters as he closed in on Babe Ruth's home run record in the mid-'70s. But black athletes like Julius Erving and tennis's Arthur Ashe moved with increasing comfort in the American mainstream, admired as much for their intelligence and sensitivity as for their on-court accomplishments.

Jordan followed the trail these men cleared, but his public acceptance is now well beyond that of any black athlete in history. With his increasing stature, however, comes a tremendous influence that Michael is just beginning to understand. That influence is greatest on young people, who view Jordan as a cross between an Eagle scout and a cartoon superhero. He, like several generations of black athletes before him, is expected to be their material benefactor and moral example, especially for those trapped in the nation's ghettos.

The presumption that regardless of their own backgrounds black athletes owe something to the inner city is a long-standing one, a remnant from the days when sports celebrities were among the only visible and affluent blacks in the country. "Try being a black athlete traded to a new team," Wilt Chamberlain wrote in his book *Goliath.* "The first thing everyone wants to know is whether you plan to help the black underprivileged kids in that city. . . . What do you want to bet that no white player gets asked if he plans to work with the underprivileged white kids?"

Not all athletes are comfortable with the burden of influence. "You can't thrust everybody into being a role model just because they can shoot a basketball or throw a football,'' Isiah Thomas says. "Being a role model is something that has to be earned, not something that can be given."

Perhaps, but success in basketball has a unique and powerful resonance in American ghettos. "In pockets of poverty today kids don't see black men with suits or with several college degrees," says civil rights activist and former assistant attorney general Roger Wilkins. "They seem as far away as the fantasies of 'Dallas' or 'Dynasty.' But they know about playing basketball. They see people all around them doing that very well. And there are stories and legends in their neighborhood about people who have gone on to play in college or in the pros. That's a ladder that is real to them. And that gives the basketball player influence that other professions don't have."

On the other hand, it is, as Randall Kennedy, editor of *Reconstruction,* a journal of black politics and culture, puts it, "the height of sentimentality" to believe that professional ballplayers can solve problems that have baffled politicians, scholars and community leaders. "I think it is a cheap way of thinking that society can be moved and changed in a good way," says Kennedy, a professor at Harvard Law School. "The social forces that bring kids to bad ends aren't going to be affected by an athlete doing one thing or another."

In the largest sense, that is indisputable. The lives of most young men and women growing up in Chicago housing projects have not materially improved since Michael Jordan came to ply his trade on the west side of town. But because he cannot cure the ills of urban America does not mean he cannot influence the behavior of the children who live there. Few other figures command their attention so completely.

"Jordan is always the talk of the day the next day back after a game," says Tremaine Pullins, a junior at St. Joseph's High School in Maywood, Illinois. "People even try to pattern his walk. One boy, James Jenkins at Proviso East [in Chicago], he has the walk down pat."

"He's emulated by every kid in the community," says Al Embry, who teaches at Cregier High School, several blocks from Chicago Stadium. "They wear Jordan clothes. They wear number 23. They've got his picture everywhere. He could marry any girl in any high school. I know girls whose kids are put into Jordan toddler clothes as soon as they are born."

But using this influence for other than commercial purposes is tricky. In 1979, several days before he was inducted into the Baseball Hall of Fame, Willie Mays returned to the site of his earliest professional glories, the Polo Grounds in upper Manhattan. A huge high-rise housing project squatted where the old stadium once stood. Each of the buildings was posted with a sign that said, "No Ball Playing." On a lot in the midst of the project Mays gave a speech aimed at the neighborhood's young people. Practice hard, he said, never give up, and when you grow up you can be just like me. There were more children living in that project than there were jobs in all of professional sports.

Athletes no longer make those kinds of speeches. "Fifteen years ago it was no problem to aspire to be a star athlete," says Gerald Early, a professor of English at Washington University, who has written extensively about boxing. "But now there is a feeling that blacks are purposefully being shunted that way."

It is a feeling perhaps most eloquently expressed by sports commentator Robert Lipsyte. "By publicizing the material success of a few hundred athletes, thousands, perhaps millions of bright young blacks have been swept toward sports when they should have been guided towards careers in medicine or engineering or business," he wrote in the winter 1982 issue of *National Forum: the Phi Kappa Phi Journal*. "For every black athlete who escaped the ghetto behind his jump shot, a thousand of his little brothers were neutralized, kept busy shooting baskets, until it was too late for them to qualify beyond marginal work."

Many scholars and community activists agree that athletics are often overemphasized and academics neglected in inner-city neighborhoods, but they are not convinced that steering children away from an activity that they love, or neglecting the few role models that the media offers them, are steps toward a solution. "If a kid comes up to you and says he wants to be Van Cliburn nobody would take issue with that, even though it's just as long a shot," Gerald Early says. "The question is should we really want to discourage any kid from pursuing excellence in that way."

Today sports stars like Jordan are asked to encourage young people to seek success in fields other than the one in which they found it themselves. "When I talk to kids I tell them there is nothing wrong with wanting to be a professional athlete," says Darrell Walker of the Detroit Pistons. "Then I tell them the odds: about 25,000 to 1 in basketball. So it is okay to want to be a professional basketball player. I don't try to shatter their goals. What if someone had come along and shattered my goals? But I tell them you better have something else in line."

The question is whether young people heed this advice, or whether the athlete's wealth and fame convince them that their only real option is a career in sports. When kids see Michael Jordan, what is it that impresses them, his character or his commercials?

"On my friends you see Nike stuff," says William Gates, who lives in Carbrini Green, the most notorious of Chicago's many notorious housing projects. "Air Jordans. I've even seen players stick out their tongues. What I see is his work ethic. How he puts his mind into the game. If he messes up he keeps going."

Jordan is a strong influence on the 18-year-old Gates, who graduated in 1991 from St. Joseph's High School in Maywood, the alma mater of Isiah Thomas. His friends used to call him "Little J" in his hero's honor. "Basketball is really my ticket out of my neighborhood," William says. "I knew I had to use that to get my college scholarship. I thought I had to base myself on somebody, and it had to be

Michael. He has everything going for him, and he is in a day and age where we can relate to him. He's 'today.' He is with us.''

For William, basketball has kept its promise. In his senior year he won a full scholarship to Marquette University. But other young players in his neighborhood were disappointed. ''There were guys who would say, 'Basketball is my life and if I don't make it with this, I'm not going to make it,' '' William says. ''They realized what they had to do, but they didn't follow through on it. They didn't get good grades, or they didn't work on their whole game.''

Or they just weren't good enough. Jordan's example has obvious power for those with a prayer of following his path. But what of those who are not in such an enviable position? Do they find the right lessons in Michael's example?

Freeman Hrabowski, executive vice president of the University of Maryland Baltimore County, says no. ''The question is, what is he being put forward for?'' he says. ''It is fame. It is the fact that he is very good on the court. It is the clothes he wears. The kids know he is getting plenty of money. He's got his degree, but is that something those young black boys focus on? No.''

Hrabowski runs UMBC's prestigious Meyerhoff program, which awards full scholarships to young black men committed to obtaining at least a master's degree in mathematics, the sciences or related fields. He spends a good deal of his time recruiting and encouraging potential candidates. ''When I ask them what they want to be, invariably you hear many talk about sports, particularly in elementary and middle schools,'' he says. ''Less so in high school, because by that point some of them haven't made the high school team. But those who are on those high school teams will still say it, and that's just so unrealistic for 99 percent of them.

''I also ask them who they look up to and I always hear either sports figures or entertainers,'' he says. ''That is who they revere.'' Hrabowski is out to change that. ''Imagine a generation of young boys whose only role models are

Michael Jordan, Michael Jackson and Michael Tyson," he says. "Why should we expect of young black boys when they become men to think about things other than fun things?"

Hrabowski understands the pressure on many young black males to succeed in sports. When the Birmingham, Alabama native was taking his master's degree at the University of Illinois in the early 1960s, people kept asking him whether he played for the football team. "The bright black male is caught between two stereotypes," he says. "Some see him as a jobless, basketball-playing dropout . . . while others may see his success as trying to act white."

The students in the Meyerhoff program illustrate this predicament quite clearly. Some feel they surrendered a part of themselves by not accepting athletic scholarships. Others are torn between wishing they had never been tempted by the dream of a career in professional sports and thinking that it was this dream that fed their self-assurance, won them friends and got them this far.

"A lot of emphasis is placed on sports when you come from a poor family," says junior Andrew Talley, a star athlete from Anne Arundel County, Maryland. "You know you don't have the money to go to college and you know you don't have the grades to get a scholarship to college. Honestly, realistically speaking, to get money you have drugs and you have sports. Now your mother, *my* mother, is going to tell you don't do drugs. So you say you are going to be the next Michael Jordan, the next Herschel Walker, the next Mike Tyson.

"I always dreamed of being a big, bad football player. If I read books they were sports books. If I watched TV it was a sports program. If I picked up a newspaper I read the sports section. I kind of regret that now because I didn't have a focus on anything outside of sports. It's good to have dreams, but I had tunnel vision."

His vision, however, was no more narrow than that of his community. "Pretty much you were put on a pedestal,"

Talley says. "You got away with murder. I was good at that. You get the big name. You get girls."

Ironically, it was his athletic success that allowed him to flex his intellectual muscles without fear of being ridiculed by his peers. "Basically my first year here I heard that if you were a Meyerhoff you must be a nerd," says Talley, who won a football scholarship to Morgan State that his mother wouldn't let him accept because of his arthritic knees. "But because I played sports and was more outgoing than most people I was able to mingle in groups. I always told people you should get to know [the Meyerhoff scholars]. You would find out they weren't a bunch of nerds. Give them a chance and you find out you would like to be around them."

But now the time has come for him to let sports go, and Talley says that won't be easy. "Sports meant so much to me and it still does now," he says. "I still think I'm as good as the guys on television. It's hard to deal with sometimes."

He, like many of his peers in the program, is searching for a way to keep competitive sports a part of his life. "I'm planning to be an orthopedic surgeon," he says. "Or an athletic trainer. I want to be the guy for the Detroit Pistons who runs up and down the sidelines and acts as crazy as Chuck Daly does. I want to be involved somehow, still have that contact."

His friend Artie Williams, Jr., a fellow Meyerhoff scholar who plays for the UMBC basketball team, wants to be an orthopedic surgeon with a specialty in sports medicine. Williams's father taught former University of Maryland star Len Bias in middle school and coached against him in summer leagues, so Artie Jr. too knows the corrosive effect that sporting success can have on a young man's character. He still keeps a poster of Bias, whom he knew as a dedicated athlete and a devoutly religious young man, hanging in his dorm room.

Williams says he has not resolved his feelings about his hero's death from a cocaine overdose in 1986, but he has drawn a few lessons from the tragedy. "Nothing is promised to you," he says. "Basketball will not always be there." Still, it is hard for him to imagine his life, or his relationship with his father, a former collegiate player, outside the context of sports.

Sitting with Talley one day in an office on the UMBC campus, Williams spoke of his uncertainty about how he will present athletics to his own children. "I'd like them to play sports, but I won't force them though," he said.

"I will," Talley put in.

"I'll buy them the balls and the equipment, but I won't make them use it," Williams responded.

"I will put it on their dinner plate," Talley said.

Neither of these young men believe they are going to grow up to be Michael Jordan. Both are keenly aware of how athletics have simultaneously enriched and impoverished their lives and those of their friends. Yet they admire Jordan, and value his example.

"I think he is great," Talley said. "Doesn't drink, do drugs. He's a great family man. He graduated from college. And right after he graduated he did this commercial about saying no to drugs. I'll never forget it. He had on a brown suit and a red tie."

"I remember that," Artie said. "It was the ugliest suit." Soon they were reciting little snatches of the appeal Jordan made almost eight years ago, and doing so with such ease it seems sure that they once had it memorized.

Perhaps not everyone who reveres Jordan is as discerning in his or her reverence as Talley and Williams, but that does not mean that Michael's fame blinds young people to his moral example. This is true, in part, because a small industry has sprung up to interpret Jordan for children. In books, videos and juvenile magazines, his virtues are exaggerated to the point of parody.

"Michael is sensitive, thoughtful, and unfazed by success," reads one children's book. "He is charming, modest, open and sincere. He always wears a smile. He is polite. . . . He encourages youngsters to read." It may be difficult to *believe* such a passage, but its message is certainly not difficult to understand.

And if conversations with children in several Chicago area schools are any indication, the message does transmit— even to older kids, who are skeptical of the heroes foisted on them by adult authority figures.

"At first I just saw a basketball player, but now I hear him speak and he's well-rounded and intelligent," says Bakiri Baker, a studious teenager from the west side of Chicago.

"Everybody wants to be like Michael Jordan," says Cristobal Guttierrez, a 16-year-old from Cicero, Illinois. "My white friends, my black friends, my Mexican friends. But you have to pay attention to what people say about him. It's not just being on television that's important. He does charity work. He loves his parents. He always does real good deeds."

Jordan has been able to sustain this image because it corresponds fairly closely to the reality of his life. On the eve of the 1988–89 season, the public Michael Jordan seemed to be living a prolonged if responsible adolescence, a life that suggested the possibility of eternal youth and easily managed fame. But in private Jordan, then 25, was confronted by vexing personal and professional developments that threatened his image and complicated his quest for an NBA title. It would be his most troubled season to date, but also, in some ways, his most impressive.

12

The 1988–89 season opened with Jordan in a familiar humor; he was angry at Jerry Krause. During the off-season, the general manager had traded Charles Oakley to the New York Knicks for veteran center Bill Cartwright and an exchange of first-round draft picks that produced Will Perdue, a stolid 7-footer out of Vanderbilt. Michael knew that the Bulls needed a center, but he didn't see why Krause had sacrificed Oakley.

The Oak Tree had grabbed more rebounds then anyone in the league over the previous two seasons. He was Jordan's protector. More than that, he was Michael's only close friend on the team. Oakley was also one of Krause's personal favorites, an overlooked talent from a small Southern college, the type of player whom he had specialized in scouting decades earlier.

But the Bulls were desperate for a center, Oakley was on the outs with head coach Doug Collins, and second-year player Horace Grant stood ready to take his place. So off Oakley went.

Jordan learned of the deal while he and Oakley were in Atlantic City attending the Mike Tyson-Michael Spinks heavy weight title fight. "Michael was real sad," Oakley said. "He said, 'No more picks. No more outlets.' He was real upset. He didn't like the trade, but it's not his team."

"We're giving up the best rebounder in the league," Jordan said. "How are we going to replace that? I don't understand the reasoning, but I guess there is some reasoning behind it." After all, he pointed out sarcastically, Jerry Krause was the Executive of the Year.

In many ways, Jordan's adult life began in the wake of the Oakley trade. The third-year player who had suggested that "Maybe I'll never grow up" was evolving into a tougher, less ebullient but more determined competitor, ready to devote himself to defeating the Pistons and winning a championship. The strong-willed star of a still-developing franchise, he found himself in regular conflict with Krause, with Collins and, occasionally, with his teammates.

When the Bulls acquired Bill Cartwright they committed themselves to installing a conventional half-court offense to supplement the free-flowing open-court game favored by Jordan, Pippen and Grant. Michael didn't like the decision, and he didn't relate well to the new center, a serious, intelligent and somewhat introverted man who was five years Jordan's senior. Cartwright was a potentially solid scorer and a cagey, if slow-footed, defender. He was also a dangerously clumsy man with a penchant for unintentionally elbowing and stomping opponents and teammates alike.

Michael doubted the new man's rebounding ability and said in training camp that he intended to pick up some of the slack created by Oakley's departure. The Bulls' chemistry could hardly have been worse, a fact that was evident in the first quarter of their season.

In some games the low-post offense worked well and Cartwright hit double figures in scoring and rebounding. Other nights it floundered badly and he seldom got good shots. Some evenings Jordan appeared willing to give the new scheme a chance. Other nights he seized control of the game and refused to relinquish it. Michael scored over 40 points four times in Chicago's first 20 games, but the Bulls were 1–3 in those contests.

Their record at the quarter pole was a mediocre 10–10, and Jordan, who was playing more than 40 minutes each game, took the unusual step of meeting with Krause to implore the general manager for some offensive help. Krause told him that the Bulls had no room to maneuver under the salary cap. Michael's own $3.125 million salary had a lot to do with that, he said. Jordan thought he heard in this explanation a hint that the team's weakness was partly his fault, and his already-chilly relationship with the man whom he nicknamed "Crumbs"—because of Krause's fondness for doughnuts—got a little icier.

While the team struggled, Michael's own game continued to improve. After a summer's worth of practice, the most-feared driver in the league was now an accurate long-range gunner as well. Jordan was hitting 35 percent of his three-point attempts, compared to just 18 percent the previous season. The newfound range helped him save a little strength. "I'm not dunking as much this season," he said. "It takes a lot of energy to do all that dunking, so I'm dunking now mostly on fast breaks."

Conserving energy had become crucial because Collins and the other Bulls seemed bent on exhausting him. In a December 27 loss to Cleveland, Michael scored 19 points in the fourth quarter and led Chicago from a 14-point deficit to a three-point lead in the space of about six minutes. But then he simply wore out. Jordan committed an offensive foul and gave up a steal as Cleveland stormed back to win 107–96.

"I'm not giving up on this team yet," said Jordan, who finished with 43 points and 12 rebounds. "I may get disappointed and frustrated sometimes, and other people have got to make some contributions, but I know there is some life out there."

That life began to manifest itself more immediately than he could have hoped. After their loss to Cleveland, the Bulls went on a surprising tear, winning nine of their next 11 games and 19 of their next 27. In retrospect, this streak is when the new Chicago Bulls announced themselves to the NBA. Scottie Pippen and Horace Grant continued to improve. Cartwright had three straight 20-point games in mid-January, and hot-shooting John Paxson emerged to challenge Sam Vincent for the starting point guard position.

On January 17, in a 103–96 victory over Indiana, Paxson led the team in scoring with 24 points while Jordan had 13 assists. "Maybe in the past he has not felt confidence in us," Paxson said. "But this [six-game] winning streak happened because Michael is showing that confidence in the rest of us."

Michael's confidence in his teammates and his organization were won and lost nightly that season. No one, least of all Jordan, would have imagined that he was already part of what, in two seasons, would become the best team in basketball. There were still difficult questions to be answered about what type of offense the team would run and who would direct its execution on the floor. Cartwright was slow in adjusting to his teammates and they were no quicker in adjusting to him. Pippen and Grant were not nearly as accomplished or as confident that season as they are today. Yet by the middle of the 1988–89 season the Bulls had all the pieces in place. The puzzle just had not been solved yet.

Jordan was also faced with a delightful new puzzle in his personal life. Jeffrey Michael Jordan was born on November 18, just a few minutes after the Bulls had beaten the Hawks in overtime. The final period was an agonizing one for Michael, who desperately wanted to be in the delivery room when his son was born. With the game tied at the end of four quarters, Jordan thought his chances of seeing the birth had passed, but after leading the Bulls to victory, he made it to the hospital with ten minutes to spare.

Michael and Juanita were not yet married. They had set a

date for the previous summer, but then canceled it. Michael was interviewed for a *GQ* profile around the time the wedding was to have taken place, and writer David Breskin found him traveling with another woman. His son's birth out of wedlock could, conceivably, have tarnished Jordan's wholesome image, but somehow it never did.

That may have been because Jordan, while promoted as a role model, neither extolled his own virtues nor criticized the values of others. Hypocrisy was not an issue. Or it may have been because Jeffrey was the product of a long, if bumpy, relationship. Michael's joy in Jeffrey's birth and his obvious devotion to the boy may also have helped curb public criticism.

Still, the companies that promoted Jordan as an exemplar of traditional values were uneasy. Several of his business associates say these firms brought subtle pressure on Michael to tie the knot and dueling rumors sprang up to explain why he had not done so. One held that Jordan's mother was leery of his getting married; another that it was Juanita who was holding back, not wanting it to appear that the couple had hurried into marriage because of Jeffrey's birth; a third that Michael simply enjoyed the freedom of single life.

"It's hard for me to trust a woman's alleged affections because it is difficult for me to know whether she likes me for me or for what I have," Jordan had once said. "That's why it's difficult for me to rush into any relationship. I realize it is hard for many people meeting me to separate the successful player from the man."

But he had known Juanita for four years at this point and they had been talking about marriage for at least two. "It [marriage] was something he wanted to do," an acquaintance says. "He was urged, but he wanted to anyway."

"He found somebody he could be comfortable with, somebody he really loved and could spend the rest of his life with," Deloris Jordan adds. "You could see the change."

One of Michael's friends remembers sitting with him in a hotel room that season while the Bulls were on the road. As they watched a television movie Jordan began to explain his changing feelings about his relationship. "It was about moving from closeness to commitment," his friend says.

Jordan used the *C* word himself in discussing his marriage during a March, 1990 interview. "You have to be mature to the point of accepting it," he said. "I was at the point of liking to provide for others. I was ready for commitment. And if you are ready for it, it is easy to accept." But while Michael may have been moving toward acceptance, he and Juanita were not about to take the final step until the basketball season was over.

After their impressive and occasionally cohesive surge through January and February, the Bulls sputtered over their final 30 games, going just 15–15. The team was deeply divided by conflicts between Doug Collins and Jerry Krause, as well as by conflicts between the coach and several of his players. Jordan, for the most part, was on the periphery of these conflicts, yet as the season progressed, they slowly drew him in.

Collins was an excellent strategist, an engaging companion, but an increasingly driven man. The task of energizing a young and sometimes tentative club had clearly worn him down and the pressure of producing a winner weighed ever more heavily upon him. He began to lose his temper with referees, official scorers, the front office and players who could not help him win immediately.

The coach, who declined to be interviewed for this book, clashed with Krause over personnel moves and belittled the general manager in front of other NBA officials. His relationship with his own staff was little better. He once banned Tex Winter from practice, and warned second-year assistant Phil Jackson not to angle for his job. His relationship with several players was so poor, reported Sam Smith of the *Chicago Tribune*, that they had plotted to catch him in a compromising situation, hoping it would lead to his dismissal.

Jordan's unhappiness with Collins was not nearly so deep-seated. He simply felt that the coach expected too much from him. In late February and early March the Bulls seemed so intent on developing other offensive options that Michael was sometimes neglected for three quarters at a time, then expected to win the game in the fourth. Assistant coach John Bach referred to this as the Archangel offense. "It's where we give Jordan the ball and say, 'Michael, save us.'"

On March 9, Collins and Jordan sat down for a two-hour meeting in which each aired a stream of grievances. After that session Michael told reporters that he had agreed to become a more vocal locker room presence, and to serve as a buffer between the sometimes overaggressive coach and the rest of the team. What he didn't say was that he had agreed to play point guard for the rest of the year. But that became obvious quickly enough.

On March 13 against Indiana, Jordan scored 21 points, pulled down 14 rebounds and handed out 14 assists in only three quarters as the Bulls cruised to a 122–90 victory. "I'm not trying to steal anybody's position, but the way I played the last two games is the way I'll play the rest of the season," he said.

On March 24 in Portland, Jordan had a career-high 17 assists to go along with 33 points in a 128–113 Chicago victory. He had begun to keep a running count of his assists and rebounds during the game, having suddenly developed an appetite for triple doubles. "I'm enjoying the point, because it is a chance to show some leadership," he said.

Collins's gamble was getting good reviews from other coaches, too. "I'd have played him there long ago and gotten a two [shooting] guard because they are easier to get," said Dick Versace of the Pacers.

"There are a few of us coaches who have asked about it for years but were glad they didn't make the move," said Don Nelson of Golden State. "It's a tremendous advantage to have him with the ball all the time."

The Bulls flourished briefly with Jordan at the point, winning nine of 11 games after the move. By early April

Chicago's scoring was up six points a game. But before the team could get comfortable in its new offense, it was racked by injuries to Paxson, Pippen and guard Craig Hodges. Jordan compiled 10 triple-doubles in one 11-game span, but Chicago limped through the final month of the season losing eight of its last 10.

The team's postseason prospects looked particularly glum. The Bulls were 0–6 against their first-round opponents, the Cleveland Cavaliers. That record included a pair of double-digit losses in the last week of the season. Many prognosticators picked the Cavs to sweep the series. Jordan was well aware of this. He had personally polled several reporters on their predictions. "It energized me," he said. Michael picked Chicago in four.

The Bulls wore black sneakers for the first game in Cleveland. It was reserve forward Brad Sellers's idea for promoting team unity. Whether inspired by the new footwear or the Cavs' loss of injured point guard Mark Price, the Bulls played like world-beaters. They took a 24–14 first-period lead and held on to win 95–88. "Sweep my butt," said a gleeful Jordan to the courtside press corps as time wound down. Michael had 31 points and 11 assists.

Over the next four games, a series that had had all the markings of a rout became one of the best and most dramatic first-round matchups in recent playoff history. The teams split games two and three. With 48 seconds remaining in game four, Jordan stepped to the foul line with the score tied 97–97. Michael was an 85 percent free throw shooter but he made just one of his two shots.

The Bulls clung to their skinny lead, however, and with nine seconds remaining, Jordan was fouled once again. He sank his first shot to give Chicago a 99–97 lead. Then with a chance to clinch the series, he fired again.

And missed.

Cleveland rebounded and tied the game on a pair of equally crucial free throws by Brad Daugherty. The Cavs won it in overtime 108–105, sending the series back to the Richfield Coliseum for game five.

"I put my credibility on the line and I didn't come through," Jordan said. "I was crushed. I'm telling you, tears came to my eyes when I thought about those foul shots. You could pin the whole thing on me because I couldn't produce."

Howard White remembers sitting in Michael's home that night and worrying about the spacey way his friend gazed at the television set. "He was like a zombie," White says. "We went home and we were going to watch a movie. And the movie hadn't started. It was just that fuzz that comes on before it starts. And he's looking at it, staring and we had to say [clapping his hands rapidly], 'Hey! Hey! Hey!' And he said, 'Yeah, I'm all right.' He was so hurt that he could have missed those free throws."

Basketball is rich in second chances, though, and Jordan got his two nights later. The Bulls struggled from behind all night. With three seconds remaining, they had the ball out of bounds in their frontcourt, trailing 100–99.

Everyone knew who would receive Sellers's inbound pass, yet somehow Jordan shook two defenders, caught the ball and dribbled frantically to his left. With one second on the clock and Cleveland's Craig Ehlo close enough to kiss, Jordan leapt into the air just inside the top of the key. Ehlo leapt too, but he landed first. Michael double-pumped and for just an instant got a clear look at the basket. He launched his jumper while leaning slightly to the left.

"I never saw it go in," he said. "But I knew right away from the crowd reaction—silence—that it had been good. Then I did something maybe I shouldn't have. I really celebrated. . . ." As the buzzer sounded, Jordan went into a fist-pumping celebration. "I yelled, 'Take that!' " he said. "All game the fans had been on me. They had been telling me to practice my foul shots and they were saying they were going to get me a tee-time. I just wanted to shut them up."

One friend has said that Michael lives his life in "stages

of accomplishment.'' His career has progressed in what might be called stages of renown. He had been the most famous basketball player on the planet for five years, yet each new season had seemed to offer some opportunity for winning greater respect from an expanding audience. His performance against Cleveland created another such opportunity. It established the narrative for the 1989 postseason: Michael Jordan against the world. So far, Michael was winning.

The joyride continued for another three weeks as Chicago took an exciting six-game series from the Knicks to earn its first trip to the conference finals since 1975. ''I think when Michael first came into the league, everybody questioned whether he made people better,'' said New York Knicks coach Rick Pitino. ''But right now, if you had to say who the best player is, you'd say Michael Jordan. Not only is he great by himself, but he is raising the play of everybody.''

The question was whether he could raise it high enough for the Bulls to beat Detroit. The Pistons had lost the 1988 NBA title to the Lakers in a heartbreaking seven-game series. They had beaten the Bulls four times in five tries and felt that this was the year they would be champions. But Jordan had enough magic remaining to make them sweat.

Game one in Detroit had about it the feel of an inspirational boys' book. The underdog Bulls scored 14 straight first-quarter points and jumped to a 24-point second-quarter lead. But the Pistons stormed back and briefly claimed a one-point lead in the fourth.

Chicago refused to fold, though, reclaiming the lead and hanging on for a 94–88 victory. Jordan had 32 points and 11 rebounds. ''I'm surprised, and you are too,'' Doug Collins told the press.

The Bulls dropped game two, but did so in a way that prolonged the promise of this enchanted postseason. Playing with the flu, Jordan scored 27 points, and teamed with Dave Corzine to stake Chicago to a slender lead with just under seven minutes to play. But the Pistons countered with an 11–1 run to even the series with a 100–91 victory.

In game three the Bulls trailed 90–80 with four minutes remaining, but Jordan led them on a surge that knotted the score at 97 apiece. With three seconds remaining he provided another minor miracle, scoring the last of his 46 points on a jumper that gave Chicago a 99–97 victory. The Bulls were just one home-court win away from taking command of the series.

"This was a stolen basketball game," Michael said. "Could be that good overcomes evil."

But the Bulls' next victory never came. Detroit took game four 86–80, as Jordan shot just 2 of 9 in the first quarter and had only two field goals in the last 41 minutes. "I can't believe that," Joe Dumars said when someone read him the stats. "That's not true, is it? Is it true? Damn. That's amazing."

Jordan's predicament deepened in game five. On the message board in the Pistons' dressing room, one of their coaches had scrawled "Remember the Jordan Rules." The Pistons did so with a vengeance. Michael took a paltry eight shots and scored 18 points in Detroit's 94–85 victory. His teammates, meanwhile, were collapsing around him. Horace Grant contributed four points and had a single rebound. Scottie Pippen got nine rebounds, but put up just seven points. The Bulls were 1–17 against the Pistons when Jordan scored 29 or fewer points.

Michael did a bit better than that in game six, but it wasn't enough. Detroit eliminated the Bulls with a 103–94 victory. Jordan scored 32 points and had 13 assists, but was virtually unaided in his forays among the Pistons' roughhousing defenders. Pippen went out in the first minute of play with a concussion from Bill Laimbeer's elbow. Bill Cartwright made only one of his eight shots.

Chicago still managed to cut a 10-point Pistons lead to just two with under nine minutes remaining, but Isiah Thomas buried the Bulls with 17 fourth-quarter points. The

Pistons' seven-point margin of victory was precisely the number of free throws missed by a dog-tired Jordan.

Jesse Jackson and Spike Lee visited the Bulls dressing room to console Michael. Jordan was particularly frustrated by his teammates' unwillingness to stand up to the Pistons' physical play. He felt that he had taken this team as far as he could take it and that barring some new developments, it might never get any further.

Jordan was uneasy too, though, about what those developments might be. He had decided that the point guard position was too restrictive for him, yet he didn't look forward to another erratic season of watching another floor leader attempting to establish a half-court offense.

Michael's own statistics had not really suffered as a result of his shifting responsibilities or the many minutes he had played. He led the league in scoring for the third straight season, averaging 32.5 points per game. His shooting percentage was up slightly. He got one and a half extra rebounds and assists per contest. While his blocks were down dramatically, he was still among the league leaders in steals. Jordan was named to the first team All-NBA, as well as the first team All-Defense. *The Sporting News* named him its Player of the Year. But for the second time in three seasons Earvin Johnson, whose Lakers lost their title to Detroit, was the league's MVP.

The off-season seemed to hold both promise and uncertainty. The Bulls had three first-round draft picks, yet the team's management was split by professional differences and personality conflicts. On July 7, Jerry Reinsdorf fired Doug Collins. He reportedly did not care for the way the sometimes hyperkinetic coach handled young players, and didn't appreciate Collins's denigration of Krause.

Rumors spread quickly that Jordan had influenced the decision, but Michael vehemently denied it. "It was not Doug Collins and Michael Jordan's relationship, because he and I were getting closer as we spent more time together," he said. "When people say Michael Jordan had something to do with Doug Collins getting fired, that doesn't have any validity to it. I just saw him last evening and I approached him as 'Coach.' ''

Collins also doubted the rumors. "I don't believe this talk about him being involved," he said. But some of Jordan's teammates fed such speculation. "Michael plays a big part in everything that goes on with the Bulls," said Horace Grant. "Who knows?"

Reinsdorf says today that he felt Collins overused Jordan, but that that was not the principal reason for the coach's dismissal. An admirer of the '69 New York Knicks, the owner named Phil Jackson his new head coach.

After the initial round of news stories about Collins's firing, Jordan kept a low profile during the off-season. The Bulls' future may have been unsettled, but the shape of Michael's was becoming increasingly clear. In the summer of 1989 Jordan began to "establish his privacy," as Fred Whitfield puts it, and to shape the life that he leads today.

He took the biggest step in that direction on September 2 at the unusual hour of 3:30 A.M., when he and Juanita were married at The Little Wedding Chapel in Las Vegas. The bride and groom both wore jeans. They were attended by Adolph Shiver, Fred Kearns and two of Juanita's friends. Jordan presented his bride with a five-carat diamond worth about $25,000 and she gave him a three-carat diamond worth about $15,000. A Chicago sports columnist reported that the couple had signed a prenuptial agreement, but Jordan wouldn't comment on that. Rather than take a honeymoon, the two flew to the La Costa Hotel and Spa in San Diego, where Michael was sponsoring a golf tournament for the United Negro College Fund.

That Michael and Juanita had made their decision some time before became clear on their return to Chicago, when Michael held a news conference to announce two major changes that would allow him to spend more time with his family. He was cutting back on his much-appreciated availability to the media because it ate up so much of his time.

Secondly, he was organizing his disparate philanthropic activities under a new umbrella—the Michael Jordan Foundation, which would raise money for children's and educational charities.

The Foundation was a creation of necessity as well as compassion. Every week, Jordan receives between 20 and 30 letters from dying children whose last wish is to meet him. He is able to oblige about 100 of those each season. Some he visits in the hospital or meets at his hotel on the road. Usually though, he arranges, through the Bulls, to have the child meet him before a game and sometimes sit on the team's bench. Every child so honored receives the pair of Air Jordans Michael wore in that night's game. A young leukemia patient who died in 1990 was buried in his.

Of all the other charity work that Jordan does, none illustrates so vividly the impossibility of meeting even a fraction of those who make profoundly moving pleas for his time. Since his rookie season, Michael has received an endless stream of solicitations. "He is asked to advocate an untenable number of causes," David Falk says. "And I told him like I tell all our clients, 'Pick two or three things that you really like to do and do those well, as opposed to becoming a spokesperson for a hundred things, being on stationery and letterheads and that kind of thing.'

Early in his career, Jordan supported the United Negro College Fund and the Special Olympics, an organization he had worked with since his days at North Carolina. He subsequently began to support Ronald McDonald Children's Charities through his work as a corporate spokesman, and the Starlight Foundation, which grants "wishes" for children who are dying or seriously ill.

He particularly enjoys meeting with children in small groups, rather than at large public events. Twice during the 1989–90 season Michael met with David Rothenberg, the California teen who was burned over 90 percent of his body after his father set him on fire. David sat with Jordan on the Bulls' bench and poked his head into all the team's huddles.

What impressed his family most about the meeting, however, was the way that Jordan, upon introduction, reached without hesitation to shake the boy's fingerless hand.

Poignant as encounters such as these are, they tap only a fraction of Michael's potential for helping others. Deloris Jordan recognized that her son's mushrooming wealth, vast popularity and extensive network of corporate contacts made him the perfect junior philanthropist. She persuaded Michael to establish the Foundation, and quickly became its driving force.

Mrs. Jordan met personally with a number of corporate chief executives to solicit their involvement in the new venture. The response was strong. Jordan's ''Founders Council'' includes American Airlines, Ameritech, Coca-Cola, Federal Express, General Mills, McDonald's, Minolta and Nike.

Perhaps more surprising was the response from the entertainment community. Many performers were eager to have their name associated with Michael's and several volunteered their services for the Foundation's first gala, in September of 1990. ''I can tell you that in the nonprofit world you don't get people calling and asking if they can do something for you,'' says Ann M. Armstrong, the Foundation's executive vice president. ''But that's what we have had.'' Kenny Rogers headlined the first gala, which raised $200,000.

The fledgling organization funded two college scholarships at Jordan's high school alma mater and distributed roughly $250,000 in its first year. Armstrong hopes to distribute twice as much in 1991 to recipients that include Edward T. Hartigan Elementary School on Chicago's south side. Jordan and his family have ''adopted'' the school, promising to monitor report cards and reward the progress of children on two grade levels, particularly those who improve failing grades. A Jordan-autographed basketball moves each week into the homeroom with the best attendance.

Michael's involvement with Hartigan is cagey as well as kind, because Jordan has been criticized, sometimes quite harshly, for his failure to speak out on issues of racial and economic justice, either in Chicago or nationwide. Several black leaders charge that he is far too cozy with the economic establishment, and that his quiescence assures whites that American society is more than fair to the "right kind" of black men.

By the eve of the 1989–90 season, these leaders, along with other critics, were evaluating Jordan's economic success and his political reticence in a new and often unflattering light. And Michael found himself drawn, much against his will, into the types of racially based controversies he had previously managed to avoid.

13

"Personally I wouldn't cross the street to shake his hand."

Robert Lucas is a neighborhood activist, president of Chicago's Kenwood-Oakland Community Organization, a man to have on your side when courting the city's black voters. He realizes that his is a minority opinion on Michael Jordan, but he thinks he has good reason to hold it. Lucas and other community activists feel that the city's most famous citizen has done little for the people who need it most. They believe Jordan has turned his back on the legacy of bygone black athletic heroes in favor of white acceptance and personal gain.

"People didn't idolize Joe Louis because he had a sharp jab and a hell of a right hand," Lucas says. "We idolized Joe Louis because at least we saw him beating up white folk who were our oppressors. Jackie Robinson, he dared to do what white folks didn't want him to. He could have been a .250 hitter and we would have idolized him. Muhammad Ali, we saw him as much as a fighter for blacks as he was in the ring.

"You can't put Jordan in with those people. Jordan is symbolic at best. Jordan can't carry Joe Louis's or Jackie Robinson's jockstrap."

During the 1989–90 season, as the Bulls labored toward another postseason clash with the Pistons, Michael was increasingly criticized for shunting what some perceived as his moral obligation to become a spokesman for black causes. In striving not to offend his white following, critics said, Michael had lost much of his meaning to his black one.

"We are a town of limited celebrity, and there is always one 'model Negro,'" says Aaron Freeman, a black Chicago-based actor and political satirist. First, he says, there was Ernie Banks, then Gale Sayers, then Walter Payton, now Jordan. "He's clean-cut, wholesome, utterly nonthreatening to white people. Even the people in Bridgeport [the Chicago neighborhood most openly antagonistic to blacks] wouldn't mind if he married their daughters."

But, Freeman adds: "He and the other 'model Negroes' achieve this *transcendental irrelevance*. When they are trying to get the mayor to do something, maybe on affordable housing, no one calls Michael Jordan to be part of the movement. There are no illusions about him. He's not going to fight for your rights or your job or anything.

"He's not a hero, but he plays one on TV."

The potential for heroism is there, some suggest, if only Jordan could be coaxed to use it. "There is a tinge of resentment that he won't get more political," Arthur Ashe says. "You hear it in ordinary conversation. He does things where you can get a pat on the back for community service but you can't get your hands dirty. You're not going to get your hands dirty with the United Negro College Fund. There are people around saying that Michael could do a little bit more."

Ashe is an admirer of Jordan's and believes in what he calls Michael's "moral right" not to be politically involved. He does not believe that politically committed athletes can save the world. Yet he is not alone in wondering whether Jordan is wasting an opportunity to help poor blacks by pleading their case to white America.

"Michael Jordan obviously could have a tremendous influence on anything he would choose to do," says Ted Shaw, former western regional counsel for the NAACP Legal Defense Fund. "While he may be the golden boy of the 1990s, how far could he parlay that if he began to speak out on political issues, the gap between the haves and the have-nots, apartheid or other systematic evils?"

It is a question that Jordan has been loath to have answered. "He's made it clear to me he is going to stay away from any and all political events," says Barbara Allen of ProServ.

"Most of these major corporations can't afford to have him be too controversial," adds Jordan's friend Fred Whitfield.

But Michael is becoming controversial, despite his best efforts to the contrary. In 1989–90, black leaders tried on three separate occasions to enlist Jordan as a voice for political change. In each instance—the so-called sneaker murders; the Nike boycott organized by Operation PUSH; and the Harvey Gantt-Jesse Helms Senate race—Michael remained all but silent.

Early in 1989, ghetto teens were assaulting and even killing one another for Air Jordans and other high-priced and prestigious sneakers. At roughly the same time drug dealers, enjoying a new prosperity since the onset of the crack epidemic, began using flashy sneakers as well as baseball caps and team jerseys as gang uniforms and recruiting incentives. School principals complained that children were so desperate for these $100-$150 status symbols that some were selling drugs or pilfering their parents' public assistance checks.

By early 1990 sports shoe manufacturers and endorsers like Jordan, Lee and Bo Jackson had come under withering criticism as the "sneaker murders" spread across the country. Phil Mushnick, a sports columnist for the *New York Post*, led the attack, arguing that Nike and other sports shoe companies were partly to blame for the violence because their advertising made poor children want something they couldn't have, and want it badly enough to kill for it. In his April 6, 1990 column "Shaddup, I'm Selling out . . . Shaddup," he wrote: "It's murder, gentlemen. No rhyme, nor reason, just murder. For sneakers. For jackets. Get it Spike? Murder."

Lee responded with an angry letter to *The National*, the now-defunct sports daily. "The Nike commercials Michael Jordan and I do have never gotten anyone killed," he contended. "The deal is this: Let's try to effectively deal with the conditions that make a kid put so much importance on a pair of sneakers, a jacket and gold."

Jordan was first informed about sneaker violence by *Sports Illustrated* reporter Rick Telander, whose May 14, 1990 cover story "Senseless" helped focus attention and sharpen debate on the issue. "I thought I'd be helping out others and everything would be positive," said a visibly shaken Jordan. He had just read a newspaper article about a Maryland teenager who was murdered for his Air Jordans. "I thought people would try to emulate the good things I do, they'd try to achieve, to do better. Nothing bad. I never thought because of my endorsement of a shoe or any product, that people would harm each other. . . . [W]hen it comes to kids actually killing each other, then you have to reevaluate things."

But in his own reevaluation Jordan had to recognize that he was closely bound to the giant sports shoe company. Michael's relationship with Nike had been solidified in 1988, when he signed a new long-term contract that reportedly paid him $2.5 million each year, plus royalties and other options.

Negotiations on the new pact had been surprisingly acrimonious, not least because Rob Strasser, the executive who helped bring Jordan to Nike, has formed his own sports marketing company and was urging Jordan to found a new sneaker and sportswear conglomerate. Michael ultimately decided to stay with Nike, but not before the company leaked a report, denied by Michael's camp, that Jordan and David Falk were looking for a $45 million, 10-year deal.

"It was a very difficult negotiation because we were asking for a commitment from them that was in a different stratosphere than anyone had ever asked for," Falk says now. "And again, there was no precedent. Nike certainly wanted to pay him a lot of money, but the question was, 'What was fair?' And neither side had much ammunition or information to base its claims on, so it got to be somewhat of a confrontational situation. But it ended up fine."

The enormously lucrative new contract made it difficult for Jordan to publicly criticize Nike, as did the fact that his parents and his brother Larry depended heavily on Nike to supply the family's "Flight" sportswear outlets in North Carolina. Initially Michael told Telander: "I'd rather eliminate the product than know drug dealers are providing the funds that pay me." But by the time that reply saw print, Jordan had already modified his answer.

"It's kind of ironic that the press builds people like me up to be a role model and then blames us for the unfortunate crimes kids are committing," he said. "Kids commit crimes to get NFL jackets, cars, jewelry and many other things. But nobody is criticizing people who promote those products."

Jordan had a point. The sneaker and sportswear murders seemed for some reason more sinister than murders committed over Chevy Blazers, one of the drug dealers' cars of choice, or gold jewelry. That is due, in part, to the fact that most Americans have an easier time understanding why someone would passionately covet an automobile or a gemstone than a pair of Air Jordans. But it stems too from the perception that selling high-priced sneakers to an impoverished inner-city clientele is a morally dubious activity.

The sneaker issue is a delicate one. How do we protect children from commercial manipulation without depriving them of the right to make economic choices? The issue is further complicated by the fact that most of the children at issue are poor and black.

Each side attempts to play the race card in its own way. The shoe companies portray themselves as champions of black self-expression, benevolent merchants selling inspiration and self-esteem, while just incidentally reaping enormous profits. The companies' critics ride an equally righteous horse, believing themselves the defenders of an unloved inner-city population helpless before the persuasive powers of television advertising.

Neither side presents the issue very clearly. Does the sneaker industry's barrage of advertising ($200 million in 1990) create demand for the product? Yes. Does the use of black athletes such as Jordan insure that these products will be popular in the inner city? Probably. And are the sneakers priced too high for those inner-city children to afford? Certainly. In the most basic way, sneaker makers must recognize that they contribute to a dangerously covetous climate in inner-city neighborhoods.

If that were all the industry's critics were charging, they would have a strong case and be on solid ground in recommending ways to alter the situation. But the remainder of their case is not only paternalistic in its attitude toward inner-city children, but insupportably conspiratorial as well.

Critics like Jesse Jackson contended that Nike and other leading sneaker manufacturers were indirectly encouraging the sale of drugs and fueling the murder rate to reap corporate profits. The charge, to which Jackson devoted one of his syndicated talk shows in 1990, is a dubious one. While it is clear that the sneaker industry profits disproportionately from the drug economy, this is primarily a function of the age of most drug dealers.

The only evidence Jackson presented to suggest otherwise was an interview with Wally Grigo, the New Haven shoe store owner who posted a sign in his window telling dealers he didn't want their business. Representatives from one sportswear company informed him that if the sign didn't come down, the company might not allow Grigo to sell its new line. Grigo's courage is admirable and his story is alarming. It illustrates how greedy some merchandisers can be, but it does not support the contention that there is a high-level, industry-wide conspiracy to turn profits through the drug trade.

Jackson and Mushnick also contended that sneaker makers have targeted inner-city children as their primary market. It is an assertion that has merit, but within very limited bounds. A few small sneaker firms—British Knights, for instance—do little national advertising, concentrating instead on the large urban media markets in which their shoes have traditionally been popular. The Air Jordan, on the other hand, like most of Nike's shoes, is supported almost entirely by a national media campaign. That would be an expensive way to reach the largely urban black population. That this is not Nike's intent is made evident by a look at the evolution of Michael's shoe and the ads used to promote it.

The first Air Jordans were ugly. Almost purposefully so. With their space-boot cut and their brutal, dull red, black and white color scheme, they had an in-your-face quality that appealed not only to inner-city kids, but to those trying to ape inner-city fashions. The second shoe was a design disaster, an Italian model that looked like the orphaned offspring of a sneaker and an alligator belt. It said "class" with the same self-defeating lack of subtlety that marks cognac commercials.

Enter Tinker Hatfield, the former architect who is now Nike's director of design. Hatfield sees himself as "a problem solver," not a fashion designer. He is a man who likes to let the new technology Nike uses in the sneaker influence the way the shoe will look. Under his hand the Air Jordan came to look decreasingly like what people in the industry refer to as "an ethnic shoe," meaning that its shape was sleeker and its style more understated. In other words, Nike was taking the Air Jordan into the mainstream, broadening its aesthetic appeal. If there was an economic motive behind the change, and Nike officials deny this, it would appear to have been the opposite of the one Jackson and others allege: an effort to chase white dollars, rather than black.

At the same time the price of Air Jordans climbed from the initial $65 to about $100 for the Italian model and about $125 today. This alone was enough to convince many sensible people that Nike was out to rip them off. Consumers in their 30s and 40s remember when it was difficult to pay *more* than about $25 for a pair of sneakers. Yet, the markup on the Air Jordan is not much greater than the markup on products industry-wide. And while it is difficult to defend a $125 sneaker as a good value, footwear analysts speak well of the shoe.

"I can honestly say that the Jordan shoes get better every year," says Tom Brunick, director of the Athlete's Foot Wear Test Center at North Central College in Naperville, Illinois. They won't make kids run faster or jump higher, he says, but they are "excellent" shoes that often include fit and cushioning advances.

"From my standpoint, kids could be buying those shoes for all the wrong reasons, but they are still doing their feet a favor," he says. Brunick, it should be noted, works for a nationwide chain of sneaker stores, but he is not enamored of every alleged innovation that comes along. Try getting him to speak on the record about the Reebok pump.

Though they are good shoes, at $125 Air Jordans are clearly a luxury. Sneaker technology has become so sophisticated that industry experts say that for $50 you can't go too far wrong. A sneaker that costs two and a half times that much is going to need a special mystique, and the Air Jordan quickly developed one. Nike marketed the shoes, which are precisely like the ones Jordan wears each night, as a kind of mass-produced Excalibur, and spent $5 million in the first two years on advertising them. These commercials were slick, often innovative and obviously persuasive, but there is very little evidence to support the charge that they took deliberate and special aim at poor black children.

The commercials flow from the baby-boom sensibility of Jim Riswold, creative director at Weiden and Kennedy. His David Robinson campaign is a spoof of the PBS children's show "Mister Rogers' Neighborhood." To believe the spot is aimed at inner-city kids alone is to believe that public television is a major force in the ghetto.

Riswold's work with Lee has a more pronounced inner-city flavor. One now-controversial spot features Lee saying: "Yo Homes, Yo Homes, Yo Homes . . . These sneakers be housin', housin' across the country. . . And every homeboy should be bum-rushin' to get some, get some." In a 1990 interview with the *Washington Post*, Jesse Jackson claimed that the use of black slang proved the ads were aimed primarily at inner-city kids.

While it is true that Riswold and Lee have infused their collaborations with a hip, urban feel, this is more a tribute to a distinctively black aesthetic than it is an attempt to "target" a black clientele. Nike has been in the forefront of American companies employing black spokesmen, and depicting them with dignity and good humor. It seems ironic, as Jordan says, that this should bring the company so much negative publicity.

Still, Nike has been oddly callous in its handling of the sneaker controversy. Publicly the company has yet to express any regret about the violence its shoes have inspired, while privately some Nike officials have questioned the motives of Mushnick, Grigo and other critics. Nike has aired an antidrug spot featuring David Robinson and a stay-in-school commercial featuring Jordan and Lee, but it and other sneaker makers could do much more to offset the corrosive materialism at the heart of the sneaker murders.

They could also be more imaginative in exposing children to young black men and women who have succeeded in fields other than athletics. Why not have Jordan and his buddy Fred Whitfield, a successful attorney, talk about friendship or loyalty? Let Bo Jackson discuss his injuries with a black bone specialist. How about piano-playing David Robinson talking music with one of the Marsalis brothers? Or Buck Williams, the student of black history, discussing that subject with a writer like Ralph Wiley or a scholar like Gerald Early?

Advertising has helped make Bill Cosby and Michael Jordan two of the best-loved and most-admired men in America. With this status come social influence and economic power, two commodities in short supply in black America. It is not too much to ask that these celebrities take note of the frenzy their endorsements create. But it is reckless to advocate that blacks ignore the engines of the consumer culture, and unfair to suggest that they bear a greater social responsibility in using them than whites.

As the debate about sneaker advertising heated up during the 1989–90 season, Nike also came under fire from Operation PUSH, which initiated a boycott of the company, calling for it to hire more black executives, name a black to its board of directors and do more business with minority-controlled banks and advertising agencies. Jesse Jackson called Jordan on behalf of his old organization and tried to enlist his support for the boycott, but Michael refused. He said that there were racial problems throughout corporate America, that Nike did better on this score than most, and that the shoemaker was being unfairly singled out. Jordan, John Thompson and Spike Lee also met with Jackson at a New York hotel after the boycott began to see if they could arrive at a solution, but the effort failed.

The boycott was a peculiar one. Before being singled out by PUSH, Nike had enjoyed the goodwill of many black Americans, who appreciated the company's use of black spokesmen and were loyal to its footwear. Nike's top officials are among the most liberal in corporate America. Company president Richard Donahue was President John F.

Kennedy's liaison to Rev. Martin Luther King, Jr. and a strong advocate of civil rights. Blacks composed 7.5 percent of Nike's work force, as opposed to just 6 percent of the population of metropolitan Portland, where the company is based. While there were few key black officials at Nike, highly visible spokesmen like Thompson, Jordan, Lee, Jackson and Robinson could easily have carried PUSH's demands to the firm's top management *before* the boycott, had PUSH given them the opportunity to do so.

The boycott began in July, 1990, and while it received extensive media coverage, it had almost no effect on Nike's sales among blacks or whites. Past supporters of PUSH boycotts had a hard time figuring this one out. One reason was that Operation PUSH, beset by internal strife and financial hardships, never successfully articulated why Nike had been singled out.

After the initial burst of publicity, reporters following the story were unable to contact authorized PUSH spokesmen and women for weeks at a time. A Nike official claims that at one point the company thought it had settled the boycott, only to learn that the PUSH representative it had negotiated with did not have the authority to strike a deal. This official says the sneaker company feared that Operation PUSH would collapse before the boycott could be settled and Nike would be known as the organization that broke PUSH, not a distinction it was eager to claim.

In another peculiar turn the boycott, though it never really materialized, did achieve many of its aims. By the summer of 1991 Nike had named John Thompson to its board of directors, appointed a black vice president, signed a contract with a minority-run advertising agency and hired minority contractors to help construct its new distribution facilities in Memphis. Company officials claim that all of these decisions had long been in the works, but a PUSH spokesman pointed out that most were not announced until well after the boycott began.

Jordan kept as low a profile as possible throughout the

boycott. Again, he was in the uncomfortable position of being a black hero siding with a white company. Even black leaders who did not support the boycott thought Michael could at least have diplomatically endorsed a few of its aims. But David Falk says Jordan's silence stemmed from Michael's determination not to be used as "an asset, as a pawn, if you will."

"If he believes in it, he'll get involved, but he has to be comfortable," Falk says. "Some people criticized him over his role with PUSH. I don't think he believed in it, so he didn't support it, and the fact that it was a black cause wasn't enough."

During the 1989–90 season, several black leaders, including Arthur Ashe, attempted to enlist Jordan's support for Harvey Gantt, the black former mayor of Charlotte who was challenging Jesse Helms for his seat in the U.S. Senate. They received no reply from Michael, although Deloris Jordan responded with a contribution to Gantt's campaign. "Anybody over Jesse Helms," she says. "He is someone who doesn't care about our school system."

Jordan, who officially resides in Illinois, has never commented on his feelings about the Senate race, but his decision not to endorse Gantt was defended by Julius Erving. "A lot of people expected him to choose a side, but it wasn't part of his agenda," Erving says. "He has to consider the downside, and in this case it was a pretty heavy downside. If my base for making my living is the general public, I can ill afford to alienate half of them or one-third of them.

"If my family and I have consciously made a decision we will go into an issue with a clear conscience and take the heat that goes with the territory. But I don't want to be pushed. I don't want to be drafted unless it is a willful choice on my part."

Erving's argument would be a persuasive one in most cases. Jordan's help is solicited by many politicians of whom his endorsement would mean little. But the Helms-

Gantt race was unique. Michael retains extremely strong ties
to North Carolina and is tremendously popular there. Though
he resides in Illinois, that would have presented little problem in a contest during which both sides relied heavily on
out-of-state endorsements and contributions. Nor could Jordan
have been ignorant of Helms's race-baiting political tactics
or the senator's abysmal record on desegregation and the
civil rights agenda. Had Michael committed himself to
Gantt—who garnered 47 percent of the vote—he might have
helped galvanize opposition to one of the most racially
divisive politicians in recent history. Such a clear-cut opportunity for a black athlete to make a political difference is not
likely to arise again soon.

Jordan has not had much opportunity to develop a political sense. Basketball and business opportunities have con-
sumed most of his time since late adolescence. He grew up
black in the segregated South but, as Fred Whitfield points
out, "By the time he was in junior high we had desegregated schools. And being as talented as he was, racial barriers
were taken down. With him being on the level he is on now,
not that much racism hits him front and center."

But it does hit. One friend tells of walking behind
Michael through a Chicago area country club and hearing
one white member ask another, "Who's that nigger?" In
dealing with these situations Michael, for the most part, has
adopted his mother's strategy of refusing to dignify igno-
rance with anger. Further, Jordan is clearly uncomfortable
speaking out on social issues when he does not completely
understand the situation.

On January 19, 1989, the Bulls played the Miami Heat in
Miami, just a few days after the city's Liberty City neighborhood had erupted in riots. Two nights earlier the Heat
had been forced to cancel a game because of the violence,
but leaders of those outbreaks promised that the streets
would be quiet while Michael was in town. The national
media was in Miami for the Super Bowl and wanted to
know if Jordan had a message for the people in the street.

"It would have been tough for me to do that, because I didn't understand the situation," he said at the time. "I wouldn't exactly know what to say to them. I was very fortunate to grow up in a very country-style background. I just never had the chance to grow up in the city life. You hate to see anybody suffer and go through poverty, especially with the riches we have in the United States. I think [the rioters] got their point across. I think people are going to start to listen, hopefully, and they can solve the problem."

In short, when it comes to politics Jordan, distinguished and bold in other fields, is ordinary and somewhat timid.

Perhaps, says Ted Shaw, he will follow the trail blazed by Dave Bing, the Detroit Pistons' Hall of Fame guard who now runs a Detroit steel and manufacturing firm and is among the nation's leading black capitalists. Until then the question of what political or economic impact he will have remains open.

"What Dave Bing is doing now is much more significant than what he was doing in the NBA," Shaw says. "It is too early in Michael Jordan's life to say what he is going to do on that count. The jury is still out."

As a stream of political and economic controversies eddied around Jordan during the '89–'90 season, he also found time to play a little basketball. The Bulls got off to a rocky 5–5 start, but won 16 of their next 20 games. Rookie coach Phil Jackson had not yet committed himself to Tex Winter's controversial triple-post offense, but he did stress working the ball inside to Cartwright "at least one out of every three times."

While the big center struggled (he averaged 11.4 points and shot just .488), the Chicago offense continued to improve and became marginally more balanced. Michael was once again leading the league in scoring, averaging 33.6 points per game, but all five Chicago starters joined him in double figures. Pippen was slowly maturing into a star in his own right, and Grant was becoming a more dominant rebounding presence.

On March 28, Jordan had the biggest single scoring night of his career, pouring in 69 points during a 117–113 overtime defeat of the Cavaliers in Cleveland. "On nights like that you feel like you can score a hundred," he said. His outburst came during a torrid streak in which the Bulls won 27 of their last 35 games. They finished the season at 55–27, the second-best record in team history. But they were also second best in the Central Division, finishing four games behind the defending champions from Detroit.

Though encouraged by their regular-season progress, the Bulls knew they still faced a single postseason question: Could they beat the Pistons? Some experts didn't think they'd get the chance. After dispatching the Milwaukee Bucks in four games, the Bulls took on the highly touted Philadelphia 76ers.

Sixers forwards Charles Barkley and Rick Mahorn played precisely the type of punishing physical game that was supposed to rattle the often-mild Bulls. But Barkley was hampered by a tender shoulder and Jordan was just rounding into his usually magnificent postseason form. Michael scored 39 points in Chicago's 96–85 victory in game one and 45 as the Bulls stormed back from an 11-point halftime deficit to win game two, 101–96.

Leading the best-of-seven series 2–0, Chicago headed for the Spectrum, and promptly proceeded to fall apart. For the first three quarters of game three, the Sixers pounded on them. Philadelphia led 93–69 with 10 minutes to play. A total Bulls collapse, one that would probably have ramifications for the rest of the series, seemed imminent.

But in the final period, Jordan staged a one-man comeback, pouring in 24 of his 49 points as the Bulls cut a 24-point deficit to six. Philadelphia managed to hang on for a 118–112 victory, but the Bulls had exposed the 76ers' inability to play aggressively with the lead. That flaw proved fatal in game four.

Once again the 76ers led late in the third quarter. This time the count was 80–66 when Chicago staged another frantic comeback. Jordan sank 18 of his 45 points in the final period and the Bulls walked off with a surprisingly easy 111–101 victory. Three nights later Chicago held Barkley and company to 36 second-half points and captured the series with a 117–99 rout.

The Bulls were one round away from the NBA finals, but the defending champions blocked their path. Chicago had lost four straight games to Detroit after an initial regular-season victory. The Pistons' aggressive, physical defense allowed them not only to contain Michael, but to demoralize his teammates, particularly Pippen and Grant, who seemed to float cloudlike through the teams' regular-season matchups. Any chance Chicago had of staging an upset rested more or less on Jordan's ability to rewrite the Rules.

Games one and two of the series were exercises in domination as Detroit claimed 86–77 and 102–93 victories over a meek herd of Bulls. At halftime of that second loss, with his team trailing 53–38, Jordan allowed himself a brief and rare temper tantrum. "We are playing like a bunch of pussies," he screamed (or words to that effect), and underlined his point by knocking over a water cooler (or maybe it was a chair). The details are fuzzy because Jordan would not talk about the incident. In fact, hoping to show his teammates that they were going to have to stand up for themselves, Michael refused to talk to the press, thus forcing the other Bulls to make their own excuses.

Whether it was Jordan's outburst or the roaring of the Stadium crowd that did it, the Bulls looked like a newly energized team in game three. Trailing 77–76 going into the fourth quarter, they went on a 23–13 tear and hung on for a 107–102 victory. Jordan, who finished with 47 points, chipped in 16 during that crucial fourth-quarter run. Scottie Pippen added 29, and he and Horace Grant each grabbed 11 rebounds.

Two nights later the Bulls evened the series, winning 108–101. Once again Michael led the way, scoring 42 points, 19 of those in the last quarter. Chicago had defended its home court, but still needed to win a game in Detroit. That wasn't going to be easy.

Game five showed why. With Michael scoring just 22 points on 7-of-19 shooting, the Pistons cruised to an easy, ugly 97–83 victory. The Bulls were one loss away from elimination.

For the first time in their long-running postseason battle with the Pistons, however, Chicago did not fold. Or at least not right away. Instead, the Bulls returned to the Stadium and won game six in a rout, 109–91. Jordan scored 18 points in the crucial third quarter and Craig Hodges came off the bench to add 19, 12 of those on perfect three-point shooting.

The convincing nature of that victory gave the Bulls hope for game seven. But it was extremely short-lived. In fact, the Bulls commenced their self-destruction before the final contest even began. During warm-ups Scottie Pippen came down with a migraine that blurred his vision and ruined his concentration. The Pistons' defense took care of Pippen's less-afflicted teammates.

For a little more than a quarter it looked as though the Bulls might make a game of it. They led 27–25 about four minutes into the second period when the collapse took hold. The Pistons' swarming defense suddenly began to force turn overs and convert them into easy baskets. Chicago's ball-handlers became increasingly frustrated and the Detroit defenders increasingly emboldened. The Bulls managed just six points in the final eight minutes of the half and found themselves trailing 48–33.

For all practical purposes their season was over. Despite Jordan's heroic second-half efforts, Detroit's lead never dipped into single digits. For all but the last two minutes of the second half, Michael scored or assisted on every Chicago basket. Still, the Bulls lost in a big way, 93–74.

A quick look at the score sheet showed how completely Jordan's teammates had deserted him. Michael had 31 points, nine assists and eight rebounds. Pippen shot one for

10 from the floor and sat out much of the game. Grant hit three of his 17 shots. Bill Cartwright chipped in a hefty six points, and Hodges, Jordan's costar in game six, hit only two of his 12 three-point attempts. Michael shot a meager .467 for the series, but his teammates managed only an anemic .382.

"You've got to accept this loss as a learning experience," Jordan said publicly. But in private, friends say, he was angry with his teammates' proclivity for disappearing in the clutch, and with the club management's inability to surround him with more able players. The fact that he disliked Laimbeer and Thomas, and felt defensive specialist Dennis Rodman got away with a welter of cheap shots, only intensified his indignation.

The loss in game seven affected each of the Bulls personally. The Pistons had not only mastered them physically, but psychologically as well. And they had done it in the most insulting sort of way, concentrating all of their defensive efforts on Jordan and daring his teammates to beat them. It was the kind of loss that provoked questions not simply about the Bulls' talent—there are always questions about the losing team's talent—but about their character. There were those who doubted that Chicago could ever break this psychological hold, particularly as long as Pippen—who seemed fearful of the Pistons—was on the team. And there were others who questioned whether any team with a player as dominating as Jordan could develop the complementary talent to help him win a title.

And so, in early October, a long season before a rematch could potentially take place, the Bulls came to training camp with the Pistons on their minds. "I'd hate to say we get obsessed about it, but you don't like to get beat that way too often, so we do think about them," John Paxson said.

"I wouldn't tell you a lie," added assistant coach John Bach. "We sit here all summer looking at tapes. We prepare to beat Detroit."

"Is there a feeling that you have to do it this year or next year?'' someone asked Jordan. ''That's my feeling,'' he answered. ''You really don't get the chances we've been getting to get to a world championship. When you get these chances you have to take advantage of them . . . I believe in making it happen in the present.''

14

At an evening practice a week before they would play their first exhibition game of the 1990–91 season, the Chicago Bulls were deep in a ball-handling drill. It was the kind of exercise familiar to anyone who has tried out for a high school team. One player tries to dribble the length of the court, the other tries to stop him. Except that there is a tacit understanding that you don't really stop him. You just make him work harder, help him sharpen his skills, don't embarrass the guy.

Michael Jordan appears to be unaware of this compact. He is playing defense against Craig Neal, a former Georgia Tech guard whom the Bulls have signed for the duration of training camp. As soon as Neal takes the ball, Jordan jumps at him, pressing close against his body, giving him no room to move. Neal turns his back, but Michael leans in, fakes right and swipes from the left side. The ball leaps from Neal's grasp and goes skittering across the floor.

Neal starts over, his back to Jordan. He manages one step, two steps, but then Jordan begins darting from side to side, threatening to reach around for the steal. Neal begins spinning from side to side himself, trying to anticipate Michael's movements. It is he who is on the defensive. Finally he loses track of Jordan, zigs when he should zag and Michael once again slaps the ball away.

This scene is reenacted several times before Neal gets the ball upcourt. By that time this confrontation has become both spectacle and embarrassment. The other Bulls don't know whether to stare or look away. What is Jordan trying to prove? Neal, to his credit, appears unruffled when the drill is over. "It's an old ACC thing," he explains, referring to the conference in which Tech and Carolina are rivals.

But Michael's undressing of the young free agent is nothing personal. His teammates, not Neal, are the intended audience for this defensive display. Jordan has come to camp hungry and impatient. This, he feels, is his year, and he wastes few opportunities to convey that sense of urgency to the other Bulls.

When he is in this frame of mind, Jordan can be a difficult man for other players to be around. Michael is the Bulls' team leader, but he does not always play that role as a speaking part. Jordan uses the example of his own intensity to set a serious tone. When he feels his message is not being received, he simply becomes more intense. His searing of Neal was a reminder to his teammates that he was going all out, even in practice, and that he expected them to do the same.

"Craig saw the fury that is Michael," says John Bach, one of Phil Jackson's three assistants. "This is the swelling pride that is in the man." Bach, one of the league's top defensive tacticians, is a connoisseur of personal confrontation and a master at facing down his own fears. His colleague, Tex Winter, the Bulls' offensive coordinator, is more the moralist, the teacher, the defender of the "team concept."

They make a fascinating pair. Each has been coaching in either a Division I college program or the NBA for more than 40 years. The oldest coaches in the league, they are a testament to Jerry Krause's conviction that "when people get older they don't get dumber." Bach and Winter share a taste for Western-style clothing, but their basketball philosophies are entirely divergent. It is as though Phil Jackson had an angel on each shoulder whispering contradictory advice in his ears. Michael Jordan's role in the Bulls' 1990-91 season is perhaps best understood as a dialectic between the two points of view expressed by Bach and Winter, one the champion of ego and brilliance, the other the proponent of submerging the self in the community.

Bach's twin brother was shot down and lost in the Pacific during World War II. John wears his twin's wings on a bracelet. He did not know how to fly when his brother was killed, but he learned, over his family's objections. He loves road trips to the Pacific Northwest because seaplanes are a particular favorite of his. This is most of what one needs to know about him.

What the silver-haired coach with the military bearing likes best about Jordan is what he values most in himself: the refusal to acknowledge limitation. "I like to say that when he leaves the locker room he starts attacking the basket," Bach says. Positioning his interviewer a hairsbreadth from the nearby bleachers, he demonstrates how Michael "runs at screens. He'll knife through there when there isn't room for a firefly." This toughness, he says, is easily overshadowed by the acrobatic elegance of Michael's game, but Bach believes it is the key to Jordan's success.

The coach especially savors Jordan's confrontation with some of the league's top guards. He remembers one game when Michael seemed to be exorcising a personal grudge against Dan Majerle of Phoenix. "I asked him what was going on," Bach remembers. "He said, 'John, I can see the fear in his eyes.' I said, 'You son of a bitch.' "

Bach takes a seat on the bleachers near the practice court and begins leafing through the Bulls' media guide, recalling Jordan's performances against every team in the league.

"Charlotte: I'd hate to tell you what he does to the kid at Charlotte at times," he says. "[Rex] Chapman. He has lit him up. The Lakers: Magic has [defended] him. And [Byron] Scott. Michael has had some very nice nights. New York: I always felt sorry for the guys who had to play him. Philly: in [Hersey] Hawkins's rookie year they tried him on Michael. What's the phrase—'cruel and inhumane punishment?' "

Jordan's slash-and-burn style is not without its drawbacks for the Bulls, Bach admits. "We have to have one guy on this team who can play him in practice," he says. "That's their contribution to the team. One year we had Elston Turner, the guy you wanted to walk down an alley with you. Michael wore him out. Wore out his confidence. You need somebody like that to guard him. Last year we had Charles Davis. He wouldn't back down an inch, but they have to be that way because of the wanton disregard that Michael has for the defender.

"I asked him one time, 'How come you are so tough on guys in practice?' He kind of chastised me. He said, 'John, I have to prepare for the next game.' "

Practice is about to resume as Bach stands up to leave. Out on the court the Bulls are engaged in casual shoot-arounds. "There isn't one player out there," Bach says, "who won't be made better by the example of the man."

Tex Winter is less comfortable with the notion that basketball is an ongoing test of one's audacity. He is milder and more circumspect than the voluble Bach, but the subject of Jordan's brilliance and its effect on the team is one he has given considerable thought. After expressing his respect for Michael and his gifts, the criticism, couched in praise, comes in a quick, quiet monologue.

"He is competitive to a fault," Winter says. "He wants to come out and dominate every practice session. He gets into the one-on-one situation too much. I think to him the game becomes a degree-of-difficulty situation. But this is not gymnastics.

"When he catches the ball, he is so talented that he figures, 'I can take this guy,' and oftentimes he can. But sometimes he gets himself into a predicament. He takes challenges sometimes that it would be better if he wouldn't.

"Not that he's a selfish player. It's a thin line. I liken it to ballet or a symphony. You have your maestro and everything is in synch. The rhythm and timing. How did it get to be that way? Everybody executes his or her role to perfection. Now I don't suppose there is an orchestra or a ballet that doesn't have a featured star, and they give an opportunity for that person to display their talent and ability as a soloist or a featured performer. That's what we attempt to do in basketball. We want to be a unit, but we want a system that features the great talents of the individuals."

That can be difficult to do with Jordan, he says. "Sometimes with Michael, the better he got, the more it distracted from team play. He is so exciting to watch he has a tendency to make spectators out of his teammates and sometimes of the coaching staff. The coaches, myself included, are reluctant to correct Michael and point out things he could do better."

Winter calls Jordan "the best athlete I've seen in the game. But he's not the best-skilled athlete." Not even *among* the best-skilled athletes, he adds. This is a minority opinion, and when pressed for details, Winter says he has been working to get Jordan to throw "a good 15-to-18-foot chest pass to an open teammate."

He is one of the few coaches in basketball who will criticize specific aspects of Jordan's highly regarded game. But as he does so, it becomes clear that his real concern is not over matters of skill but matters of style. "I think we would be a better team and he would be a more effective player if he didn't try to score every time he touched the basketball," Winter says. "Michael can say in his own mind, 'With the kind of money I make and the success I've had, the most successful basketball player in the world, I'm not changing my style of play.' He may be right. I can't say I blame him. He may be right.

"Why should he change? He should change, in my mind, in order to make the team good enough to win a championship. He may have to change.

"You can sum all this up in one line," Tex Winter says. " 'This guy is an old-fashioned basketball coach.' But that's what I believe."

Taken together, the two veteran coaches' remarks illustrated the central tension of Jordan's career. How much individuality should the greatest individual player in the game be allowed to display? To what degree did Michael's magnificence elevate his teammates, and to what degree did it inhibit them? Would the Bulls win the NBA title because Jordan had learned to trust his teammates or because they had become worthy of a trust he was already willing to bestow?

What they came to know for sure in Chicago was that something clicked. After a few false starts, and the occasional outbursts of intramural ill will, the Bulls became the best team in basketball.

In the four seasons before the 1990–91 campaign, Michael Jordan accounted for nearly one-third of Chicago's points. He, Scottie Pippen and, to a lesser extent, Horace Grant flourished in a wide-open game that thrived on the fast break. They favored an offense built around isolating one player man-to-man against a defender and letting him create scoring opportunities. But there was little place in that style of game for the Bulls' other starters—John Paxson, a steady but slow-footed guard with a deadly outside shooting touch, and Bill Cartwright, the solid interior defender with the awkward but once-reliable turnaround jumper.

The Bulls' reliance on the fast break also made them vulnerable to teams that could force them into their erratic half-court offense. This weakness was accentuated in the playoffs, when teams could concentrate on stopping Jordan's forays and force the other Bulls to create their own offensive opportunities. The Pistons' ability to do this had twice helped make them NBA champions.

Phil Jackson's goal before the 1990–91 season was to improve Chicago's half-court game without hampering the fast break or robbing Jordan and Pippen of their creativity. To accomplish this he adopted Winter's complicated triple-post offense, a system the assistant coach had first outlined in a book published in 1962 while Winter was head coach at Kansas State. The offense is based on crisp passing and constant, tightly patterned movement and resembles a collegiate "motion" offense.

In an ideal world, the triple post creates so many offensive options that the ball-handler always has one appealing choice no matter how the defense responds. But the Bulls were slow in adjusting to the new strategy, and the world in which they began the season was far from ideal. Chicago dropped its first three games, including one to the lowly Washington Bullets.

"We didn't seem like we had the chemistry and continuity that we had in practice," said Jordan after scoring 29 points in the 103–102 loss at Washington. "I think we better develop it quick, before we find ourselves in a hole. We don't know how, instinctively, to get ourselves in position on offense. You find yourself with the clock running down, having to force the issue."

This was particularly true of Michael. In most of the Bulls' early games he hung back in the first quarter, wanting to give his teammates a chance to get untracked offensively. Some nights they did, but most they didn't. Often Chicago found itself trailing in the fourth period and suddenly turning to the previously underused Jordan to save the game.

"Don't judge us by the way we look now," Phil Jackson said privately just before his team was thrashed 125–112 by the Portland Trail Blazers during a road trip in late November. "Portland is really in synch," he said. "They know each other. They are where we want to be."

Throughout the season the Bulls lurched in that direction. After a 109–107 loss to the Phoenix Suns, Chicago went on a seven-game winning streak that transformed the team from a 5–6 disappointment to a 12–6 contender in the space of two weeks. "Obviously we are playing much better," said Bill Cartwright before the Bulls beat the Knicks 108–98 for the seventh of those victories. "Everyone is more involved. There is a greater recognition of one another."

It was true that the Bulls' new offense showed promise, at least on paper. The team was averaging about three points more per game than it had the previous season, and Jordan was doing only about a quarter of the scoring. But in action it seemed less that the Bulls had mastered the triple post than that they had learned how to win while struggling with it.

Part of the reason was an adjustment on Michael's part. Fourteen games into the season, he decided to concentrate on scoring first-quarter points, rather than waiting for his teammates to get untracked. For the first time since his rookie season he began shooting around before games, in hopes of getting off to faster starts. It worked. In the next five games, which coincided with the heart of Chicago's winning streak, he averaged 14 points in the first quarter.

But Tex Winter wasn't completely happy with Jordan's commitment to the new offense. "He has accepted it, and he hasn't," Winter said. "I still think he thinks he has to score. And he *does* have to score. But there are points for him in the offense. He's getting his 30-point average, but he's getting it more easily than he ever did before."

Michael admitted to misgivings about the new scheme in an interview with Jack McCallum of *Sports Illustrated*. "I fight the offense when we lose close games and I haven't given the output I could've given because of the system," he said. "On nights we win, obviously, it's fine. I only want to win. I think the offense can work. But one of the problems is that the offense takes time to perfect, and we still make a lot of mistakes."

Those mistakes were particularly obvious against good teams. The Trail Blazers ended Chicago's winning streak with a 109–101 victory in the Stadium in early December. Three nights later the Bulls lost to the Central Division-leading Milwaukee Bucks, 99–87. In that game the triple post produced just 10 third-quarter points.

Against substandard opposition, however, Chicago continued to wreak havoc. On one mid-December weekend the Bulls beat the Clippers by 40 points and the Cavaliers by 18, after outscoring Cleveland 36–5 in the first period. Jordan was out of that game so early that he spent much of the second half sitting at the end of the Chicago bench joking with season-ticket holders about the ragtag action out on the court. It was a moment's calm before an extremely taxing 10 days during which the Bulls played the Pistons twice and the Lakers once and Jordan dealt with a personal emergency.

On December 19, Chicago took its usual shellacking at the Palace of Auburn Hills; the Pistons crushed them 105–84. That embarrassing defeat dropped the Bulls' record to 15–9, but it also helped turn their season around. Two days later they beat the Lakers 114–103 in Chicago, starting a streak in which they would win 12 of 13 games.

For Michael, the most memorable of those victories came on Christmas Day against the Pistons. But what had recently happened off the court was more momentous than what happened on. Juanita Jordan was due with the couple's second child in late January, but very early on Christmas eve morning she went into labor.

"I came down that morning and he was sleeping on the couch," remembers Fred Whitfield, who spent the holidays at the Jordans' home. "I said, 'Where's Juanita?'

"He said, 'I took her to the hospital at 2:30.'

"And I didn't believe it, because I had been talking with her at midnight. And he said, 'Yeah, she had the baby at 5:30.'

"And then there he is—sleeps on the couch, and he's ready to roll the next day."

With his son Marcus James Jordan safely in the world,

Michael celebrated with a 37-point performance against Detroit and the Bulls won a nationally televised victory, 98–86.

Two weeks later in Philadelphia, Jordan was again in a celebratory mood. With 25.2 seconds to play in the first quarter, he sank a free throw for his 15,000th career point. It had taken him 460 games to amass those points. Only Wilt Chamberlain, who did it in 358, had managed the feat more quickly. As the ball fell through the hoop, the Spectrum crowd rose to its feet and erupted in cheers.

"I got some chill bumps," said Jordan, who had also scored his 5,000th and 10,000th points at the Spectrum. "To do it on the road and see people respect you that much, it really inspires me." Michael scored 40 points in the Bulls' 107–99 victory, and when a reporter asked Hersey Hawkins what it felt like to guard Jordan he replied: "I can't answer that question. I don't know."

The Bulls' hot streak ended during an indifferent road trip on which they lost to the dreadful New Jersey Nets as well as the Lakers and the San Antonio Spurs. But no sooner was one streak over than another began. Just before the All-Star break they beat the Pistons—who had lost Isiah Thomas to a thumb injury—in the Palace, 95–93. It was the second victory in what would become an 11-game skein. But the Bulls were fighting among themselves as they flourished.

Jordan and Jerry Krause were at the center of this contention. Michael perceived, correctly, that Dennis Hopson—who had come from the Nets in exchange for two draft picks—had not strengthened the Bulls' bench offensively. In fact, the second unit, embarrassed by the Pistons in the previous year's playoffs, was having a much harder time learning Winter's offense than the first. Jordan felt the team needed to acquire a veteran guard who was a proven scorer, and he had just the player in mind.

The Denver Nuggets were shopping former Tar Heel Walter Davis, a deadly outside shooter whom Jordan felt could enter a game and produce instant points. But Krause was not alone in wondering if Davis could help the team. Chicago already had a designated outside shooter on its bench in Craig Hodges. Like Hodges, Davis played miserable defense, and though he'd once been a brilliant athlete, at 36 he no longer ran the floor with quite the same aggressiveness.

The Bulls management and coaching staff voted 6–0 against dealing for Davis. But Jordan, who was apparently unaware of the vote, aimed his anger almost exclusively at Krause. When the trading deadline passed without the acquisition of Davis or another veteran guard, he made his already well-chronicled complaints even more pointed. "If I was general manager I would not be in this position," he told the press. "My team certainly would be much stronger."

Michael's criticism of the general manager was remarkable not so much for its force—he'd lashed out at Krause before—as for its duration. On All-Star weekend in Charlotte, several weeks after the trading deadline, he was still easily drawn into a discussion of the controversy, and still suggesting that the Bulls were at least one player short of being a championship-caliber team. "I just felt we could have made a stronger push to get this guy," Jordan told a large circle of reporters in a ballroom at the Omni Hotel. "It can be seen that our bench still lacks offense. And that the guy was still available. I would have liked to see us get him."

His judgment on the issue, he implied, was better than Krause's. "I've got a good sense of players I play against . . . better than general managers who never played the game of basketball, who got started in baseball." Was he referring to anyone in particular, someone asked. "No," Jordan said, chuckling. "Michael, can I ask a question about the [All-Star] weekend?" another reporter broke in. "Yeah, yeah, get back to this weekend," Jordan said.

Michael's impatience with Krause had been compounded by the general manager's year-long negotiations to bring Toni Kukoc to the Bulls. Kukoc was regarded as the best player in Europe, and many scouts felt he would be a surefire star in the NBA. At 6-foot-10, Kukoc was quick and strong, an excellent ball-handler, a deadly shooter and a brilliant passer. But it was not at all clear he wanted to play in the NBA, and not at all clear he would fit well into a team with Jordan and Pippen, two players whose need for the ball rivaled his own. Krause felt these obstacles could be overcome and made Kukoc's agent an extremely attractive offer.

Unfortunately for the general manager, his overture found its way into the press. The Bulls had reportedly offered the Yugoslavian star more than $2 million, a sum that angered several Bulls whose contracts expired at the end of the season. Chief among those was Scottie Pippen.

The Bulls' second star was enjoying his finest season. He had added range and reliability to his jump shot, confidence to his floor game, and was slowly picking up the finer points of an offense that had bedeviled him early in the season. Pippen made just $865,000 a year, below the league average and a paltry sum for a man of his accomplishments. He thought the Bulls were being extremely slow in offering him a new contract and couldn't help but see Krause's pursuit of Kukoc as part of the problem.

John Paxson and Bill Cartwright were also in the final years of their contracts, and realized that to some extent their earnings might be influenced by the success of the team's quest for Kukoc. Added to this mix were a few players disgruntled by their lack of playing time, one of whom, Stacy King, went briefly AWOL in the second half of the season. It made for an uneasy locker room atmosphere.

Whether these feuds had any effect on the Bulls, other than distancing a few of them from the general manager, is hard to say. It didn't seem to be affecting their play. After the Houston Rockets snapped Chicago's 11-game February winning streak, the Bulls won nine straight in March.

Their best opponents, meanwhile, were wracked with injuries. In Boston Larry Bird was beset by back pain. Isiah

Thomas had missed a huge chunk of the season, and though he'd be back for the playoffs, he wouldn't be at the top of his game. The Bulls, on the other hand, were 50–15 and becoming increasingly confident in the triple post. They were surer of each other's movements and clearer about when to pass and when to shoot.

But despite their growing confidence, the Bulls continued to struggle against good teams. In the last month of the season they lost twice to Philadelphia and once each to Houston, Boston, San Antonio and Detroit. Their only victory over a top playoff contender in that span came on the final day of the season when they beat the Pistons 108–100.

Chicago finished the regular season with a 61–21 record. It was the best in franchise history and the best in the Eastern Conference, yet they remained a mysterious team. They had outscored their opponents by an average of 9.1 points per game, best in the league. They had held other teams below 100 points 46 times, second best in the league. Yet, against opponents with records of .500 or better, the Bulls were an unimpressive 21–18. Questions about their postseason fortitude lingered.

None of this was supposed to keep them from making quick work of their first-round opponents, the New York Knicks, a team that finished at 39–43 and owned the worst record in the playoffs. All the Bulls could do in this series was demonstrate to their detractors, and to each other, how well-prepared they were for the postseason. They accomplished that immediately.

The Bulls beat the Knicks 126–85 in game one of their series, the largest margin by which a Bulls team had ever won a postseason game. The remaining two games of the series were a bit more competitive, but the outcome was the same. Craig Hodges hit a three-pointer that ignited a 9–2 Chicago surge late in the third period of game two and the Bulls won it 89–79.

Playing on their home court, the Knicks built a 12-point second-quarter lead in game three, but the Bulls' swarming defense forced a host of turnovers that led to easy baskets and allowed them to pull within one point at halftime, 54–53. That turnaround took the fight out of the Knicks. Behind Jordan's 15 third-quarter points, Chicago spurted to an 83–71 lead and coasted the rest of the way. The final count was 103–94.

Their victories over the Knicks demonstrated how dominant the often-overlooked Bulls defense could be. New York had averaged just 86 points per game in the series, and had shot a meager .443. Patrick Ewing, the Knicks' splendid center, had managed just 16.7 points per game, 10 off his season average.

The defense depended on sheer athleticism and a willingness to gamble, and was the perfect extension of John Bach's personality. Jordan and Pippen were quick enough to harass opposing guards, but big enough to double-team front-court players. Horace Grant had the speed to double-team on the outside, then hurry back to his man without getting burned. Bach called these three his "Dobermans," and used them to perfection in a disruptive defense that gave Chicago's games the feel of a jailbreak, with the Bulls busting out on one fast break after another.

Of course, this dominance had been displayed against the worst team in the playoffs and might count for nothing against the Philadelphia 76ers. The Sixers, led by Charles Barkley, were an inconsistent team without a true center, but they had beaten the Bulls three times in four meetings. Two of Chicago's six losses at the Stadium had come at the Sixers' hands.

Any notion that Philadelphia might repeat those victories in game one was extinguished immediately. Chicago leapt to a 34–14 lead late in the first quarter, thanks to a dozen points from Bill Cartwright, and Philadelphia never cut its deficit to single digits. The Bulls, led by Jordan with 29 points and Pippen with 24, took an easy 105–92 victory.

Chicago was not so dominant in game two. After trailing by nine at the half, the Sixers closed to within five at

103–98. But with just under two minutes to play, Horace Grant broke through two defenders to stick in Jordan's errant three-point attempt and spark a closing rush that gave Chicago a 112–100 victory.

Game three was the best of the series as Jordan and Hersey Hawkins engaged in a second-half shoot-out, scoring 24 points apiece. Jordan gave the Bulls a 96–93 lead with just under a minute and a half to play when he drove on 7-foot-7 Manute Bol, soared toward the basket and drew a foul. Bol argued the call and picked up a technical foul for his trouble, but Michael hit only one of his free throws.

The Sixers quickly shaved the lead to 96–95. With 15 seconds left, the Bulls once again went to Jordan, who once again tried the lane and was fouled. Once again, he hit just one of his two free throws. The Bulls led 97–95.

Five seconds later, Barkley drove through the middle of the Chicago defense. Jordan left Hawkins to stop Barkley's drive. As he did so, the Sixers' forward zipped a pass to the man Michael had abandoned. Hawkins, who had been on the losing end of so many duels with Jordan, won this one. He swished a three-pointer with 10 seconds to play and the Sixers hung on to win 99–97.

That was the Sixers' moment. The Bulls routed them methodically in game four behind a defense that held Philadelphia to just 57 points in the first three quarters. Chicago had opened up a 16-point lead by then, getting extremely balanced scoring, including 25 from Jordan, 22 from Grant and 20 from Pippen. The final tally was 101–85.

Game five began as though it might be nearly as easy. For the first three quarters Scottie Pippen drove the lane at will, hitting 13 of his 14 shots and staking the Bulls to a 13-point lead. But the demanding task of guarding Barkley landed him in foul trouble. He watched much of the fourth period from the bench as the Bulls frittered away their advantage. A pair of free throws by Armon Gilliam tied the score at 92 with just over three minutes to play.

Jordan had not been shooting well, hitting just six of his

16 first-half shots. But with victory about to elude him, Michael's touch suddenly returned. He scored his team's last 12 points, played suffocating defense and controlled the backboards in a bravura three-minute performance that gave Chicago the series with a 100–95 victory.

After the game Jordan, who scored 38 points and pulled in 19 rebounds, was asked if he felt any sympathy for his friend Charles Barkley. Michael's answer said as much about his shifting perception of his Chicago teammates as it did about Barkley. "I really feel there are some great similarities in our system and Philly's," he said. "[T]he guy goes out there and plays an all-around game. He plays his heart out and sometimes it looks like he's doing all the work.

"It used to be that way here, but things have changed. A few guys have emerged, a few guys have matured and we're a team now. That was a team effort at the end. Guys were diving for loose balls. Somebody had to get me the ball. Somebody had to set screens. That wasn't all me, that was a team effort."

He was, for a change, describing what was, rather than what he wished would be. Pippen had emerged as almost as great an offensive and defensive threat as Jordan himself. He was averaging 22 points and nine rebounds a game in the playoffs. Grant was performing solidly on offense, Cartwright solidly on defense. The Bulls, as always, were killing opponents with their quickness, but, for a change, they were not being manhandled on the backboards.

No team was better designed to test their new ruggedness and growing composure than the Pistons.

Detroit was not as strong a team in 1990–91 as it had been in the two preceding seasons. Thomas's thumb injury was still delicate. James Edwards was having painful back problems. In fact, most of the Pistons' starters hobbled into the Eastern Conference finals with one ailment or another. Still, this was the most physically aggressive and defensively accomplished team in the league, and one with a hexlike hold over the Bulls.

The series ahead was played out partially in the press, with the Bulls talking bravely about how they had matured and the Pistons reminding Pippen and his mates how they had folded in game seven the previous season. This combativeness found expression on the court in an almost comic way, as the Pistons looked for opportunities to provoke the Bulls and the Bulls looked just as hard for opportunities to stand up to the Pistons' provocation. Jordan, who is generally loath to be caught talking trash, openly goaded Dennis Rodman, Detroit's superb if sometimes dirty defensive forward.

The Bulls set a pattern in game one as they had against the Knicks and Sixers, roaring to a 20–8 first-quarter lead. But the Pistons were a more resourceful team than Chicago's earlier opponents. Reserve guard Vinnie Johnson poured in 14 second-quarter points and brought Detroit to within eight at the half, 45–37.

Chuck Daly went to his bench again in the third period, sending Mark Aguirre in for the struggling Bill Laimbeer. Aguirre, who finished with a game-high 25 points, gave Detroit a 54–53 lead with just under five minutes to play in the third period. But this is when the role reversal that would characterize this series first took hold.

In seasons past it had been the Bulls—led by one player, almost always Jordan—who would make a valiant run at the Pistons, only to have Detroit's greater offensive balance and defensive intensity thwart their comebacks. This season Chicago played like the more seasoned and confident team, retaking the lead 68–65 at the end of the third period.

What Phil Jackson did next might have led to calls for his resignation had it not worked out so well. He sent his second unit—B. J. Armstrong, Craig Hodges, Cliff Levingston and Will Perdue—out to start the fourth quarter with Horace Grant. It was the same group, save for Levingston, upon whom the Pistons had preyed so enthusiastically in playoffs past. For perhaps the five and a half most crucial minutes of the game, Jackson left this bunch on the floor. And when Jordan, Pippen and Cartwright returned to action, the Bulls led 81–72. The first team managed not to squander this lead, and Chicago won 94–83.

It got easier from there. In game two the second unit teamed with Scottie Pippen to stretch a five-point first-quarter lead into a 16-point bulge late in the second. Detroit never really got back in the game. Jordan made sure of that, saving 15 of his 35 points for the final quarter. Chicago won it 105–97.

"They stole our playbook," said the Pistons' John Salley. "Talking junk, talking garbage, their intensity on defense, making sure there is only one shot, keeping people out of the middle, making us beat them with the jump shot. That's what we usually do."

That's what the Bulls thought the Pistons might do when the series moved to the Palace. Chicago had lost six straight playoff games there. Because they had the home-court advantage, the Bulls didn't need to win in the Palace to clinch the series—but the job might have felt half-done if they hadn't.

In the early going game three was not unlike game one. Chicago leapt to a 24–8 lead after just 10 minutes, but Vinnie Johnson brought the Pistons back, shooting Detroit ahead 38–36 early in the second quarter. Once again, though, the better-balanced Bulls withstood the charge. Jordan, who finished with 33 points, Pippen (26) and Grant (17) gave Chicago a 51–43 halftime lead that the Bulls extended to 77–63 late in the third period.

But the Pistons had one last comeback in them. In a furious fourth quarter, they narrowed the gap to 103–98. With two minutes remaining, Mark Aguirre, the least likely of defensive heroes, swiped the ball from Pippen and fired it to a streaking Vinnie Johnson.

The Pistons' explosive guard had Joe Dumars on his right and only Jordan to beat as he bore in on the basket. But

Michael lunged at him, forcing Johnson to lob a soft pass toward Dumars. The pass was so weak that Jordan had time to recover. When Dumars caught the ball, Michael was all over him.

Dumars threw up an off-balance shot as he fell out of bounds. It bounced off the rim, Jordan snatched the rebound and the clock ran out on a 113–107 Chicago victory. The series was just about over.

"I thought we took their best shot today," Phil Jackson said.

He was right. The Pistons played an extremely well-disciplined first quarter in game four, and trailed just 25–24 when Chuck Daly and assistant coach Brendan Suhr were hit with technicals. In a matter of seconds Chicago led 32–24. The defending champions whittled a point off that lead in the second quarter and trailed 57–50 at the half.

But that was it. With their title on the line, the tired and injury-tattered Pistons failed to show up for the second half. The Bulls began the third period with an 11–4 run. With 19 minutes still to play, they led 68–54.

The lead was 103–80 when Daly sent in his subs with four and a half minutes remaining. The final tally was 115–94. Several of the ever-classy Pistons, including Thomas and Laimbeer, slunk off the court with a few seconds still on the clock and refused to shake hands as they passed the Chicago bench.

The Bulls couldn't quite believe how easy it had been. "We surprised ourselves," Jordan said. "Unexplainable," added Jackson.

Chicago had dominated what had been the most dominating team in the league for the last two seasons. And they had done it by stealing Detroit's own strengths. The Pistons shot just .456 for the series. The Bulls outrebounded them by more than six boards per game. The Jordan Rules were never a factor, partly because Scottie Pippen had redeemed himself with 22 points and almost eight rebounds per contest. Even the second unit distinguished itself, as Levingston and Perdue combined for nine rebounds each game.

Three days later the Los Angeles Lakers defeated the Portland Trail Blazers to win the Western Conference championship four games to two and set off a fortnight of sports media hysteria. More than any other team sport, basketball can be dominated, night after night, by a single outstanding player. More than any other major sports league, the NBA markets itself as the showcase for such outstanding individual talents. In the 1991 NBA Finals, the league, the NBC television network, and a nation of basketball fans were blessed with the perfect pairing: Michael Jordan versus Magic Johnson. The two best players in the game, as well as the two best-known.

Here were two men of abundant but divergent gifts. Jordan's style was slashing, confrontational, acrobatic, while Johnson, in the Lakers' new half-court offense, was a sleight-of-hand surgeon dissecting the opposing defense, or a basket-bound battering ram when the need arose. While most observers conceded Jordan's athletic superiority, there was an undertone both in the press coverage and the comments of other players suggesting that Magic was smarter, that his game was truer to the essence of basketball. The Bulls, according to this thinking, had been stunted by Michael's selfish brilliance, while the Lakers had flowered under Magic's tender care.

The two principals paid little attention to this type of argument. Jordan had originally suspected Johnson of supporting his humiliation at the 1985 All Star game, but at Magic's initiation the two had become friends. It was Johnson who helped persuade Jordan to put aside his initial reluctance and agree to play on the 1992 U.S. Olympic team. By the fall of 1991, their relationship was a warm one, and Jordan was one of the first people Johnson called to impart the devastating news that he had contracted the AIDS virus.

Despite their friendship, however, the two superstars remained intensely competitive. Going into the 1991 finals, Jordan realized that after seven seasons—playing against the master of a style supposedly superior to his own—he had a chance to silence his basketball critics for good. "I am not going to pay any attention to it," he told reporters about his personal matchup with Magic. Then he winked, to make sure they knew he was kidding.

15

With just under a minute to play in the fifth and deciding game of the NBA Finals, Michael Jordan drove into the lane. A clutch of Lakers awaited him—Vlade Divac on his left, Magic Johnson on his right, and Sam Perkins behind them. But Jordan spun and found John Paxson where he knew he would be, 10 feet behind him, without a defender in reach. Paxson caught the pass and buried the shot, as he buried four others in the last three and a half minutes of play. The Bulls led 105–101. In a moment, they would be champions.

For sheer virtuosity this move was no match for the breath-stealing maneuver Jordan executed in game two, when he soared down the lane with the ball held high in his right hand, spotted Perkins in a position to contest the easy jam, shifted the ball quickly to his left hand and kissed his scoop shot off the glass and into the net just as gravity was beginning to reassert its claim on him. For audacity, his pass to Paxson was not in the same class as his single-handed stop of Vinnie Johnson and Joe Dumars on their fourth-quarter fast break in game three of the Pistons series. But the pass to Paxson was a sign that Jordan and his teammates, after a season of experimentation and discord, had become a community on the court.

"On national television, in the finals, we did it as a team," Jordan said. "All season long we did it as a team."

The ease with which they had done it surprised even the Bulls themselves. They won 15 of their 17 postseason contests, losing only when opponents hit three-pointers in the waning moments. And they swept the last four games of the finals despite a wrenching loss in game one, a defeat they all agreed was a product of their nervousness.

It was difficult not to be nervous. This was the most heavily hyped NBA Final in recent memory. NBC had scheduled all the weeknight games for prime time. The series was being broadcast in more than 70 foreign countries. And the city of Chicago, whose residents slept outside the Stadium for two nights for a chance to buy tickets, had gone slightly mad.

In that frenetic atmosphere, the Bulls took the court in game one and became the Ghosts of Playoffs Past. Jordan, on the strength of brilliant first and fourth quarters, scored 36 points and grabbed eight rebounds. But Paxson, Grant and Cartwright managed only six points each.

Still, the Bulls led 91–89 when Jordan, a sizzling 14 of 22 from the field at that point, missed a 15-footer with 24 seconds remaining. Magic Johnson led the Lakers back downcourt looking for a chance to tie, but with 17 seconds left he saw Sam Perkins untended, just behind the three-point line. Perkins swished his shot to give Los Angeles a 92–91 lead, but its victory was not safe until Jordan's 18-footer rattled in and popped out in the closing moments.

"We had every opportunity to win," Jordan said. "I missed my last two shots." Michael was blunt about his teammates' performance as well, singling out Paxson for criticism after the usually deadly shooter missed four open jumpers. It seemed that the Bulls might revert to their old ways, leaving Michael—who, with 12 assists, had figured in two-thirds of Chicago's scoring—virtually alone against the opposition.

Game two eased Bulls fans' fears. Jordan was his brilliant self, scoring 33 points and hauling in 13 rebounds, but on this night the other Bulls were nearly as lustrous. Pippen and Grant (who hit 10 of 13 shots) scored 20 points each. Cartwright went six of nine from the floor and Paxson shot a remarkable eight for eight as Chicago, behind a 38-point third period, routed the Lakers 107–86. The Bulls also set a playoff record by shooting almost 62 percent.

Jordan, who made 13 straight shots, picked up a few early fouls trying to guard the taller Johnson. But he got defensive relief from Pippen. The Bulls' forward harassed Magic throughout the rest of the game, applying length-of-the-floor pressure and forcing him to give up the ball early. "They are trying to wear me out or take the ball out of my hands," said Johnson, who made just four of his 13 shots. "Take your pick."

The series moved to Los Angeles for game three, where, it was written, the untested Bulls would come undone before the Forum crowd. The Bulls, Jordan included, played the first two-thirds of the game as though trying to bear this out. Michael was mired in his worst shooting performance of the series (11-28). Meanwhile, Magic (22 points and 10 assists) picked apart the Bulls' defense. Late in the third period, Chicago trailed 67–54. But, paced by no one in particular, the Bulls went on a 20–7 surge that tied the score at 74 with just over six minutes to play. Eight different players contributed to that run, including Jordan, though he scored only two points.

Once matters became more urgent, however, Michael took the game in hand. He hit a 13-footer over the outstretched hand of Terry Teagle to knot the score at 92 with three seconds remaining. Moments later he poked the ball away from Vlade Divac to insure overtime.

The next five minutes all but broke the Lakers' spirit. Jordan scored six of Chicago's 12 points and hit Paxson for an open jumper. Horace Grant, who finished with 22 points and 13 rebounds, scored a clutch basket off the offensive board. From a 96–96 tie, Chicago pulled away to win 104–96.

The Bulls won more convincingly in game four, steam rolling the Lakers 97–82 in the Forum. Again Jordan was marvelous, scoring 28 points and handing out 13 assists, but again the Chicago attack was a balanced one. Paxson stayed hot, hitting seven of his 11 shots for 15 points. Every Bulls starter netted at least a dozen. Michael played with a bruised right toe, an injury he had sustained hitting the game-tying shot 36 hours earlier, but he didn't seem much affected.

"This is like a nightmare," Magic Johnson said. "I never dreamed that this would happen. I never even thought about it, us being dominated like this."

Lakers coach Mike Dunleavy said his team was in a ditch: "Not a hole. A ditch." He didn't know it yet, but neither James Worthy, who was having a somewhat subpar series on a sprained left ankle, nor Byron Scott, who had bruised his right shoulder, would be available for game five. In the case of Scott, who had hit just five of his 19 shots, that may have been a blessing.

Without their two starters, the Lakers played a gutsy final game. Johnson had 20 assists, Perkins put in 22 points, and rookie substitutes Elden Campbell (21 points) and Tony Scott (12 points) played with a spirit their older teammates lacked. Los Angeles rallied from a 70–62 third-quarter deficit to take a 93–90 lead with six and a half minutes to play.

But Scottie Pippen, who led the Bulls in scoring with 32 points, nailed a three-pointer to tie it. Then, as Magic Johnson put it, "John [Paxson] got crazy on us." Beginning at the three-and-a-half-minute mark, the Bulls guard drilled three long-range jumpers and scored on a fast break. Jordan tossed a driving layup—through three Lakers—into the mix as Chicago scored 10 points in a two-minute span.

But Sam Perkins countered with eight consecutive Laker points, and with one minute to play, Los Angeles trailed by just 103–101.

On the Bulls' next possession, Jordan fired the pass to Paxson that came to symbolize the season. Pippen would add a pair of free throws and Michael, fittingly, would score the last point on a free throw of his own. The final score was 108–101.

When the buzzer sounded, Jordan embraced Cliff Levingston, then John Paxson, and together they began pushing their way through the jubilant throng of Bulls fans who had flown out for the game. At the mouth of the hallway that led to the tiny dressing room, the sea of people parted and Jordan sprinted down a corridor thick with well-wishers and television wires. He grabbed a few towels from an attendant who stood near the door of the dressing room, then suddenly collapsed to his knees and began sobbing for joy.

American sports fans are accustomed to victory celebrations, to the waving fingers of fans proclaiming that their team is number one, to the boorish boasts of athletes reminding us that they are the greatest. This had nothing in common with those. This was a glimpse of a man humbled by his own achievement. Jordan was not so much exultant as at peace. In a moment when he could have been excused for feeling full of himself, Michael instead felt emptied out, purified.

He joined his teammates in saying the Lord's Prayer and then, as the champagne corks popped, watched Commissioner David Stern awarding the championship trophy to Jerry Reinsdorf. When next the cameras found him, he was sitting in the corner of the dressing room. His father sat at his right hand, his wife at his left. There was a hat on his head; there were tears in his eyes, and he held the gold-plated trophy as though it could feel his tenderness. Jordan seemed all but oblivious to the champagne spray that had made his skin sticky and the shouts of the television announcer asking repeatedly where he was.

"I never thought I'd be this emotional," Jordan would say later. "I've never been this emotional publicly, but I don't mind. This is a great feeling, a great situation to be emotional."

After seven seasons, Jordan had his championship; after 25 seasons, the Chicago Bulls had theirs. "It means so much," he said to Bob Costas and a national television audience. "When I first got to Chicago we started at the bottom and every year we just worked harder and harder 'til we got to it. I've appreciated so much in my life from my family, from my kids, everything, but this is the most proud day I've ever had."

Even after the Pistons had been so easily exorcised and the finals had begun, there were those who asked whether any squad dominated by a talent as rare as Jordan's could win the NBA title. The basketball gods, they said, would never bless a man who flew so close to the sun. The implication lingered that somehow Michael's greatness would assure his team's defeat. At least it lingered until the clock ran out on game five and it was clear that Icarus still lived.

"I think what [the championship] is going to . . . get rid of is the stigma of a one-man team," Jordan said at the postgame press conference. "We have been trying to get rid of that stigma for a while. A lot of you guys say it's my fault because of the way I play offensively. Maybe it is. Who knows? But we can't live on that stigma anymore. We've got players surrounding myself who give a contribution and make us an effective basketball team."

The party that began in the Bulls' dressing room continued at the team's hotel, the Ritz-Carlton in Marina del Rey. Jordan, though, didn't spend much time with his teammates, none of whom he is particularly close to, repairing instead to his rooms with family and friends. Earlier, at Michael's insistence, the other starters had been included in his Disney World commercial. That, combined with his absence from the party, provided a telling commentary on Jordan's relationship with the other Bulls. Michael can be a teammate and a benefactor, but he lives in a world apart and cannot really be their friend.

One gets the sense, sometimes, that Jordan has wearied of his fame. Yet he continues to pursue the endorsements that feed it. Before the summer was out he had his own chewing gum, Hangtime, and had switched his soft-drink allegiance from Coke to Gatorade (in a multiyear deal worth $18 million). He also found himself criticized in a *Sports Illustrated* roundtable on the status of the black athlete.

"What has Michael Jordan ever said, other than how much money he makes?" asked Bill Walton.

"I think that Michael needs to speak out, and I think he'll find himself even stronger if he does," said Henry Aaron.

These remarks touch on the great unanswered questions about Jordan: How has he affected the world? How might he affect it still?

It may be that there are white children growing up with a broader and more benign sense of what black men are like because of Michael's example. It may be that there are black children who find it easier to believe that a world which welcomed Michael will welcome them. But Jordan has neither encountered the circumstances nor taken the risks that would make him a truly forceful actor in the nation's racial drama. Indeed, he seems willfully to have avoided doing so.

Michael does not live in a society as segregated or a culture as bigoted as earlier black sports heroes, and so he has had the chance to charm rather than fight his way into the nation's affections. He does not move on a landscape barren of black elected officials, and so he has not been forced to be a spokesman for his race. Instead he has had the opportunity to carve his own considerable niche in American culture and make himself extremely comfortable there. It may be a sign of racial progress that Jordan feels no greater need to involve himself in social controversy than, say, Arnold Palmer. There is something to be said for allowing a black athlete to be nothing more than an athlete.

Yet, even should he never utter a compelling remark, Jordan will not be allowed the fate he may well crave. His athletic and commercial successes have enshrined him as one of the few cultural heroes shared by blacks and whites alike. As such he argues, simply by existing, that Americans share a common culture, that in a society increasingly characterized by extremism and reaction, certain virtues—clichéd virtues like hard work, personal rectitude, devotion to one's family and a willingness to share the fruits of one's gifts—still exert an almost universal appeal. At the same time, his dazzling style on the court speaks of a uniquely black contribution to American culture, and constitutes a nightly reassertion of a particular sort of racial pride. In Jordan the tension between assimilation and the loss of cultural identity seems somehow reconciled. And that makes him too compelling a presence to be left alone.

For many people Michael's status as America's best-loved athlete is evidence that the American dream is still working, a symbol that blacks, who have shared less fully in that dream than any other group, are making their way in greater numbers into the economic mainstream. To others, though, Jordan's ascendancy is little more than a diversion, a way for white Americans to feel good about how tolerant they are of blacks without addressing larger questions of racial and economic injustice. "I admire him tremendously," says Ted Shaw. "But he doesn't tell us a bit about the way black folks are being treated, or even the way black athletes are treated. He plays at a level above everyone else and he lives at a level above everyone else."

Like Bill Cosby, Jordan illustrates simultaneously that a black man can capture the affections of the white mainstream and how singularly talented, charismatic and solidly middle-class he must seem to do so. Also, how irrelevant to people's everyday lives. "One of the reasons people accept Bill Cosby and Michael Jordan and will invite them into their living rooms and make them part of their life is because they are in a place you will never get to," Julius Erving says. "People have less security when black people come into their own arena. You say, 'Wait a minute. This is my territory and it is only big enough for one.' It's easy to accept when somebody is not competitive with you. You say, 'Go for it,' because they are entertaining you.''

But the stature these men have attained as entertainers puts them in a position to be so much more. Jordan seems incompletely aware of this. He understands charity, it seems, but not change.

For nearly a decade Michael has been this democracy's idea of a crown prince—young, handsome, virtuous, charismatic and powerless in all but symbolic ways. It is a wonderful role, but not one that lasts a lifetime. Jordan has already begun to ponder what he will do when he retires from basketball after another four or five seasons. Trying out for the Professional Golfers Association tour is an option about which he is more serious than people suppose. But it is not his only alternative.

''I think Michael will have limitless freedom of choice when his career is over to do almost anything he wants,'' says David Falk. ''I think he can go into politics. He can go into business. He can stay in basketball. He could develop a much closer relationship with one of his corporate partners. He could become a broadcaster. He could become a goodwill ambassador for the NBA. He could become a pro golfer. He can do almost anything that he wants, and I think he really wants to understand better each of the different opportunities before he makes a decision.''

Falk realizes that when Jordan stops playing basketball, Michael will lose the principal platform from which he addresses the public. But he does not believe that Jordan will, or will want to, fade into obscurity. ''It is assumed that when you stop playing the impact dramatically goes away,'' he says. ''Quickly. Because you are not in the public eye. In his case I don't think that is going to be the situation at all. I think he is going to be very much before the public eye. I think he is still going to be doing Nike commercials, maybe [other] commercials. He will be in a different phase in his life. Almost maybe more as a Bill Cosby, as a family guy who is well-known and popular and espouses good values. And that, in theory, may never end.''

''A family guy who espouses good values.'' For a figure of Jordan's stature, it seems both an admirable and insufficient goal. With so many people willing to listen to him, one can't help wishing he had a more distinctive voice—that he understood more clearly than he does now that under the right circumstances he could wield the power to change long-entrenched attitudes. Perhaps his decision to work with Magic Johnson in promoting AIDS awareness will drive the point home.

Jordan will retire enormously wealthy and will have the opportunity to use that wealth in creative ways. Dave Bing put his more meager resources into a pair of manufacturing ventures in inner-city Detroit and has become a leading black capitalist. ''You can give somebody satisfaction because of the way you play or a particular move that you made, but that passes real quick,'' Bing says. ''American athletic life is really day to day. 'What have you done for me lately?' There's much more meaning and permanence attached to a job. You are giving meaning and substance to a person's life and to a person's family. If I can help somebody pay the rent or get a car or educate their kids, I feel that's much more substantial than anything I did as an athlete.''

Implicit in Bing's remarks is an understanding of the duality at the heart of American sports. The games we watch are both real and imaginary. Real because they are not prescripted; they unfold before our eyes. Imaginary because they are intrinsically meaningless, depending for their significance on a collective act of will, a national exercise in mythmaking. Athletes live with one foot in the real world and one in the land of make-believe, but only rarely make contributions to both. Some, like Willie Mays, perhaps the greatest baseball player of all time, enrich the national imagination without ever paying much attention to the national reality. Others, like Joe DiMaggio, embody so fully the style of an era that they attain a significance that transcends sports, yet remains primarily symbolic. The rarest of athletes—Louis, Robinson, Ali—achieve both of these feats and then something more. They change people. They make a history other than that recorded in baseball annuals and preseason guidebooks. Our understanding of the world is different for their having lived in it.

The era in which it was possible for an athlete to achieve this may well be past. There are few present-day injustices quite so obvious as segregation. It may also be that the best of modern athletes are so much a part of the American establishment that they dare not criticize it. Yet the legacy of segregation endures even if the institution itself has largely vanished, and confrontation is not the only way to effect change. For Michael Jordan, who has enriched the national imagination and achieved a significance that transcends his sport, there are a myriad of options that would enable him to affect the national reality. He may make his mark as Bing has—as a capitalist. Or, regardless of his next career, he may use the Michael Jordan Foundation to become a more active proponent of children's rights. Or, he may decide that he has done enough.

Across the street from the building in which Michael has written his legend stand the Henry Horner Homes. The children there grow up accustomed to the sounds of gunfire. Jordan is the project's hero. It is sentimental to pretend that he can solve the many problems that beset this place, irresponsible to imagine that he owes a greater responsibility to these kids than one owes them one's self. But he could focus attention on these children's problems simply by crossing the street. These kids, and others like them, are not Jordan's obligation, but they are his opportunity. And with so much on the line, who would you rather see with the ball?

INDEX